Seóirse Bodley

Seóirse Bodley

Gareth Cox

Field Day Music 4

Series Editors: Séamas de Barra and Patrick Zuk

Field Day Publications
Dublin, 2010

ISBN-978-0-946755-48-6

Published by Field Day Publications in association with the Keough-Naughton Institute for Irish Studies at the University of Notre Dame.

Field Day Publications
Newman House
86 St. Stephen's Green
Dublin 2
Ireland

www.fielddaybooks.com

Set in 10.5pt/14pt Quadraat
Designed and typeset by Red Dog Design Consultants
Printed on Munken Lynx

Contents

Field Day Music

This series of monographs was conceived to provide a scholarly and readable account of the careers and creative achievements of some of the most significant figures in Irish composition. Each volume will provide the reader with some idea of the nature and extent of a composer's work and the context in which it was produced. The monographs are aimed at the general reader as well as at the specialist and will appear in pairs, one devoted to an historical figure and the other to a living composer. Forthcoming volumes will survey the careers of Ina Boyle and James Wilson, and it is envisaged that every major figure will be covered in due course.

Séamas de Barra and Patrick Zuk

Acknowledgements

I am indebted to Seóirse Bodley for allowing me unrestricted access to his private collection of scores, programmes and scrapbooks, for his unfailing help and extremely prompt responses to numerous queries, for his encouragement over the last few years, and for the hospitality which was extended to me by Seóirse and his wife Lorraine on my many visits to their home. I wish to thank the Research Office in Mary Immaculate College, University of Limerick, for funding at various stages of this project and the library staff of Mary Immaculate College, RTÉ and Contemporary Music Centre, Ireland, for their invaluable assistance. I am also very grateful to Paul Collins, Ronald Cox, Axel Klein, and Michael Murphy for reading various drafts of the manuscript and for their helpful observations; to Karen Power and Laurence Beard for their precise work preparing the music examples; to the general editors of the series, Patrick Zuk and Séamas de Barra for their many perceptive suggestions and attention to detail, and to Ciarán Deane of Field Day Publications for his meticulous copy-editing. Extracts from Bodley's works are reproduced with the permission of the composer and the Contemporary Music Centre, Ireland.

Gareth Cox
Limerick 2010

Seóirse Bodley (1982)
© RTÉ Guide collection

Preface

This book presents an overview of the career and creative achievement of one of Ireland's foremost living composers, Seóirse Bodley. It documents the context from which his work has emerged over the course of the last sixty years, considers its reception and discusses its most significant features. I wish to acknowledge those who have previously written on Bodley's music, including Malcolm Barry, Axel Klein, Pádhraic Ó Cuinneagáin and Lorraine Byrne Bodley. I have also drawn extensively on Bodley's own explanatory writings and on concert reviews and articles on his work in national newspapers.

My own experience of Bodley's music has been quite a long one, stretching from the 1970s to the conference papers and articles of the last ten years in which I discussed specific technical aspects of his compositions. His music has been for me not only a source of pleasure, but also a multifaceted challenge. I hope that this first full-length study of his life and work will appeal to a wide range of readers and musicians, both specialist and amateur, and most importantly, will encourage more performers to study, play and record Bodley's music.

1. Studying in Dublin and Stuttgart

Over a period of six decades, Seóirse Bodley has established himself as one of Ireland's best-known composers. He has been integral to Irish musical life since the second half of the twentieth century, not just as a composer, but also as a teacher, arranger, accompanist, adjudicator, broadcaster, and conductor. His long and distinguished career has been recognized in many ways, most notably by his election as the first composer to the title of *Saoi* by his fellow artists in Aosdána in 2008, Ireland's highest artistic award. On the occasion of the conferring of this honour at the Arts Council in Dublin on 24 November 2008, the President of Ireland, Mary McAleese, declared that Bodley 'has helped us to recast what it means to be an artist in Ireland'.[1]

Seóirse Bodley was born George Pascal Bodley in Dublin on 4 April 1933 at 90 Phibsboro Road, between Dalymount Park and the Royal Canal. He had an older brother, Dermot (1922–99). His mother Mary (*née* Gough) (1891–1977) worked for the Guinness brewery and his father, George James Bodley (1879–1956), was employed at the London Midland & Scottish Railway Company at their Dublin offices on the North Wall Quay and later worked for the Port and Docks Board. Bodley recalls that there was a great emphasis on education at home during his childhood and that his artistic aspirations were always encouraged. He was enrolled at a private junior school in Phibsboro at the age of six, and after a year moved to the primary school at the Holy Faith Convent in Glasnevin, Dublin. From the age of nine he was a pupil at the Irish-speaking Christian Brothers School at Coláiste Mhuire in Parnell Square, where he succeeded in winning a highly prized Corporation Scholarship for his secondary school education.[2] He subsequently transferred to the

---

1   Cited on the President of Ireland's website www.president.ie (26 November 2008)
2   See Daniel Murphy et al., 'Seóirse Bodley', *Education and the Arts: The Educational Autobiographies of Contemporary Poets, Novelists, Dramatists, Musicians, Painters and Sculptors, A Research Report* (Dublin, 1987), 232

School of Commerce in Rathmines and with the help of a private tutor for the subjects not taught there, Bodley attained his Leaving Certificate in Irish, English, Mathematics, Latin, Drawing and Geography.

There was little music in the various schools he attended, and although with the Christian Brothers he did play violin a little, it was 'just a question of "who in this class has a violin at home". And if you put up your hand you got about half a dozen lessons on the fiddle, enough for you to finger it.'[3] Music was encouraged at home. His father, who played in a mandolin band, taught Seóirse how to play the instrument. His mother played the piano and, with her encouragement, he started lessons at nine years of age with a local teacher, Sheila Delaney. However, for a short period between the ages of eleven and thirteen, he developed 'an intense hatred for music'[4] and gave up the piano, but later resumed lessons of his own accord at the Royal Irish Academy of Music (RIAM) in Westland Row. This time he embraced the piano more enthusiastically, recalling that he would practise up to six hours a day, often entertaining 'the thought of being a very romantic and dramatic concert pianist, somewhere halfway between Liszt and Chopin'.[5] He also studied at the Brendan Smith Academy of Acting from about thirteen, while reading the works of Stanislavsky on acting and regularly attending productions at the Gate Theatre. Bodley recalled that, although neither of his parents had strong literary interests, he remembered his mother taking him to see *Twelfth Night* at the Gate: 'In a funny sort of way there may not have been a great knowledge of the arts [at home], but there was a respect for them in a general, abstract sort of way.'[6] In fact at that very young age he felt that he had to choose between the theatre and music: 'I had an ambition to write plays, at this stage. I'm afraid it never materialised, except for private plays we used to produce when we were kids.'[7] He also recalls that having spent some time at drawing classes he realized that he could not work in a medium where there was no sound.

He began composing in his early teens; there was apparently an early piano piece called 'Snowdrops'.[8] He had already enrolled for harmony and counterpoint lessons at the RIAM when he also began to study composition privately with the German conductor, Hans Waldemar Rosen (1904–94), while still at school. Rosen had arrived in Ireland in 1948 from Leipzig via a Welsh prisoner-of-war camp and began his Irish career as chorus master of the Dublin Grand Opera Society. He later became conductor of the professional chamber choir maintained by the national broadcasting station, Cór Radio Éireann (which was later reorganized as the Radio Éireann Singers), as well as of its larger semi-amateur choir, the Radio Éireann Choral Society (in which Bodley sang bass for a time). Rosen

3   Murphy et al., 'Seóirse Bodley', 233
4   Charles Acton, 'Interview with Seóirse Bodley', *Éire-Ireland*, 5, 3 (1970), 119
5   Acton, 'Interview', 119
6   Murphy et al., 'Seóirse Bodley', 230
7   Acton, 'Interview', 118
8   Acton, 'Interview', 119

was also highly regarded as a vocal coach and composition teacher. Bodley's lessons with him continued until late 1956. He is particularly indebted to his teacher for being one of the first to recognize his talent, as well as for his remarkable generosity in refusing to accept payment for much of the period of study with him.[9] He repaid this encouragement by making rapid progress. Under Rosen's supervision, he completed two part-songs for male voices to texts by Milton, 'Ring Out Ye Crystal Spheres' and 'Song on May Morning'. These were heard in broadcast performances given by the Radio Éireann Men's Octet, conducted by Rosen, on 25 December 1950 and on 26 May 1951, respectively. He also had some of his early songs performed by the well-known baritone Tomás Ó Súilleabháin on Radio Éireann (RÉ) on 23 February 1952.

During this time he would often go to Pigott's music shop in Grafton Street in Dublin to hire various wind and brass instruments on a short-term basis in order to explore their basic technical possibilities:

> I made an arrangement with them to pay five shillings a week for the loan of an instrument. So I would take out a wind instrument, for maybe five to six weeks, buy a tutor for it and teach myself to play it. It wasn't so much for the sound, but just to get the feeling of how the instrument worked. During this time I taught myself the basics of the flute, clarinet, trumpet, trombone and French horn.[10]

He also sang, and at the School of Commerce in Rathmines in May 1952 he took the part of the Sheriff in the students' Choral Society production of Flotow's Martha. His main instrument, however, was the piano, and he became sufficiently proficient to be awarded the Licentiate diploma from Trinity College, London. He participated in concerts held under the auspices of the Students' Musical Union in the RIAM in 1951–52, playing works by Beethoven and Bartók. He also appeared in chamber music recitals and as an accompanist, often contributing solo items. He performed with the distinguished Dublin musicians Joseph Groocock and John O'Sullivan, in a performance of Bach's Concerto for Three Claviers and Strings at a concert given by the Dublin Orchestral Players on 3 December 1953. This practical experience of performing in public stood Bodley in good stead and he continued to make regular appearances subsequently both as solo pianist and as accompanist, often performing his own works.

His early music education was further augmented by regular attendance at the two concerts given every week during its seasons by the Radio Éireann Symphony Orchestra (RÉSO) in the recently built Phoenix Hall in Dame Court (between Dame Street and Exchequer Street, Dublin). At these, he had the opportunity to hear leading foreign

---

9   Over twenty years later, in 1974, Bodley took the opportunity to mark the occasion of Rosen's retirement as conductor of the RTÉ Singers by writing a short piano piece entitled Planxty Rosen, which he dedicated to the conductor. This piece was first performed privately, but Bodley subsequently recorded it for RTÉ radio.
10 Murphy et al., 'Seóirse Bodley', 231

conductors such as Carlo Franci, Jean Martinon, Carlo Zecchi, Hans Schmidt-Isserstedt, and Jean Fournet conducting a very wide repertoire of works. Not surprisingly, the standard works of the classical and romantic periods, such as Dvořák's *New World Symphony*, made a vivid impression on him, but he also heard much twentieth-century music, including works by composers of the Second Viennese School conducted by Winfried Zillig, who had studied with Schoenberg.

In the autumn of 1952 Bodley began his three years of undergraduate music studies at University College Dublin (UCD). The Department of Music was then housed in rooms in Newman House, St. Stephen's Green. The well-known composer John Larchet (1884–1967) occupied the Chair, and was the department's only full-time member of staff. He was assisted by Mairead Pigott, who taught Irish Music, and by Rita Broderick from the RIAM, who taught harmony. The student cohort was very small. Bodley's father initially disapproved of him studying music, fearing, not unreasonably, that the outcome would be an uncertain career as a musician. However, both his parents eventually proved very supportive. Bodley threw himself enthusiastically into student life and was active in the UCD Music Society, which organized concerts and promoted other musical events on campus. He also began studying the German language as he recognized that it would be useful for his future plans in that country. Most importantly, perhaps, for the development of his orchestral skills, in his final two years at UCD he completed many arrangements of Irish music (usually one or more a month) for Radio Éireann, which, he recalled, helped towards his upkeep at home.[11] Arranging Irish folk-songs for small orchestras was practically the only way for a composer to earn an income in the early 1950s.[12]

Bodley had continued to compose quite steadily during his late teens, completing a number of songs and chamber works, including two charming Capriccios for violin and piano, which were composed for the virtuoso violinist François d'Albert, who taught at the RIAM. A *Cradle Song* appears to be his very first solo song, written when he was aged seventeen. It is an attractive setting of Yeats's poem from the collection *The Rose* (1893) and is reproduced in Ex. 1.

The poet sighs in resignation that he cannot retain the present moment. Bodley sets the text to a lilting 6/8, making frequent use of open fifths moving chromatically from A minor via B major and C sharp minor to E major. The middle verse depicts the 'Sailing Seven' — the Pleiades constellation visible during the sailing season in antiquity — in the rolling arpeggiated figures in the bass.

---

11   Murphy et al., 'Seóirse Bodley', 234
12   Denis Donoghue, 'The Future of Irish Music', *Studies* 44, Spring (1955), 111. Patrick Zuk notes that such arrangements are 'representative of a kind of light music which has now disappeared altogether, but which was once published in abundance and formed the bulk of popular concert fare and, later, music broadcast on the radio.' Zuk, 'Words for Music Perhaps? Irishness, Criticism and the Art Tradition', *Irish Studies Review* 12, 1 (2004), 20.

Ex. 1 *A Cradle Song*

Bodley composed his first significant work, *Music for Strings (Ceol do Théada)*, at the age of nineteen. He commenced this in January 1952 and completed it eleven months later. It was first performed on 10 December 1952 in the Metropolitan Hall, Dublin, by the Dublin Orchestral Players (which had a policy of playing works by Irish composers), conducted by Brian Boydell, in a programme that included Haydn's *London* Symphony and Bach's Violin Concerto in E major with d'Albert as the soloist. Encouragingly for Bodley, the work received largely favourable notices. The critic for the *Irish Times* noted that the piece

> showed that this young composer can express himself with sincerity and definite purpose, [though] ... his knowledge of string technique is, however, still rather hazy, and he would be well advised to obtain some scientific and authoritative instruction upon the complex harmonic technique which he employs. The free use of modern harmony is rather dangerous unless one has either a sure knowledge or a superlatively sensitive ear.[13]

The *Irish Press* agreed, suggesting that Bodley 'would do well to study modern harmony and orchestration with one of our more eminent composers, as he is undoubtedly a promising musician',[14] while the critic for the *Evening Herald* noted that Bodley had 'a fine grasp of the structure and range of an orchestra, which knowledge he uses to great advantage'.[15]

The first movement, *Alla marcia*, is interrupted twice by an *Adagio rubato*, once over open fifths in the bass gradually settling back into the march via a cello solo and the second time with imitative entries over a sustained pedal. The second movement, an *Adagio non troppo*, opens with solo violin over slowly pulsating D major chords (Ex. 2) and is clearly indebted to Shostakovich. According to Bodley, he experimented here with combining the diatonic modality characteristic of Irish melody with dissonant elements, with results that struck many contemporary listeners as rather daring.[16] A senior colleague, the Irish composer Frederick May (1911–85) noted that these harmonies, 'while frequently bold and daring, are never perverse and the texture is always clear with a strong feeling for counterpoint'.[17] This movement has a number of imaginative touches, such as the countermelody on a second solo violin which accompanies the principal thematic material on its return. It ends serenely in D with oscillating B flats and As which recall the opening of the movement before dying away. The final two movements, a Scherzo (*Allegro molto*) and Rondo (*Allegro vivo*), continue the use of similarly shaped melodic material and are well crafted, with good use of violin solos over sustained chords at the end of both movements.

13   'B' [Walter Beckett], *Irish Times*, 11 December 1952
14   'R. J.' [Robert Johnson], *Irish Press*, 11 December 1952
15   *Evening Herald*, 11 December 1952
16   Acton, 'Interview', 120
17   Radio Éireann programme booklet, 15 January 1956

Ex. 2 *Music for Strings*, II, 1–9

Music for Strings remains one of Bodley's most popular works and has been played frequently since its premiere.[18] It was included in programmes performed by the Douglas Cameron String Orchestra during its Irish tour in 1956 and was subsequently taken up by other ensembles such as the New Irish Chamber Orchestra who included it on an American tour. The work was also recorded for commercial release in 1958 by the RÉSO under Milan Horvat on the Decca long-playing record *New Music from Old Erin*.

Bodley was taught his subjects at school for many years through Irish, becoming proficient in the language in his teenage years. He often took his holidays in various areas of the Gaeltacht (the Irish-speaking districts of Ireland) and was involved in musical activities as accompanist and conductor in the Keating Branch of the Gaelic League; he rehearsed in its headquarters in Parnell Square. In 1952, his enthusiasm for the Irish language led him to adopt the Irish version of his Christian name, Seóirse, and he changed his name officially on his birth certificate. Quite apart from an early aspiration to establish an Irish identity for himself for artistic reasons, it might have been difficult for him to make his way as an Irish composer with the Christian name of the patron saint of England. He had already signed himself 'Seóirse Bodlaí' in some of his early pieces (with 'Seóirse Bodley' in brackets) and in quite a few manuscripts of the early 1950s he subsequently overwrote 'George' with 'Seóirse'. Bodley's competence in the language was such that in January 1954, while still an undergraduate, he was asked to present 'Broadcast Music of the Week' in Irish on Radio Éireann every third week. He also wrote short articles for Irish language periodicals such as *Comhar* (contributing a monthly feature entitled 'Nótaí Ceoil' [Music Notes]).

His interest in his native language naturally led him to set texts in Irish. An early choral work from this period, *Trí h-Amhráin Grá* [Three Love Songs] for SATB, sets three poems by seventeenth-century poets: 'Taisig agad féin do Phóg' ['Moist is your kiss'], 'Dar liom is galar é an Gradh' ['Love, in my opinion, is a disease'], and 'An Macalla' ['The Echo']. This set was first performed on 7 January 1953, directed by Rosen, in an Irish Musical Arts Society concert. It was performed subsequently in Germany after a German conductor, Hermann Wagner, heard the songs while on holiday in Ireland.[19] Wagner conducted the songs in a concert of new music by Der Junge Chor of Schleswig-Holstein on 21 October 1953 at the Volkshochschule in Oldenburg in Holstein. Wagner and Rosen translated the texts of the songs and they were published privately as *Drei altirische Liebeslieder* [Three Old Irish Love Songs] in an attractive booklet with a picture of Bray Head and the Sugarloaf Mountain in Co. Wicklow on the cover. All three songs have the same opening character as the sopranos and altos descend first in thirds, then sixths and in the last song in a mixture of intervals, each opening imitated a bar later by the tenors and basses. In the songs Bodley handles some unresolved dissonance within a tonal-modal setting.

---

18   See Richard Pine, *Music and Broadcasting in Ireland* (Dublin, 2005), 144, 456.
19   *Irish Press*, 18 September 1954

In 1953 Bodley composed nine solo songs for baritone and piano. He set texts by Shakespeare and by three highly regarded contemporary poets who wrote in Irish, Séamus Ó Néill (1910–86), Seán Ó Ríordáin (1916–77) and Liam S. Gógan (1891–1979). All of these early songs are quite individual and varied in mood and tempo, ranging from the humorous to the reflective. As such they do not constitute a collection or cycle, although the three settings of texts by Ó Néill, the Co. Down writer, could possibly be grouped together. Almost 30 years later, Charles Acton, the senior music critic with the *Irish Times* from 1955 to 1987, was to bemoan the fact that Bodley in his teens was writing songs to Irish words 'that deserve far better of our singers than the neglect they have suffered'.[20] None of the eleven songs carries a key signature and they display a mixture of extended tonality, modality, some quite dense and dissonant chromaticism, and also, in places, a certain deliberate simplicity. They are through-composed and the piano part is often quite independent of the vocal line, with little word painting.

It was clear that Bodley's talent was beginning to be recognized by his more established colleagues. On 14 November 1953 a recording of his 'Four songs for voice and piano' (a selection of the above-mentioned songs) was played and introduced by the composer himself at the quarterly meeting of the Music Association of Ireland (MAI) held at Brian Boydell's house at 85 Anglesea Road in Ballsbridge, Dublin. Boydell had been one of four (with Edgar Deale, Olive Smith and Frederick May) who had founded the MAI five years previously to promote music and music education in Ireland. Other composers who played recordings of their works that Saturday night were Boydell himself (*In Memoriam Mahatma Gandhi*), Deale (*A Pageaunt of Human Lyfe*), A. J. Potter (*Concerto da chiesa*), and May (*Songs from Prison*). The circular advertising this recital also stated that 'the formation of an Irish Composers' Centre will be discussed after the recital'.[21] James Wilson recalls hearing recordings at Brian Boydell's house at that time and 'being impressed by some songs by a young man, considered promising, named Bodley'.[22]

Eight of these songs were also performed at a public concert the following year on 26 November 1954 by Tomás Ó Súilleabháin, accompanied by Bodley, in the Graduates' Memorial Building in Trinity College Dublin. The programme consisted entirely of Bodley's own music. Before the performance of the songs, the poems were recited by the journalist and broadcaster Seán Mac Réamoinn (1921–2007). This concert was the third in a series of music by Irish composers organized by The Composers' Group of the Music Association of Ireland and it was well attended.[23] Although these attractive early songs have been for the most part forgotten, some of the short piano pieces which Bodley wrote around this time have stayed in the repertoire as children's pieces. At this concert Bodley

20 *Irish Times*, 9 January 1981
21 Copy in Bodley Private Collection
22 *Soundpost*, 1 (1981), 30
23 *Evening Mail*, 27 November 1954

also performed *Scherzo* (c. 1953), *Movement in B* (c. 1954)[24] and *Ceithre Píosaí Beaga* [Four Little Pieces] (1954) — the latter were published separately in four issues of *Feasta* in 1960[25] and again by the Dublin firm of Walton's in 1985. He also accompanied Ruth Ticher in his two Capriccios for violin and piano. Bodley's *Ceithre Píosaí Beaga* resulted from experimenting with writing some short melodies and deciding that four of them could be used as the basis of piano pieces.[26] The *Irish Times* critic reported that this recital

> was certainly the most impressive contribution so far to the series ... . Here is a young Irish composer who is neither another late plodder in the footsteps of the folk-song enthusiasts, suffering from chromatic fever, nor a creaking imitator of fashionable models. From his music it is clear that he has learnt from Hindemith and Bartók, but what he has learned has served merely to feed and cultivate his own musical thinking. There was a fluency, coherence and sense of purpose in most of the pieces which were offered which suggest that we now have a young musical talent which has something original to say.[27]

In the same issue, 'Quidnunc' (Patrick Campbell) in 'An Irishman's Diary' reported that Bodley was 'generally thought to be the most hopeful recent arrival on the contemporary musical scene in Ireland'.[28]

In 1954, Bodley set another text by Seán Ó Ríordáin for SATB chorus, *Cúl an Tí* [The Back of the House], which was first performed by the Radio Éireann Singers conducted by Rosen in a radio broadcast on 9 July 1955. The poem describes the fairy-tale wonderland which, in Louis de Paor's phrase, can be conjured up out of 'the orderly chaos of a back garden'[29], as the imagination transforms ordinary everyday objects such as a kettle, an old hat and familiar domestic animals into a fantastic scene. In the poet's mind, these objects and animals appear to communicate in a mysterious language, which only Aesop would have understood. Bodley sets its six short stanzas as sections of about a dozen bars in length, which are to be sung without a break in a jaunty *Allegro moderato*. The piece is structured in ternary form, each component section of which combines two verses. It commences in E minor with a dotted rhythm figure in the sopranos over a sustained vowel

24 Listed on the programme as 'Sonata in B (First Movement)'. The review in the *Irish Times* of 27 November 1954 referred to it as 'an unfinished Piano Sonata'. A few years later Bodley played the piano pieces again on an RÉ programme, *The Piano Music of Seóirse Bodley*, broadcast on 4 January 1957. A recording of this performance has been preserved in the RTÉ Recording Library.
25 *Feasta*, January, March, June, and September 1960
26 See Pádhraic Ó Cuinneagáin, *The Piano Music of Seóirse Bodley*, unpublished dissertation, National University of Ireland, Maynooth (1992).
27 *Irish Times*, 27 November 1954. Earlier this year there had also been a profile of 'Seóirse Bodlaí' in *Indiu*, 18 June 1954.
28 *Irish Times*, 27 November 1954
29 Louis de Paor, 'Contemporary Poetry in Irish: 1940–2000', in Margaret Kelleher and Philip O'Leary, eds., *The Cambridge History of Irish Literature*, 2, 1890–2000 (Cambridge, 2006), 329

Ó on the pitch E in the basses, which subsequently shifts onto the open fifth, F sharp–C sharp. In the second verse, the soprano and alto lines proceed in parallel fourths over repeated Bs in the bass before the dotted rhythm comes to a halt on the line 'Is tá sé siúd sa chré anois' ['And he is now in the earth'], referring to Aesop, who, unfortunately is long dead and hence unable to interpret the backyard's magical language for the poet. This line is set as a short *doloroso* passage, in which the phrase 'sa chré' is coloured dramatically with a dissonant soprano D against an alto D sharp in bar 23. The central section of the ternary structure, comprising stanzas 3 and 4, sets both openings imitatively. The setting of the fifth stanza is an exact repeat of the opening and while the sixth commences in the same way as the second (both verses allude to Aesop), it ends differently. Here, the poet describes his pleasure in being 'ar chúl an tí' in the darkness late at night when he can see the spirit of Aesop, who is described as being 'ina phúca léannta' — a 'learned pooka' (hobgoblin or puck). At this line, the music moves to E major, and Bodley adds a final flourish on the syllable Ha!

Bodley spent a few months in late 1954 working on his *Sonatina for Five Wind Instruments*, which he finished in early January of the following year. Under its original Irish title, *Sonáidín do Chúig Gaothúirlisí*, this score was first recorded on 14 December 1955 by the wind ensemble Les Amis de la Musique for Radio Éireann. It is an attractive and very melodious four-movement work, scored for flute, oboe, clarinet, horn and bassoon. It displays conventional formal techniques such as sonata form, fugato, and ostinato accompaniments within a tonal-modal harmonic framework using similar thematic material across the piece.

Bodley graduated from UCD in the summer of 1955 with a first class honours B. Mus. By this stage his music was so well-known in Dublin that the music critic for the *Irish Times*, Denis Donoghue, in a much-quoted article 'The Future of Irish Music' (1955), suggested that the name of Seóirse Bodley could now be added to the list of established Irish composers given in Aloys Fleischmann's 1952 book, *Music in Ireland*.[30] However, in 1956 after a Radio Éireann performance of *Music for Strings*, Charles Acton, whilst forecasting great things for Bodley, stressed that he had much to learn 'before he becomes, as he certainly should, Ireland's equivalent of Sibelius or Bartók'.[31] Clearly there was sufficient confidence in his professional competence at this early stage of his career for Radio Éireann to continue offering him work arranging Irish folk music for its various ensembles. During the 1950s he arranged a considerable quantity of Irish airs, mostly for the RÉ Singers, but also some for orchestra (see Appendix I), which were broadcast on various programmes that featured

---

30 Donoghue, 'The Future of Irish Music', 109. Fleischmann had restricted his list of composers to the period 1935–51. Aloys Fleischmann, ed., *Music in Ireland: A Symposium* (Cork, 1952). See also Séamas de Barra, *Aloys Fleischmann* (Dublin, 2006), 112.
31 *Irish Times*, 16 January 1956

this repertory.[32] One orchestral arrangement, 'The Palatine's Daughter' (1956/57), became particularly well-known when it was subsequently used as the signature tune for a popular Irish television soap opera, The Riordans, which was screened during the 1960s and 1970s.[33]

In April 1955 Bodley had commenced work on a short piece, Movement for Orchestra (to which he gave the Irish title Gluaiseacht do'n gCeolfhoireann). This was first broadcast in March 1956 and was subsequently performed in public a few months later on 21 July 1956 by the RÉ Symphony Orchestra under Milan Horvat in the Phoenix Hall, Dublin, in a programme that included Beethoven's Symphony No. 7 and Brahms's Violin Concerto. Following a repeat performance on 4 November 1956, Acton wrote in the Irish Times that

> Bodley is an Irish composer who is not afraid to write a memorable tune. His Movement for Orchestra is a serious and lyrical work of great beauty and a very individual quality ... the harmonic resources are restrained, and in parts surprisingly unmodern. ... [T]he one real fault is that Mr. Bodley has not yet the craftsmanship to join his sections quite as well as I would like.[34]

This one-movement work is in ternary form with the gentler and more pastoral Adagio outer sections framing (from letter H) a faster and more dramatic agitato central part which is underpinned by long timpani rolls and punctuated by fff climaxes. Canonic and motivic techniques are used to develop the thematic material and effective use is made of quartal and quintal gestures and sonorities. The handling of the medium foreshadows many features of Bodley's later orchestral writing, particularly in the symphonies, in its employment of chorale-like passages for the brass, the use of a solo violin, as well as prominent passages for the piccolo and timpani. Understandably one looks for influences in the music of a young composer, and it is hardly surprising to hear many echoes of

---

32 See Richard Pine's extensive research into the Radio Éireann programming of the time when arrangers such as Bodley 'were busily involved, in mining the wealth of folk song in order to translate it into "art-music"'. Pine, Music and Broadcasting in Ireland, 382. These arrangements were broadcast on such popular radio shows as 'Round the Counties', 'Music at Eleven', 'On Wings of Song' and 'A Musical Bouquet'. Pine also mentions various songs and arrangements by Bodley which were sung by the RÉ Singers both in Ireland and on tour abroad. See Pine, 382–89.

33 This arrangement was recorded on a long-playing record made by the RÉ Light Orchestra of folk-music arrangements by various Irish composers entitled 'Ceol na h-Éireann/Music of Ireland', which was released by the Irish-language organization Gael Linn (1958).

34 Irish Times, 5 November 1956. This new composition from the young composer commanded attention and the work was widely reviewed. 'The music is episodic and rather short-breathed, but advancing years will enable Mr. Bodlai [sic.] to strengthen his already surprisingly sure grip of his medium' (Evening Press, 5 November 1956). The Irish Press felt that it 'commands instant attention, and sustains it mainly because of its intellectual character [using] a full orchestra expertly' (5 November 1956), while the Irish Independent noted the 'intellectual rather than emotional' character of the piece. The Irish-language journal, Comhar, considered it to be one of the most important works to be composed for orchestra in the country until then and noted its maturity of ideas, despite some formal weaknesses, and concluded by forecasting great things for the composer (December 1956, 30).

Vaughan Williams in the harmonic idiom and melodic writing, as well as in the scoring for strings (Ex. 3). And one suspects that Bodley was also susceptible, unconsciously or otherwise, to the characteristic effects of the Mantovani orchestra, as he employs an occasional cascading string passage. *Movement for Orchestra* proved justifiably popular and was programmed by Radio Éireann a number of times subsequently.

In 1956 Bodley wrote what can be regarded as his first major choral work, *An Bhliain Lán* ['The Full Year'] for tenor solo and SATB chorus. It is a setting of a text by Tomás Ó Floinn (1910–97) based on an eleventh-century Irish poem. The opening section of the piece is entitled 'Preludio: Turas Athairne' [Athairne's Journey]. This *Andante mosso* is a vocalized four-part fugue on the vowels Ó, Á and Ú which depicts the wanderings of the legendary poet Athairne on his way to visit his pupil and foster-son, the equally renowned poet Aimheirgin. Athairne only intended to stay for one night, but when the time came for him to depart, Aimheirgin composed a compelling poem on the beauty of autumn (*Allegro con spirito*) which persuaded his foster father to stay until winter. But when he made a second attempt to leave, Aimheirgin recited another poem, this time on the melancholy nature of winter (*Adagio*) (Ex. 4).

> In the black season of deep Winter a storm of waves is roused along the expanse of the world. Sad are the birds of every meadow plain, except the ravens, who feed on crimson blood, at the clamour of harsh winter: rough, black, dark, smoky. Dogs are vicious in cracking bones; the iron pot is put on the fire after the dark black day. [35]

Aimheirgin resorts to the same strategy when winter comes to an end, reciting a poem on the chilly springtime weather (*Allegro*) which successfully discourages Athairne from leaving. He is finally allowed to depart at the end of the summer, a peaceful season, according to the poet, which brings warmth to the earth. This section features a reprise of the fugal material which opened the work. In the end, therefore, Athairne finds that he has stayed for 'the full year' of the title. The solo tenor, who acts as a narrator and links the various sections throughout the piece, brings the work to a close with a short recitative describing Athairne's eventual departure — *Do ceadaíodh dó ina dhiaidh sin imeacht sa Samradh* [After that, he was permitted to leave in the summer] — which is accompanied by a rich F major seventh chord. The choir resolves this onto an A major triad, which dies away in a serene *ppp*.

---

35 Kenneth Hurlstone Jackson, *A Celtic Miscellany: Translations from the Celtic Literatures* (London, 1967 [1951]), 69

Ex. 3 *Movement for Orchestra,* 98–107, strings only

An Bhliain Lán was first heard in a broadcast performance by the RÉ Singers under Hans Waldemar Rosen on 1 February 1957. The work was subsequently published by the Irish state publisher, An Gúm, and was awarded a prize in a competition organized by An t-Oireachtas, a national festival of Gaelic culture similar to the Eisteddfod in Wales. It received its first public performance at a concert given jointly by the RÉ Singers and the RÉ Symphony Orchestra on 9 May 1958, on which occasion Brian Boydell's orchestral work In Memoriam Mahatma Gandhi was also featured in the programme.

Bodley has often recalled that he was well aware at the time of the need to develop his control of larger scale works. It was time to study abroad, and Bodley had to consider where to go and with whom to study. He first considered approaching Paul Hindemith — an unsurprising choice, as he had written in Comhar that he had studied Hindemith's pedagogical volumes Unterweisung im Tonsatz (published as The Craft of Musical Composition) in great detail and that they had influenced his recent compositions.[36] Hindemith's former composition student at Yale, the distinguished Irish musicologist, Frank Llewelyn Harrison (1905–87) was very supportive of Bodley's plans and showed Hindemith some of Bodley's

---

36 See Bodley, 'Cúrsaí Ceoil in Éirinn', Comhar, 13 (1954), 8. In Bodley's view, Hindemith's books also gave by far the best understanding of contemporary music and should, he felt, be used as textbooks in music schools. He mentioned Hindemith's teaching again in 'Fadhb an Chumadóra Éireannaigh', Feasta (March, 1957), 4.

scores in person — at the time, Harrison lectured at Oxford University and acted as external examiner in UCD during Bodley's final year. Bodley duly wrote to Hindemith, who sent a gracious reply in English on 23 April 1955, but declined to accept him as a student:

> Dear Mr Bodley,
> When I was in London, Prof. Harrison gave me your manuscripts. I read them with interest and was pleased with your talent and good intentions. Unfortunately I must disappoint you. I am giving up teaching altogether and thus there would not be any opportunity of your studying with me. I am sure you will find another — and probably even better — teacher somewhere who will give you the advice you need and want.
>
> With best regards, yours sincerely,
> Paul Hindemith [37]

Disappointing as this must have been, such a response from one of the most important living twentieth-century composers must have been nonetheless extremely encouraging. Rosen then suggested that he should apply to study in Stuttgart with the Austrian composer, Johann Nepomuk David (1895–1977), whom he knew personally. David had been professor of composition at the Staatliche Hochschule für Musik in Stuttgart since 1948 and had established a considerable reputation by this stage in his career. Bodley was delighted to receive an extremely positive reply from David a month later accepting him as a student:

> Dear Mr Bodley
> Thank you for kindly sending me your compositions. I have studied them very closely and am pleased with the progress that I detect in them. I would be delighted of course to accept you as a student and I look forward to helping you further such a fine talent. The pieces which you sent me are almost all well structured and are in their own way technically quite satisfactory. They demonstrate the result of a solid and talented output which will become more secure with further studies. I would be grateful if you could let me know before the end of July whether you are able to come to me. I am returning your compositions with thanks and I wish you luck and every success in your ventures.
>
> With best wishes,
> Yours
> Joh. Nep. David.[38]

37 Bodley Private Collection
38 David to Bodley, 24 May 1955, Bodley Private Collection (author's translation)

Ex. 4 *An Bhliain Lán*, 168–84

In order to finance this prospective period of study abroad, Bodley applied successfully in 1956 for a National University of Ireland (NUI) Travelling Studentship awarded for graduate study outside of Ireland. This, together with an Arts Council Prize for young composers which he also received, enabled him to go to Stuttgart in early March 1957 to study for two years with David. When he arrived first, Bodley lived briefly in Sielmingen on the southern outskirts of the city, before moving to the north-eastern district of Bad Cannstatt. His initial experiences of living in Germany were somewhat disconcerting:

[You] were speaking a different language, with no real opportunity to speak English. And not alone was it a different language, but it was a 'different' language from German: Swabian, the dialect from the Stuttgart area. Second, if you came from Ireland you might as well have come from Mars as far as a lot of local people

were concerned, it was so far away. "Where are you from?" "I'm from Ireland."
"Ah, Holland." "No. Ireland." "Oh! Iceland?" "No. Ireland." "Oh! Ireland. Isn't that
somewhere in England?" [39]

Bodley also recalls that Ireland seemed very remote. The cost of phoning or travelling
home to Dublin was prohibitively expensive. He immersed himself in the concert life
of the city, attending concerts given by the Sinfonieorchester des Süddeutschen
Rundfunks and various series devoted entirely to contemporary music, such as 'Musik
unserer Zeit' and 'Tage Zeitgenössischer Musik'. He also made some public appearances
as an accompanist and chamber musician. In addition to his compositional studies, he
availed of the opportunity to enrol for classes in conducting with Hans Müller-Kray and
Karl-Maria Zwissler and in piano with Alfred Kreutz.

Many commentators have noted that the compositional style of Bodley's new teacher
defied easy categorization. Josef Häusler notes his frequent use of monothematicism,
quartal harmony, pervasive polyphony, and extended tonality, and summed up his
achievement as being 'a highly individual blend of inherited tradition and the musical
thinking of his own generation'.[40] Hans Stuckenschmidt remarked that, although David
had been labelled a representative of the Neo-Gothic, the Neo-Baroque, or as a synthesis
of Bach and Bruckner, he did not belong to any school as such.[41] In the year that Bodley
came to study with him, David completed two major works, his Symphony No. 7 and
Violin Concerto No. 2. The latter is a serial work in which, as Häusler points out, David
'did not succumb to the Schoenbergian orthodoxy, in that the series are built around tonal
centres of gravity and function as principal motifs, although they lead to an extension of
harmonic resources'.[42]

According to Bodley, David 'did not try to recreate himself in his pupils' — something
he came to feel that Hindemith might have done[43] — it is nevertheless not surprising
that David's influence is discernible in some of his works from this period. Bodley
knew David's recent orchestral compositions quite well but David did not use or
discuss his own works in class. He based his analytical teaching on works such as
Mozart's *Jupiter* Symphony and Bach's Inventions, Sinfonias and the *Well-Tempered Clavier*.

39 'Seóirse Bodley: Michael Dungan talks to the composer', *New Music News* (September 1996), 9
40 Josef Häusler, 'Johann Nepomuk David', *The New Grove Dictionary of Music and Musicians*, 2nd edition, ed.
    Stanley Sadie (London: Macmillan, 2001), vol. 7, 52
41 Hans Heinz Stuckenschmidt, *Johann Nepomuk David: Betrachtungen zu seinem Werk* (Wiesbaden, 1965), 57.
    See also Rudolf Klein, *Johann Nepomuk David: Eine Studie* (Vienna, 1964).
42 Häusler, 'Johann Nepomuk David', 52
43 Axel Klein, 'Irish Composers and Foreign Education: A Study of Influences', in *Irish Musical Studies IV: The
    Maynooth International Musicological Conference 1995, Selected Proceedings Part I*, Patrick F. Devine and Harry
    White, eds. (Dublin, 1996), 278. See also Peter Hölzl, *Der Lehrer Johann Nepomuk David: Aus dem Unterricht
    bei Johann Nepomuk David an der Stuttgarter Musikhochschule* (Vienna, 1992) vii, where the author states
    unequivocally that David did not try to teach his pupils to imitate his own style.

Significantly for Bodley, David also emphasized the importance of a thorough knowledge of and engagement with folksong.[44] As part of their technical studies, students were expected to play from figured bass and execute complex keyboard harmony exercises with modulations to distant keys. Composition lessons for majoring students were conducted on a one-to-one basis. Bodley progressed well and enjoyed a very cordial relationship with his teacher, and was often invited to David's house, on which occasions his composition lesson would be followed by lunch.

While in Stuttgart he also encountered the music of Stockhausen, Boulez and Luigi Nono and although he was impressed with the 'extreme technical competence' their works demonstrated, his initial reaction was 'not particularly favourable'.[45] One of his fellow students at the time was Helmut Lachenmann, who left Stuttgart in 1958 to study with the more progressive Nono in Venice. Bodley was only one of many students who came from abroad to study with David. On the latter's retirement in 1962, *Der Jahresbericht der Stuttgarter Hochschule* noted the large number of foreign composition students that David had taught, many of whom had gone on to make a name for themselves.[46]

Shortly after moving to Germany, Bodley commenced work on his first major orchestral work, *Salve, Maria Virgo*, which was commissioned by the priests of the Franciscan Order at Adam and Eve Church, Dublin to commemorate the tercentenary of the death of the Waterford-born theologian and author of the *Annals of the Franciscan Order*, Father Luke Wadding (1588–1657). The tercentenary was marked by a series of major events held between November 1956 and November 1957, and new works were specially commissioned from John Larchet and Éamonn Ó Gallchobhair (1906–82) as well as Bodley. These commissions were organized by Fr. Cassian Byrne (1916–99), a priest of the order who had a strong interest in music and was a capable musician (he had previously conducted Bodley's *Cúl an Tí* at the Cork International Choral Festival).[47] *Salve, Maria Virgo* was completed in July 1957 and was first performed on 27 October 1957 by the RÉ Symphony Orchestra under Milan Horvat in the Gaiety Theatre, Dublin in a concert that included Bruckner's Symphony No. 4 and Glazunov's Violin Concerto.

Like the *Movement for Orchestra* of the previous year, *Salve, Maria Virgo* lasts about eight minutes and is scored for full orchestra. An *Adagio maestoso* opens the piece dramatically with the first theme outlined in brass fanfares. At letter B this theme is presented by a solo flute gently over a pulsating double-dotted rhythm articulated *pianissimo* in the strings (a rhythm which was also introduced in the opening) in a passage reminiscent of the first movement

---

44 Hölzl, *Der Lehrer Johann Nepomuk David*, 21. See also Karl Michael Komma, 'Johann Nepomuk David, Mensch und Musiker: Erinnerungen an seine Stuttgarter Zeit', *Mitteilungen der Internationalen Johann-Nepomuk-David Gesellschaft*, 11 (Wiesbaden, 1996), 4–5 and Wolfgang Witzenmann, 'Bei David im Unterricht', *Mitteilungen der Internationalen Johann-Nepomuk-David Gesellschaft*, 5 (Wiesbaden, 1987), 12ff.

45 Acton, 'Interview', 122

46 Stuckenschmidt, *Johann Nepomuk David*, 55–56

47 I am grateful to Paul McKeever, organist at Adam and Eve Church, for confirming this information.

of Shostakovich's Fifth Symphony. A short solo clarinet flourish leads into the *Allegro* where the violins take up this theme repeatedly. After a short quiet passage featuring a new idea on the clarinet to the accompaniment of tremolando violas, horn, cymbal and timpani (which subsequently forms the basis of an ostinato accompaniment), the second theme of the work — a plainchant melody associated with the words, 'Is maith an bhean Muire Mór' [Good and great is Our Lady, Mary] — is presented by the oboe. The theme is repeated with the clarinet before breaking forth *forte* in unison strings as the ostinato moves into the brass. The thematic material is contrasted and developed contrapuntally with the plainchant theme singing out in the trombones in crotchets and then presented in augmentation (Ex. 5) against the first theme in the woodwind. The work ends in E major with a crescendo to *fff* in the last bars for the trumpets and trombones.

The harmonic language of the work is firmly tonal, though effective use is made of quartal and quintal sonorities. It is nonetheless a score of considerable complexity, as Bodley's elder contemporary Frederick May pointed out in his programme note for the premiere, singling out the work's 'contrapuntal ingenuity' for special mention.[48] After the premiere Acton noted that it showed Bodley's 'further development and greatly increased command of orchestration [in] a short work which gripped and held my interest throughout'.[49] However, a year later, he was less enthused after another performance under Eimear Ó Broin suggesting that 'perhaps it is still promise rather than full achievement'.[50] Full achievement it could not be, but it is nevertheless a well-constructed and very attractive piece, if at times slightly repetitive. The work found a place in the Irish repertoire and has been performed or broadcast several times since, notably selected by Radio Éireann three years later to share the programme with Isaac Stern playing Beethoven's Violin Concerto under Constantin Silvestri on 30 June 1960 in the Theatre Royal.

The other important work completed by Bodley in Germany was his *Sonata for Violin and Piano*, dated 'Stuttgart Oktober 1957 – März 1959'. It received its first performance on 2 November 1959 by Margaret Hayes accompanied by Bodley in the Radio Éireann studios in Dublin. The work received its first concert performance five years later on 5 March 1964 in Dublin, on which occasion it was played by violinist Hugh Maguire and pianist Joyce Rathbone, who subsequently included the piece in their tour around Ireland. The sonata is in three movements, which are marked *Allegro moderato*, *Adagio* and *Allegro*. The first movement opens with a statement of a four-note motif (Ex. 6) which is used extensively throughout the sonata as a whole (influencing in particular the shape of the plaintive theme of the second movement) and appearing as a link in the final movement where 28 bars of the *Adagio* section (now transposed a semitone higher) interrupt the *Allegro*.

48 Radio Éireann programme booklet, 27 October 1957
49 *Irish Times*, 28 October 1957. The *Evening Herald* (28 October 1957) commented that it was 'a work of dignity and deep feeling'. The *Evening Press* (28 October 1957), however, suggested that Bodley had not 'been able to produce enough matter for his manner'.
50 *Irish Times*, 13 October 1958

Ex. 5 *Salve, Maria Virgo, 339–46*

Ex. 6 Sonata for Violin and Piano, I, 1–23

In a highly enthusiastic review of Maguire's performance, Acton claimed that Bodley composed 'as clearly, acceptably and attractively as the best of Shostakovich, Hindemith or Prokofiev'. He singled out the closing *Allegro* for particular praise, describing it as being 'as serious as a Beethoven finale, and as spirited', while sounding 'indefinably Irish'. Acton concluded his remarks by declaring, 'This is an important work.'[51] Despite Acton's rather hyperbolic comparison with Beethoven, the sonata as a whole is indeed well-crafted. Unlike *Salve, Maria Virgo*, which Bodley completed before he went to Germany, and thus could not have been influenced by David's teaching, this sonata was written during his period of study abroad. As in his *Movement for Orchestra* and *Salve, Maria Virgo*, the influence of Hindemith is readily discernible, which is perhaps surprising, given that Bodley has often stated that David tended to steer him away from Hindemithian techniques. Acton refers above to the 'indefinably Irish' nature of the work and, quite apart from the inclusion of a jig-like finale, there are certainly melodic contours which recall Irish folk music, not least in bars 39–41 in the second movement and alluded to again in the interpolated *Adagio* section of the finale. Indeed, before he left for Stuttgart, Bodley had been in open correspondence with Acton in the *Irish Times* about the possibility of using Irish folk music as a basis for a sophisticated compositional idiom, as Bartók had managed to do with Hungarian folk music. In a letter which was published on 13 February 1957, Acton contended that Ireland had 'perhaps the richest folk music of Europe, but, alas, no one has yet found out the nature of its roots … .We await an Irish Bartók.' For his part, Bodley envisioned a new Irish art music in which the influence of Irish traditional music would be confined to the melodic contours of the thematic material, and which would use neo-classical forms and modern techniques: 'We have an excellent tradition of melodic curve (particularly in the slow songs) that begs for exploitation.'[52] In his reply, Acton expressed the hope that Bodley would make a detailed study of the recordings of Irish traditional music made by the Irish Folklore Commission when he returned from Germany to learn 'the grammar of our folk music'.[53] Bodley in his turn pointed out that Acton had omitted to mention that 'one of the requirements for a true appreciation of Irish folk music […] is a knowledge of the Irish language […] one cannot properly appreciate the spirit of the songs unless one can understand the words.' [54] He also clarified that by 'melodic curve' he was not thinking of the ornamentation which he felt was

51 *Irish Times*, 6 March 1964. Anthony Hughes in 'Bodley, Séoirse', in *The New Grove Dictionary of Music and Musicians*, Stanley Sadie, ed. (London, 1980), vol. 2, 838, describes it as having 'taut melodic lines and clear textures [which] recall Hindemith'. See also Kitty Fadlu-Deen, *Contemporary Music in Ireland*, unpublished dissertation, University College Dublin (1968), 112–16.
52 *Irish Times*, 20 February 1957
53 *Irish Times*, 25 February 1957
54 *Irish Times*, 6 March 1957

largely incapable of further development and least easy to assimilate into a contemporary musical style [but rather] the basis on which these external trappings hang, and develop melodic lines, modern yet Irish from that which is most fundamental in the traditional music — namely, the style of melodic curve which forms the basis of the tunes.[55]

Bodley was to elaborate on these views in 1958 when he was invited as one of the youngest of seventeen Irish composers to contribute to a 'Composers at Work' series on Radio Éireann. In this series, each composer selected some of their own works for performance and recorded a short statement ('Composer's Viewpoint') outlining their views on what it meant to be an Irish composer.[56] Richard Pine notes that while some of the contributions addressed the status of the composer in mid-century Ireland, others considered how an Irish composer might incorporate Irish ethnic material into their compositions.[57] Bodley's presentation fell into the latter category:

One of the main problems facing the contemporary Irish composer is that of musical nationalism, in particular the relation between traditional Irish music and contemporary European art-music. Since I feel a great deal of sympathy with both types of music, I have attempted to come to grips with the problem of combining them. ... I would be most interested, for instance, to hear an Irish folk-song combined with electronic sounds in the manner employed by Stockhausen in his *Gesang der Jünglinge*. The greatest danger which faces the Irish composer is that of false nationalism. In other words, he must not write music in an Irish style out of a sense of duty. ... The Irish composer who wishes to avoid false nationalism must be careful that he does not substitute another false ideal for it. ... I should like to compose music that would be well constructed, reflect my own experience and background, and be written in the contemporary idiom without regard for passing fashions. This is the ideal against which I would wish the value of my music to be estimated.[58]

Although Bodley was quite content in Germany, he remarked that 'probably the knowledge that at some stage I would have to involve myself with Irish music was the deciding factor in my return home'.[59] Bodley's decision to move back to Ireland was also influenced to some extent by personal circumstances. Eighteen months previously, in September 1957,

55 *Irish Times*, 6 March 1957
56 Radio Éireann, 13 November 1958. The Bodley works performed were his Capriccio No. 1 for violin and piano (played by Margaret Hayes, violin and Rhoda Coghill, piano) three songs (Tomás Ó Súilleabháin, baritone and Richard Cooper, piano) and *Four Little Pieces for Piano* (Rhoda Coghill). RTÉ Recording Library.
57 Pine, *Music and Broadcasting in Ireland*, 218
58 RTÉ Recording Library; also cited in Pine, *Music and Broadcasting in Ireland*, 233–34.
59 Axel Klein, 'Irish Composers and Foreign Education', 282

he had married Olive Murphy (1934–99).[60] She came over to live with him in Stuttgart and the first of their three children, Blánaid, was born there on 22 June 1958.[61] The Bodleys and their young daughter returned to Dublin in March 1959 and shortly afterwards Bodley was offered a lectureship in music at his *alma mater*, UCD. An aspiration attached to the award of the NUI Travelling Studentship was that recipients might return to teach at the university's constituent colleges. The position, which was initially on a contract basis, soon became a permanent one. Only a few years earlier, the *Irish Press* expressed the hope that Seóirse Bodley or an Irish musician of comparable stature would become professor of music in the National University.[62] In 1960, Bodley was awarded the degree of DMus, for which he submitted his first symphony.

The manuscript score of Symphony No. 1 is dated 'Stuttgart 1958 – Dublin 1959' and the work was written mostly under the tutelage of David. His conducting teacher, Hans Müller-Kray, who had been conductor of the Süddeutscher Rundfunkorchester in Stuttgart since 1948 and had given the first performances of several of David's symphonies, accepted RÉ's invitation (organized through Bodley) to come to Dublin especially to conduct the Radio Éireann Symphony Orchestra for the premiere of his former student's work. This took place in the Gaiety Theatre on 23 October 1960. The programme for the concert also included Brahms's Second Piano Concerto and Beethoven's Seventh Symphony. In his programme note, Brian Boydell emphasized the significance of such a premiere in Irish musical life at this period:

> The first performance of this symphony will provide a unique experience in Irish musical life; for there are very few symphonies by Irish composers, and none of such proportions and seriousness of intent as this new work by Seóirse Bodley. ... In it, the composer has undoubtedly achieved a characteristic and personal idiom emancipated from the more obvious influences which could be observed in his earlier orchestral works. The harmony is astringent, arising from a closely knit contrapuntal texture, and the scoring is economical. ... With its avoidance of mere 'effects' to attract the superficial ear, its astringent and individual language, and its deep seriousness, this is undoubtedly a work which will not reveal its full power and beauty to many listeners in one performance; though few should fail to be struck by its great sense of momentum and drive, culminating in the impressive climax of the final bars.[63]

60 *Irish Independent*, 12 September 1957
61 Their other two children, Evelyn (b. 1961) and Ronan (b. 1962), were born in Dublin.
62 *Irish Press*, 13 March 1957
63 Brian Boydell, programme note, Radio Éireann programme booklet, 23 October 1960. Although the critics were present at this important premiere, they were prevented from publishing their impressions by a newspaper strike.

The symphony is in many ways Bodley's journeyman piece. It lasts about twenty minutes and its four sections are performed without a break. Despite Boydell's contention that Bodley had achieved a more personal manner of expression, the influence of Hindemith is still clearly perceptible, particularly in the writing for brass. The intervallic material of the opening ostinato in the bass and the first two bars of the first violins (bars 3–4) is subjected to extensive motivic and contrapuntal elaboration throughout the piece which demonstrates how much he had learned in Stuttgart, and the whole piece flows easily. The least persuasive section of the score is perhaps the *Adagio* movement, much of which is based on a motif that is developed in ascending sequences in the strings. After the third section, which Boydell described as a 'Scherzo and Trio' (beginning in bar 323 after a long fermata and a dramatic outburst on the solo timpani which rises from *pp* to *ff* within seven bars), the opening ideas return from bar 726 in the final section, which is marked 'Tempo I' (Ex. 7). Here, Bodley combines the thematic ideas convincingly in a *crescendo* to a dramatic close. Bodley recalled that people commented at the time that the symphony was not particularly Irish, yet people outside Ireland had said that it was a very Irish work.[64] Axel Klein detected both Austrian and Irish influences in its 'direct line from Bruckner via David, adding melodic tinges of Irish traditional music [featuring] aspects of *Urmotiv* and fugato techniques very clearly.'[65]

After his return to Dublin, Bodley settled into a busy routine of teaching, performing and composing. Between 1960 and 1962 he completed three new scores: two short choral works, *An Bás is an Bheatha* [Death and Life] (1960) and *Trí Aortha* [Three Satires] (1962) and an orchestral work, *Divertimento* (1961). *An Bás is an Bheatha*, for mixed choir was first performed on 22 January 1961 by the RÉ Singers under Rosen in the Gaiety Theatre during an orchestral concert. For this work Bodley set five Irish-language proverbs on life and death. The text of the first proverb contrasts the happy lot of a man of means with the unenviable lot of a pauper. Bodley's setting, which is marked *Allegro*, falls into two sections, the first of which describes the fortunate man who is snug in his house and loved by everyone. This features material based on two descending perfect fourths, D–A and B–F sharp, each accented and presented in unison. The interval of a fourth is crucial to the melodic and harmonic structure of much of the piece. As the upper voices hold open fourths from bar 40, the tempo slackens and we are introduced to the unfortunate man who has nothing and is universally regarded with impatience. The second song (*Andante un poco rubato*) is set for female voices only and tells expressively of the old man, weary and grey, who will pass on like the song of the lark on the mountain that fades in the sky. It is structured as a theme with three variations, with the theme introduced in canon a fourth apart and with each variation corresponding to a line of the verse. The last line, 'Imeóig

---

64 Acton, 'Interview', 121–22. Acton restated this opinion later: 'Bodley's symphony is German rather than Anglo if it is centred anywhere but Ireland'. Charles Acton, *Irish Music and Musicians* (Dublin, 1978), 1–2.
65 Axel Klein, 'Irish Composers and Foreign Education', 278. See also Axel Klein, *Die Musik Irlands im 20. Jahrhundert* (Hildesheim, 1996), 239–42.

a bhfuil beó's dtáinig riamh' [Whatever has lived or is living must learn to die] is presented on suspensions and the movement ends *pianissimo* on the word 'riamh' [passing]. The more humorous third song (*Allegro*) offers an effective contrast to the sombre mood of the second, describing how the deceitfulness of women will persist until ducks cease to swim on lakes or dogs desist from gnawing on bones. Bodley wrote of this central song that 'its rather cynical context does not, I feel, conflict with the other poems which share with it a similar style of masculine *Weltanschauung*. It makes use of the only onomatopoeic effect in the whole work, namely, the barking of the dog in line three of the text.'[66] Word painting is also evident in the melismatic use of '*Go sgaraig an lacha le linn do shnámh*' [Till the duck ceases to swim on the lake]. The fourth song (*Adagio*), for male voices, mirrors the second in its structure but reverses the order of entries with the lower bass first and uses the opening fourths inverted in the fourth line of the song. The final song (*Allegro*), like the opening song, is structured as a double fugue which treats two subjects in turn. The first subject highlights the word 'Fínis' and is based on the opening four notes of the piece, and the second is a theme derived from part of the *Dies Irae* melody on the words '*Is Críosta dár ndídean ar Shliabh Síon*' [And Christ protect us on Mount Sion]. Both fugal subjects are combined dramatically as the cycle builds towards a unison *fff* climax on these words (Ex. 8).

The *Divertimento* for string orchestra was completed in October 1961 and was first performed by the RÉ Symphony Orchestra under Tibor Paul on 15 June 1962 in the Phoenix Hall in Dublin (Bodley's colleague in UCD, Anthony Hughes, was the soloist in Mozart's Piano Concerto in C minor, K. 491). It is in five movements: *March, Pastorale, Gigue, Cavatina,* and *Rondo*. The first of these opens 'Alla Marcia' in a similar style to the *Music for Strings* almost ten years earlier, with a walking bass in crotchets. The material is similar across all the movements and mostly treated contrapuntally, the contrasts in the piece lying more in the mood of each movement. The instrumental writing is notably more experimental than in Bodley's previous orchestral works, with its frequent recourse to colouristic string effects. Its musical language is also more adventurous, and the piece also displays his first tentative foray into using all twelve notes of the chromatic scale within a theme (i.e. Gigue, bars 50–54). The work was very well received. Acton noted its 'impalpably Irish feel', despite the absence of 'folksiness or obvious nationalism', and warmly praised the 'passionate beauty' of the *Cavatina*.[67] There were many subsequent performances or broadcasts of this work under either Tibor Paul or Bodley himself.

66 Bodley, analytical remarks in the facsimile score, Contemporary Music Centre, Ireland
67 *Irish Times*, 16 June 1962

Ex. 7 Symphony No. 1, 726–37

Ex. 8 *An Bás is an Bheatha*, V, 114–25

In 1961, Bodley took over the conductorship of one of Dublin's leading amateur choirs, the Culwick Choral Society, which had been founded in 1898 by the composer and conductor James Culwick. Bodley conducted the choir for ten years until 1971, and it was widely acknowledged that under his direction that choir attained new heights of artistic excellence.[68] During this decade, the choir presented the Irish premieres of Michael Tippett's cantata *Crown of the Year* in December 1963, Carl Orff's *Catulli Carmina* in December 1966, Britten's *War Requiem* (with RTÉ personnel under Paul) in April 1967 in St. Patrick's Cathedral, and Stravinsky's *Les Noces* in May 1969. The choir regularly performed with some of the most distinguished Irish artists of the period, including the mezzo-soprano Bernadette Greevy and the pianist Charles Lynch.[69] In 1968, the Irish poet Brendan Kennelly, with whom Bodley would later collaborate on a number of works, evoked the atmosphere at one of these concerts in a poem he presented to the composer:

The Singers

They take their places on
The stage. Shuffling into
Symmetry, it seems they
Hardly know what to do
In their coloured disarray.

They begin to be a form;
Ordered in their silence now
They wait. He comes from the right.
A dark manipulator,
Dramatic in the light

That drowns us into one
And shows him in command,
A certain harmony in his head,

68 An essay in the publication prepared to mark the choir's hundredth anniversary characterizes the period of Bodley's tenure as having marked 'a new era in the choir's music-making': see Jane Clare, Magdalen O'Connell, Ann Simmons, eds.,*The Culwick Choral Society Celebrates One Hundred Years: 1898–1998* (Dublin, 1998), 17.
69 The list of singers, guest artists and accompanists which Bodley worked with constitutes a snapshot of musical performers active in Dublin during the 1960s: singers William Young, Frank Patterson, Hazel Morris, Richard Cooper, Gerald Duffy, Mabel McGrath, Patrick Ring, Carmel O'Byrne, Peter McBrien, Mary Sheridan, Minnie Clancy, Marie Frewen, Arthur Moyse, Molly Reynolds, Ann Moran, Joseph Dalton, June Croker, Reggie Lawless, and Tomás Ó Súilleabháin; guest artists Doris Keogh (flute), The Testore Quartet, John Beckett (harpsichord), The Prieur Ensemble, The Stedfast Band, Veronica McSwiney, Mercedes Bolger (harp); and accompanists Deirdre McNulty, Gerard Shanahan, Gerard Gillen, David Lee, John O'Conor, Gillian Smith, Audrey Carr, and John O'Sullivan.

Raising a controlling hand,
Expressing what cannot be said.

The singers celebrate
The world that moves
Inexorably among
Its hates and loves,
Praise is at the heart of the song.

The clumsy city tolerates
Human words and cries of birds,
Concord radiates his face
As he leads the singers towards
Pinnacles of grace.

Nothing can be separate now
All is unified
Orion and Mars join hands with us
Tyrants time and space are dead
The hour is marvellous

And then it's over. There's
A silence eloquent as death;
As harmony withdraws
Hundreds seem to catch their breath.
Applause, applause!

Smiling singers bow and break,
He bows upon the stand,
They (good ladies, gentlemen)
Seem the happiest in the land.
Confusion spawns and teems again.

Only a year after being appointed conductor of the Culwick Choral Society, Bodley was commissioned to write a short unaccompanied choral work for the Seminar on Contemporary Choral Music as part of the 1963 Cork International Choral Festival, which, though founded only a few years before, had rapidly established itself as one of the most notable international festivals of its kind. These Seminars had been inaugurated the previous year by Aloys Fleischmann, the founder of the Festival, and were held under the auspices of the Department of Music at University College, Cork. They were designed to give contemporary music a prominent place in the festival and to encourage contemporary composers to participate in the performance and discussion of modern choral writing, particularly for amateur choirs.[70] Bodley recalls the seminars as being one of the highlights of the event, largely due to Fleischmann's gift at communicating his analytical insights to the audience.[71] The other composers commissioned that year were Egon Wellesz and Flor Peeters. Zoltán Kodály had also been commissioned to write for the 1963 festival but could not attend. The score that he contributed, *Ode for Music* was consequently not included in the Seminar, although it was performed on another occasion during the Festival.[72] Peeters was present to hear the premiere of his *In Convertendo Dominus*, a setting of Psalm 125, as was Wellesz for his *Laus Nocturna*. Bodley supplied *Trí Aortha* [Three Satires] for mixed-voice choir, settings of humorous old Irish texts, which he completed in October 1962. They were analysed at the seminar on 18 May 1963 by Fleischmann in a morning session, before receiving their first public performance by the Culwick Choral Society under Bodley's direction that night in the City Hall. The Cork musician Seán Neeson, in a report for the *Musical Times*, wrote that Bodley's 'fine economical craftsmanship' achieved 'titillating effects',[73] with the *Irish Times* reviewer also using the words 'fine craftsmanship' whilst noting, however, that its performance 'scarcely matched its imaginative quality'.[74]

Bodley enjoyed the challenge of writing for amateurs, noting that 'it is one skill to write for a professional choir that is highly trained and can sing anything or very nearly anything, but it is quite another to be able to write interesting music that can be sung by a really good amateur choir.'[75] His intimate understanding of choral music and his experience he gained from earlier works written for professional choirs such as *An Bás is an Bheatha* is in evidence throughout. In the *Trí Aortha*, he uses major and minor triads juxtaposed and superimposed within contrapuntal contexts to generate some dissonant effects while still keeping the music simple enough for an amateur choir to sing confidently. The title of the first satire, *Mug, cupán, agus píopa* ... is a truncated version of the opening three lines 'Mug, cupán, agus píopa | tá annso sgríobhtha ar a leabaidh; | is olc a bpáirt re Maoilre' [A mug, a cup and a pipe | are inscribed on Maoilre's grave]. It describes the three 'characters' who discuss Maoilre and declare frankly that they don't think much of him. 'It would suit me', says the mug, 'if he never woke again. He often left my belly

---

70 See de Barra, *Aloys Fleischmann*, 112–14, for an outline of the history and aims of the Seminar on Contemporary Choral Music, and also Ruth Fleischmann, ed., *Cork International Choral Festival 1954–2004: A Celebration* (Cork, 2004).

71 Interview with Anne Fleischmann in Ruth Fleischmann, ed., *Cork International Choral Festival 1954–2004: A Celebration* (Cork, 2005), 296–97

72 See de Barra, *Aloys Fleischmann*, 114

73 *Musical Times*, 104, 1445 (July 1963), 495

74 *Irish Times*, 21 May 1963. The *Cork Examiner* disagreed, however, describing it as 'a first-class performance' (20 May 1963). The work was subsequently recorded by the RÉ Singers under Hans Waldemar Rosen for an LP made by the New Irish Recording Company, but this was never released.

75 Ruth Fleischmann, ed., *Cork International Choral Festival*, 297

empty long days and nights.' 'Me, likewise', says the pipe. 'Though he kissed me often enough he burned my mouth each time, and I lost my head in his pocket.' 'Quiet!' says the cup, 'you foolish, deluded pair. He'll rise in his health again — it's only a touch of drink.'[76] The piece ends with an A major root position chord superimposed over a 6/4 D minor triad set to a derisive 'ha ha ha'. The note in common between these two superimposed triads, A, serves as a link to begin the slow middle satire, 'Do Bhádhasa Uair' [The Lament of a Bald Man for his Departed Hair] (Ex. 9), a text that Bodley had already set in the early 1950s for baritone and piano:

> Once I was yellow-haired, ringleted; now my head puts forth only a short grey crop. I would rather have locks of the raven's colour grow on my head than a short hoary crop. Courting belongs not to me, for I wile no women; tonight my hair is hoar; I shall not be as once I was.[77]

This gentle piece is mostly imitative and at the close settles in a mood of wry resignation on a quiet unison E (at the words 'I shall not be as once I was'). Again the link to the third and final satire, the lively Laoi Cháinte an Tobac [Song of Complaint about Tobacco] is conceived pragmatically for an amateur choir and it opens in a similar fashion to the first piece. Here, changes of time signatures generate the syncopation for most of the song. Ironically, the commission was sponsored by the tobacco firm of W. D. & H. O. Wills.[78]

Within the space of a single year, Bodley would display quite a dramatic change of style, as a comparison of these moderately advanced Trí Aortha of October 1962 and his more avant-garde Prelude, Toccata and Epilogue of autumn 1963 shows clearly. Although he was now a highly regarded composer at home, as he entered his thirties he sought a fresh creative stimulus which would enable him to develop a more modernist and international musical language. He would find it in Darmstadt.

---

76 Translation by Thomas Kinsella in An Duanaire 1600–1900 Poems of the Dispossessed, ed. Seán Ó Tuama and Thomas Kinsella (Mountrath, 1981), 39
77 Translation from Gerard Murphy, ed., Early Irish Lyrics: Eight to Twelfth Century (Oxford, 1956), 169. Murphy notes that the poem probably dates from 1200 (240).
78 This final song was recorded separately by Corkfest Records on CD in 1994 by Cór Naomh Mhuire under Fiontán Ó Murchú (see Appendix II).

Ex. 9 Trí Aortha: Do Bhádhasa Uair

2. Embracing Modernism

In 1962 Bodley was the recipient of the Macaulay Fellowship, a bursary awarded annually on a competitive basis by the Irish Arts Council to enable young creative artists to advance their liberal education. At the time, this bursary was worth £1,000, a sum of money which enabled Bodley to attend various new music events in Germany and Holland, as well as travel to London to see the Hamburg Staatsoper's productions of Alban Berg's operas *Wozzeck* and *Lulu* (he recalls attending every performance of the latter). Most significantly for his future creative development, however, this bursary made it possible for him to attend the renowned Internationale Ferienkurse für Neue Musik [International Summer Courses for New Music] in Darmstadt each summer from 1963 to 1965. At these courses, which were generally regarded as one of the most significant educational initiatives of their kind, he was exposed to the most complex forms of integral serialism, aleatoricism, and electronic music. He also had the opportunity to hear many of the leading composers of the day — including Pierre Boulez, Henri Pousseur, Luciano Berio, Karlheinz Stockhausen, Milton Babbitt, György Ligeti, Mauricio Kagel, and Bruno Maderna — analyzing their works and expounding the techniques on which they were based. Amongst the lectures he attended were an analysis by Ligeti of his *Apparitions*, *Atmosphères*, and *Aventures* and by Stockhausen of his *Gruppen*. Many of these composers presented academic papers at the concurrent conferences, which also featured eminent performers, musicologists and philosophers such as Earle Brown, Carl Dahlhaus, Aloys Kontarsky and Theodor Adorno. The various frank opinions which he noted in his copies of the programme booklets from 1963 to 1965 testify to his close engagement with the talks, workshops, and the many concerts of contemporary works held during the two-week courses. Bodley recalls that Darmstadt seemed 'a totally enclosed world' for the duration of the summer school. He remembered 'on one occasion having to go into the nearest village to buy a needle and thread to sew on a button. As I entered the everyday world of the shop I remember thinking: people do exist after all who care nothing about series or structures or aleatoric music.[1] He has also described his period at Darmstadt as 'a most exciting and stimulating time', which led him to think that 'serial and post-serial music was almost the only way that music could develop'.[2] However, looking back on his experiences there, Bodley feels he was not so much influenced by other composers' music, but rather by aspects of their techniques and the lectures by composers explaining and analyzing their works.[3] In an interview in 1979, he recalled that

> in Darmstadt there had to be a new 'ism' each year [but] what has really mattered in the long run is less the style in which a particular piece was composed than whether it is good or not in terms of that style. It's how you use an 'ism' rather the 'ism' which you choose that's important.[4]

It was therefore more the spirit of Darmstadt that inspired him rather than any specific composer or musical idiom. His encounters with the music of the post-1945 avant-garde led him to embark on a series of modernist works which have been described as the 'most adventurous Irish music of the decade'.[5] Bodley's knowledge of contemporary techniques and composers also informed his teaching, and he played an important role in raising wider awareness in Ireland of international musical developments. He started to give lectures on the music of figures such as Xenakis, Lachenmann, Cage, Boulez, Cardew, Ligeti, and Berio at UCD, and had a particular interest in Spectral Music and the music of Gérard Grisey. He was also the first person to introduce courses on electro-acoustic and computer music into the curriculum of an Irish music department. Bodley's enthusiasm for new music communicated itself to many of his students, a number of whom became distinguished composers in their own right. Raymond Deane, one of the most successful Irish composers of his generation, recalls that an abiding memory of courses taken as a music student in UCD in the early 1970s was that on twentieth-century music given by Bodley.[6] The Irish musicologist Bernard Harris noted that 'the philosophical and aesthetic influences of [Bodley's] music have been far-reaching for other, younger, Irish composers and will no doubt remain so'.[7]

In the autumn of 1963, after returning from his first visit to Darmstadt, Bodley wrote a short solo piano piece, *Prelude, Toccata and Epilogue*, which explores for the first time a more avant-garde musical language in its experimentation with pianistic textures

1   Klein, 'Irish Composers and Foreign Education', 282
2   Klein, 'Irish Composers and Foreign Education', 282
3   Bodley in conversation with the author, 12 April 2000
4   *Sunday Independent*, 25 March 1979
5   Hughes, 'Bodley, Seóirse', 838
6   Patrick Zuk, *Raymond Deane* (Dublin, 2006), 2
7   Bernard Harris, 'Contemporary Irish Music: A Survey', in Birgit Bramsback and Martin Croghan, eds., *Anglo-Irish and Irish Literature: Aspects of Language and Culture* (Stockholm, 1989), 209

and sonorities. This was first performed, in UCD in 1964 by Deirdre McNulty, and has been played regularly since, having been taken up by a number of distinguished pianists including John O'Conor and John McCabe.[8] The outer movements, the Prelude and Epilogue, should both last a maximum of one minute and feature seconds and thirds played tremolando, gradually rising and fading from ppp to fff to ppp, and performed rallentando and accelerando in opposition with crossed hands. These end with a pedal trill followed by a single bar (Adagio in the Prelude; Allegro tempestuoso in the Epilogue) of five major thirds widely separated and a soundlessly depressed 'sonority' with the right hand of all the notes between middle C and the G above (in the Epilogue this also requires a pedal trill). Bodley describes the central Toccata as

> a brilliant piece using both themes and fragmentary interjections. Though the style is basically linear it exploits a wide range of piano sonority. Throughout the Toccata special use is made of dramatic contrast of ideas but all linked together by the intervals on which the music is based.[9]

In her analysis of the work, Hazel Farrell notes that it reveals 'a fascinating and perhaps unconscious reluctance to totally eschew tonality as exemplified in his consistent use of quasi-tonal intervals ... to imply a tonal basis within an atonal context'.[10] She identifies various interval classes and some instances of pitch centricity to underpin her argument. On the basis of her findings, she suggests that the Toccata falls into three main sections, each of which features recurring pitch-class sets. The tremolo thirds from the Prelude are much in evidence, particularly from bar 43 in the bass, a tremolo C–E which can be played ad libitum as accel-cresc or dim-rall. The Toccata has a lively rhythmic drive and some of the energetic syncopated writing at times recalls Hindemith's Ludus Tonalis. Its forward momentum is occasionally interrupted by brief passages of a more gentle and reflective nature, and the keyboard writing features numerous grace notes and spare pointillistic textures. In the context of this material, however, the glissandi over the entire compass of the instrument which Bodley introduces later sound somewhat incongruous (Ex. 10).

---

8   The work was recorded by the Irish pianist Charles Lynch on an LP issued by the New Irish Recording Company in 1971, which also featured piano works by Aloys Fleischmann, Brian Boydell, Gerard Victory, and James Wilson. This LP was reviewed by Frank Dawes in the Musical Times, 114, 1566 (August 1973), 802; and also by Acton who considered Bodley's piece to be 'a convincing marriage of modern ideas and musical excitement' (Irish Times, 31 January 1972).

9   Bodley, programme booklet, Dublin Festival of Twentieth-Century Music, 1972

10 Hazel Farrell, Aspects of Pitch Structure and Pitch Selection in Post-War Irish Composition: An Analytical Study of Tonal and Post-Tonal Referential Collections in Selected Works by Irish Composers, unpublished dissertation, Mary Immaculate College, University of Limerick (2002), 19–20. See also Klein, Die Musik Irlands im 20. Jahrhundert, 244–49.

Ex. 10 *Prelude, Toccata and Epilogue, 72–118*

The influence of Webern is pronounced in Bodley's next work, the Chamber Symphony No. 1 of 1964, whose textures are distinctly reminiscent of the Austrian composer's Symphony Op. 21. Certain Neo-classical and syncopated features of Stravinsky's *Dumbarton Oaks* are also evident, another composer who was clearly an influence on Bodley around this time. Originally called 'Symphony for Chamber Orchestra', this is the first of his two chamber symphonies (the second was written in 1982). The work is in four movements and is scored for flute, bassoon, horn, harp, piano, percussion (timpani, xylophone, vibraphone, tambourine, snare-drum, cymbals, hi-hat, tam-tam and tubular bells) and string quartet. Twelve-tone techniques are employed in all the movements except the third, the *Elegy*, and are used exclusively in the second movement.[11] The work opens with an eighteen-bar *Largo* (which is recalled very briefly at the end of the work). This leads to an *Allegro* which contains much writing for string quartet alone and uses imitative and canonic procedures. The row is presented at the outset in the first two bars of the *Largo* between the first violin, harp and vibraphone (Ex. 11).

Bodley told Acton in 1970 that it was 'the rhythmic thing [...] that really sent me in the *avant garde* direction'. In the first movement of this Symphony, the character of the main *Allegro* theme becomes 'more and more frenetic in an effort to get away from the rhythmic straightjacket [sic]'.[12] Extensive use is made of changing time signatures and cross-rhythms to generate excitement. The energetic second movement (also an *Allegro*) is cast in ternary form. An inversion of the row is heard at the outset, being presented on the second violin (with the B and D sharp both being repeated three times consecutively). Frederick May, who wrote the programme note for the premiere, considered the third movement *Elegy* (*Adagio*) to be the most striking movement of the work. Bodley had suggested to May that the movement may have been unconsciously influenced by the film, *Hiroshima, mon amour*, which he had recently seen.[13] This film, which has a screenplay by Marguerite Duras and was directed by Alain Resnais, tells the story of a French actress who performs the role of a nurse in a film shot in Hiroshima after the Second World War. While there, she falls in love with a Japanese man who reminds her of her first love, a German soldier, with whom she had become involved after the German occupation of Nevers. Certainly the opening has a hauntingly oriental flavour with its quiet use of suspended cymbals played with a soft stick and the tam-tam and the prominent use of harp and flute later in the movement. The *Elegy* (Ex. 12) is built on a short plaintive melody characterized by a repeated-note opening followed by wide leaps, which is developed imitatively and later returns insistently in the timpani. The movement ends with repeated notes in the horn, flute, bassoon and cello, accompanied by the cymbals and a final *ppp* tam-tam note. The tension of the *Elegy* is maintained by a *lunga pausa* which leads *attacca* into the final movement, a lively and jaunty *Allegro*. This is also somewhat Stravinskian in its neo-classical contrapuntal textures. It features prominent flute, horn, bassoon solos and a long cello solo which leads at letter G to the unexpected entry of the tubular bells, which have been reserved throughout the piece for this moment. At letter J, a fermata on the note G in the cello introduces a brief *Largo* passage which repeats the opening two bars of the Symphony, but in a slightly altered rhythm. The tempo then picks up again for the final 13 bars, which recall the opening of the movement. It concludes with string *glissandi* that culminate on a *sforzando tutti* chord.

---

11 Malcolm Barry also noted that along with a 'tendency towards episodic construction is an ear for sonority that established the composer as a willing acquiescent to the demands of a language that can, all too easily, become anonymous. To establish an identity in this idiom, as Bodley discovered, the material demands some distinctive character' ('Examining the Great Divide', *Soundpost*, 16 (1983), 17).

12 Acton, 'Interview', 121. Bodley added, 'The trouble with all works which are based on motor rhythms is the difficulty of stopping the motor once you have got it going. Eventually I found that I had landed myself beyond the field of metrical rhythms as such into the field of irregular rhythm.'

13 May, RTÉ programme booklet, 7 February 1965

Ex. 11 Chamber Symphony No. 1, I, 1–9

Ex. 12 Chamber Symphony No. 1, III, 1–32

Chamber Symphony No. 1 was first performed in 1964 by members of the RTÉ Symphony Orchestra conducted by Bodley, having been selected by Radio Éireann to represent Ireland at that year's International Rostrum of Composers organized by the UNESCO Radio Station conference in Paris.[14] Tibor Paul conducted the same orchestra in the first broadcast performance on RTÉ radio on 6 October of that year, and also gave the first public performance on 7 February 1965 in the Gaiety Theatre, Dublin.

In April 1965, Bodley completed another major work, *Never to Have Lived is Best*, a cycle of W. B. Yeats settings for soprano solo and orchestra. This was commissioned by RTÉ to celebrate the Yeats Centenary and was first performed on 11 June by Veronica Dunne and the RTÉ Symphony Orchestra under Tibor Paul in the St. Francis Xavier Hall, Dublin. The poems trace the passage of life from childhood to death. Bodley selected the five poems from the collections *The Green Helmet and Other Poems* (1910), *Responsibilities* (1914), and *The Tower* (1928). When he was featured in the Radio Éireann series 'Composer's Workshop' on 13 February 1969, Bodley described the cycle as 'a sort of a satire', but added that it was 'a satire in depth'.[15] The work was written very quickly within the space of six weeks. Bodley worked closely with the soprano Dunne who gave a splendidly committed and dramatic performance. Dunne made the part her own, and was the soloist again in January 1971 at another performance in the St. Francis Xavier Hall under Pierre Michel le Conte.

The first movement, 'The Dolls', displays the characteristic angular features of the vocal line, which is predominantly syllabic. High B flats appear at critical moments: at the words 'looks at the cradle and *bawls*', 'out-screams the whole *shelf*', 'head upon shoulder *leant*' (with 'My Dear, my dear, O Dear' repeating this central pitch). The busy orchestral accompaniment emphasizes dark instrumental timbres, yet remains quite sparse. Unlike many of Bodley's later vocal works, considerable use is made of word-painting to point the text: for instance, in the second movement, 'The Friends of His Youth', the

---

14 The work was subsequently recorded in 1974 by the New Irish Chamber Orchestra with Bodley conducting and again in 2009 with the RTÉ National Symphony Orchestra under Robert Houlihan (See Appendix II).
15 RTÉ Recording Library

opening reference to 'laughter' is illustrated by a manic melismatic outburst. In the third movement, 'The Mask', the solo singer must depict both voices of an emotionally intense dialogue between a man and a woman, requiring her to characterise them by singing in different registers and with different timbres. The vocal line is highly taxing, ranging from an A below middle C to a high B flat:

[Man:]	Put off that mask of burning gold
	With emerald eyes.
[Woman:]	O no, my dear, you make so bold
	To find if hearts be wild and wise,
	And yet not cold.
[Man:]	I would but find what's there to find,
	Love or deceit.
[Woman:]	It was the mask engaged your mind,
	And after set your heart to beat,
	Not what's behind.
[Man:]	But lest you are my enemy,
	I must enquire.
[Woman:]	O no, my dear, let all that be;
	What matter, so there is but fire
	In you, in me? [16]

The man is accompanied by strings and the woman, in contrast, by percussion, harp, piano, celesta, glockenspiel, vibraphone and solo cello. The fourth movement, 'The Coming of Wisdom with Time' lasts a mere twenty-one bars and accompanies the voice with wind and brass alone. It opens with a quotation on the oboe of the famous BACH motif (the German musical letter names B–A–C–H corresponding to the pitches B flat–A–C–B), repeated by the soprano on her opening words, 'Though leaves are many' (Bodley invokes the name of Bach here to symbolize 'wisdom' perhaps). Bodley's annotations in his copy of the Yeats poems reveals that he gave careful thought to the possibilities for expressive word-painting afforded by the text. In the energetic final movement, 'From *Oedipus at Colonus*', a line from which Bodley chose as the cycle's title, the soprano's 'toneless' words are picked up and sustained by various instruments. When the soloist enunciates the word 'kiss', for example, Bodley has the suspended cymbal take over the concluding sibilant consonant with soft sticks (Ex. 13).

16 W. B. Yeats, *Collected Poems* (London, 1976), 106

Ex. 13 *Never to Have Lived is Best, V, 79–end*

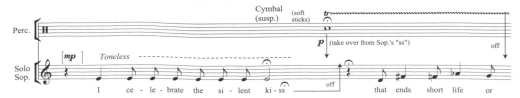

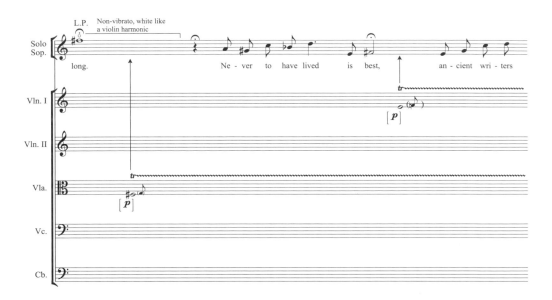

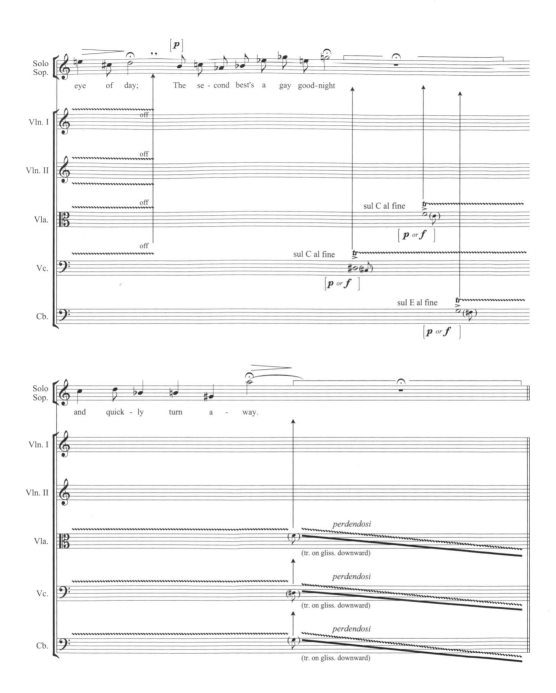

Bodley's command of dramatic vocal writing and orchestral colour in *Never to Have Lived is Best* suggests that his gifts would also have been well-suited to writing music for the stage.

However, he never wrote an opera, although he had considered at one point setting Yeats's final play Purgatory, which depicts the tragic relationship between a father and his son.[17]

Bodley recalls feeling that he had made a significant breakthrough with the composition of this song-cycle, but it was followed by a protracted period of uncertainty:

> I actually stopped composing for about nine months ... and I spent the time studying new techniques, all sorts of serial techniques. ... I wrote a number of studies and various pieces that I have never released. Perhaps this is partly because they are not so terribly good — at least I've never wanted them to be heard in public, so they remain lying in my desk.[18]

So, in the autumn of 1965, after his three summers in Darmstadt, Bodley ceased composing for six months to reflect on the avant-garde techniques which he had studied. He would emerge from this period of self-reflection to write Configurations, a piece which Acton deemed to be 'probably the most avant-garde music ever presented live in Dublin'.[19] Responding to a commission from RTÉ for the subscription concert series 1966/67, Bodley submitted this new orchestral piece, Configurations, in early November 1966. This was premiered on 29 January 1967 by the RTÉ Symphony Orchestra under Tibor Paul at the Gaiety Theatre, Dublin.[20] Configurations is scored for an expanded orchestra which included two harps, piano, celesta and electric guitar, as well as a large percussion section comprising chimes, Chinese box, two sets of handbells, sleigh bells, tom-toms, xylophone and vibraphone. Bodley supplies detailed indications of how these large forces are to be disposed on the stage (Ex. 14). The string section is divided into two separate string orchestras, the second of which is placed behind the first but in a reversed seating arrangement (i.e. first violins on the right of the conductor, etc.). The electric guitar, celesta and piano are placed at the front of the stage and the two harps on opposite sides towards the back of the ensemble. The leaders of each string orchestra should also be provided with stopwatches. In Darmstadt, Bodley had had the chance to hear Stockhausen analyse his spatially organized Gruppen for three orchestras of 1955–57 and this undoubtedly had a profound influence on his own score.[21]

---

17 Acton, 'Interview', 118
18 RTÉ Recording Library: interview, 13 February 1969
19 Irish Times, 30 January 1967
20 Later that year a recording of the work was played on a continuous loop in the musical section of the Paris Biennale Exhibition at the Musée d'Art Moderne.
21 At a performance at the RTÉ Living Music Festival on 27 October 2002 in Dublin's Helix Centre with the National Symphony Orchestra of Ireland conducted by Zsolt Nagy (the recording used for distribution by the CMC), Bodley's integral spatial instructions were not adhered to, which compromised the intended effect.

Ex. 14 *Configurations*: Disposition of Orchestra

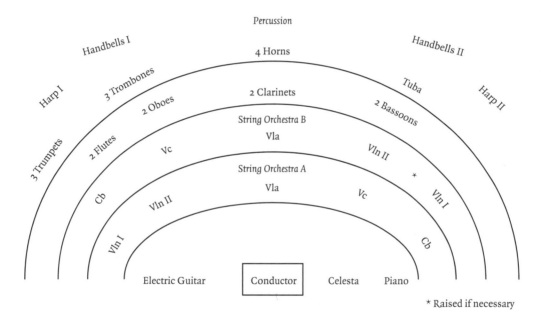

Ex. 15 Configurations, III, 1–23

* ◄—► = play the note anywhere within the indicated time-length

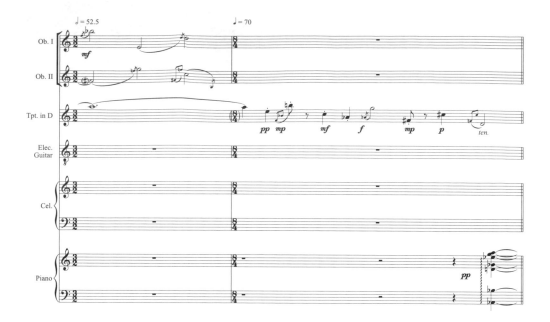

Bodley recalls that the work was written following a period of intense study of the music of the avant-garde and he applied serial technique 'to all aspects of the composition, including the rhythmic structure and dynamics'.[22] However, he recalled that at the time he 'deliberately avoided joining the group of composers who gave [integral serialism] total allegiance; I felt a need to retain my own individuality, not to become just another member of a group.'[23] Given that a 'configuration' is the structural arrangement of constituent elements and the form as determined by the arrangement and interconnection of these elements, the title of the work seems most apt. Within its five short movements, lasting approximately twenty minutes in total, the entire piece is made up of a succession of linked, yet apparently discrete multiple elements. The striking orchestral sonorities of the work's opening movement owe much to the post-Webern Darmstadt school, employing a wide variety of colouristic effects, dramatic brass and wind punctuations and sudden pauses. The opening *Allegro* establishes this fragmented sound-world. The second movement opens with a tenor saxophone flourish, followed at letter A by horn *glissandi*. Here Bodley makes, in his own words, 'extensive use of free rhythm' and the

22 Bodley, programme booklet, RTÉ Living Music Festival, 27 October 2002. In a recent article he commented on this period: 'One of the interesting aspects of this experience was the positive effect of the destructive aspects of working with total serialism. Once I engaged with the irregular rhythmic procedures that resulted from this method I realized the benefit of being forced away from evenly balanced construction and obliged to confront the irregular structuring of musical compositions.' Seóirse Bodley, 'The Claims of Conformity', in Patricia Flynn, ed., *Teaching the Unteachable? The Role of Composition in Music Education* (Waterford, 2009), 37.

23 Bodley, 'The Claims of Conformity', 37

'inner tension' created leads to a conclusion with very dramatic brass chords played *sfp* with a crescendo to *fff* which almost drown out the handbells, triangle, cymbals and sleigh bells. Malcolm Barry suggests that in this movement the 'several moments of great expressive potential [which are] cut off brutally by percussion … is successful both in itself and, interestingly, as a metaphor for the clash Bodley obviously felt between "the system" and his own natural lyricism'.[24]

The third movement (Ex. 15) opens with the lower strings of string orchestras A and B exchanging fragmentary rhythmic and melodic ideas and two oboes present staggered serial lines. The solo trumpet leads with a note-row into an aleatoric passage at letter C where four sections are to be played by trumpet, electric guitar, piano and celesta in any order within exactly forty-two beats of crotchet = 46.6 (whereby the latter two instruments, however, are instructed to play their sections in the same order). At letter D, while the two oboes engage in four bars of duet, the leader of string orchestra A must direct the chord for the first and second violins to be sustained anywhere between nine and eighteen seconds. The players may switch at random to any other note within the sonority and back immediately. This is followed in the third bar of the passage by the first and second violins of string orchestra B also sustaining a chord which this time must be held for $2x + 18$ seconds, x being equal to the number of seconds between the start of the chord and the end of Orchestra A's chord, hence the requirement for stopwatches. Again the players may switch notes at random. The solo trumpet and oboes end the movement as they began it in dialogue. The fourth movement is mainly characterized by clusters played *glissandi* in the strings and trombones under some jagged flute passages. The bustle of this movement is suspended for a short almost static middle section where the strings explore subtle sonorities of low clusters in a *pianissimo* passage marked 'sul pont./norm./sul tasto/pizz.(little)' ad libitum. The fifth and final movement features tuba solos with interpolated aleatoric passages. As the piece nears the end the gestures become ever more fragmented and pointillistic, particularly in the piano and vibraphone, before three *sforzando* chords bring the work to a close.

Configurations is an highly effective score. It was widely recognized as a major achievement by an Irish composer and indeed a milestone in the history of Irish music. In his programme note for the premiere, Gerard Gillen remarked:

> Bodley has consolidated his position as a composer who has a unique and compelling language, an impressive technical mastery with which to convey his ideas, and a lively imagination ever questing for new and unexplored avenues of expression. … [He] has decidedly taken his place among the most avant-garde of contemporary composers.[25]

24 Barry, 'Examining the Great Divide', 17
25 RTÉ programme booklet, 29 January 1967

One of the most notable features of Bodley's scores from this period onwards is his concern to evolve new types of musical notation. Many of them make use of a variety of symbols, which are usually explained in a preface to the score.[26] Some of these are used to indicate relative durations. Bodley uses diagonal strokes through note-stems, for example, to indicate notes of short duration (the greater the number of strokes, the shorter the duration), while square note heads on minims and semibreves are used to indicate longer durations. The approximate lengths of pauses are indicated by a series of semicircles or half-boxes containing a dot (see Exs. 17 and 18); and tails on pauses are used mainly where an attack enters in another part during the pause. He also uses N to indicate normal vibrato and the symbol ⊥ for non-vibrato whereby diagonal lines on either side of ⊥ are added to indicate *molto vibrato* (Ex. 16). These can be combined to indicate a sudden *crescendo* with vibrato. The end, or in some cases, the beginning, of a note is marked with arrows relative to other parts (Ex. 13). He uses numbers in diamond boxes to indicate conductor's beats in bars without time signatures or to show how an event takes place at any point within a time limit specified by horizontal arrows.

In 1968, Bodley was invited to attend the International Music Congress, which was held in New York and Washington between 6 and 15 September. He heard concerts featuring the music of Aaron Copland, Milton Babbitt and Ravi Shankar during a very full programme of events for the Congress, which was jointly hosted by the International Music Council, the International Association of Music Libraries, and the US National Commission for UNESCO. Later that year, he completed another major work, his String Quartet No. 1,[27] which was written at the suggestion of David Lillis, the leader of the recently formed RTÉ String Quartet.[28] This ensemble gave the first performance on 6 January 1969 at a concert held during the Dublin Festival of Twentieth-Century Music. The premiere of Bodley's first essay in the genre of the string quartet was a very significant occasion and many reviewers evidently experienced difficulty in evaluating the score. Acton, while freely admitting that he was out of his depth in attempting to come to terms with its musical idiom, conceded, however, that there were 'a few moments and passages of quite lovely illumination of an otherwise misty prospect'.[29] Felix Aprahamian, who had come to Dublin to review the Festival for the *Sunday Times*, was less impressed, however, and found the work as 'tiresome [and] as frustrating as flickering traffic lights'.[30] Ronald Crichton, writing in

26 See, for example, the table of signs for the three piano pieces, *Prelude Toccata and Epilogue*, *The Narrow Road to the Deep North*, and *Aislingí* given in Ó Cuinneagáin, *The Piano Music of Seóirse Bodley*, 127–30. A three-page summary of many of the signs specific to his music which he developed in the mid to late 1960s appears in the preface to his scores for *Meditations on Lines from Patrick Kavanagh* (1971) and *September Preludes* (1973).
27 The following discussion of the quartet draws on the present writer's article 'An Irishman in Darmstadt: Seóirse Bodley's String Quartet No. 1 (1968)', in Gareth Cox and Axel Klein, eds., *Irish Musical Studies 7: Irish Music in the Twentieth Century* (Dublin, 2003), 94–108.
28 Bodley in correspondence with the author, 22 February 1999
29 *Irish Times*, 7 January 1969
30 *Sunday Times*, 12 January 1969

the *Financial Times*, confessed to finding the quartet 'long and grim', but conceded that it gave the impression of 'a serious if partly misguided attempt at communicating genuine experience'.[31] Although other reviewers responded more favourably, these reactions are to some extent comprehensible given the extreme complexity of this score, which as Malcolm Barry has remarked, represents 'a peak of abstraction unique in Bodley's output'.[32]

In his programme note for the premiere, the composer stated that he thought of the first movement as 'September Music No. 1' and that he intended it to be 'the first of a series of projected works which somehow reflect the significance of that month [for him], not only that month externally [but] also an attitude'.[33] During an RTÉ radio programme in February 1969 Bodley further noted a certain resemblance between his working method in the quartet and *Never to Have Lived is Best*, in the sense that he was attempting to explore the potential of the voice and the string quartet.[34] Bodley placed the 'accent on process and activity' rather than form, claiming that 'it's perhaps the "what" and the "how" rather than the end result which are important'.[35] The quartet is essentially linear and melodic, and it is interesting to note that Bodley has stated that, although his radically different second string quartet written almost twenty-four years later in 1992 differs in style and texture from his first, both share 'beneath the surface disparities, a common emphasis on melody, and rejoice in the ability of strings to carry a singing melodic line'.[36]

The String Quartet is in two sharply contrasted movements of unequal length, the first lasting two and a half minutes and the second eleven minutes. The first movement, which is only sixty-four bars long, falls into five formal sections displaying 34 changes of time signature. Each section has a different metronome marking which gets faster as the section proceeds (slowing, however, in the final section) and Bodley's sketches indicate exact timings in minutes and seconds for each subsection of beats. The pitch material is derived from a note-row which, as Bodley's sketches reveal, was designed to form three tetrachords. However, he allows himself some freedom in manipulating the row, while retaining a large measure of serial rigour. Thus, although the first and last four pitches do not vary, Bodley allows himself to omit or move pitches 5 and 8, as well as omit or reverse the order of pitches 6 and 7 thus yielding more serial possibilities.[37] The dyad of a major third features prominently in the entire movement which, despite the serial nature of the pitch selection, lends a quasi-tonal feel to some sections. Bodley appears to be allowing his ear to guide his pen, writing in many

31 *Financial Times*, 8 January 1969

32 Barry, 'Examining the Great Divide', 18. Mary MacGoris in the *Irish Independent* noted that its 'remote and often mournful poetry is punctuated by starts of fitful gaiety and determination', *Irish Independent*, 8 January 1969. See also *Irish Times*, 12 February 1969.

33 Programme booklet, Dublin Festival of Twentieth-Century Music, 1969

34 RTÉ Recording Library: interview, 13 February 1969

35 RTÉ Recording Library: interview, 13 February 1969

36 RTÉ programme booklet, 21 May 1993

37 For a more detailed discussion of Bodley's handling of serial technique in the String Quartet, see Gareth Cox, 'An Irishman in Darmstadt: Seóirse Bodley's String Quartet No. 1 (1968)', 94–108

ways intuitively and governed by what Malcolm Barry has succinctly described as the tension between his ear and his historical consciousness.[38]

The structure of the first movement could be interpreted as a Webernesque variation form with the five sections corresponding to five variations on the row material with the theme being the row itself (no section can therefore be designated as a theme as such). The variations become more substantial as the movement progresses, with each being clearly separated from the next (with the exception of variations IV and V) by either a fermata or rests. Bodley's exploration of a wide range of timbres throughout the work should also be noted: the first violin begins with a minim (tied to a semiquaver) started *non-vibrato* leading to *molto vibrato*, followed by two semiquavers played *col legno battuto*, a semiquaver (with acciaccatura) *sul ponticello tratto*, and a final semiquaver (of the quintuplet) plucked *pizzicato* (Ex. 16). These playing techniques are also employed across the other parts in approximately the same order (although the slide up a quarter-tone in the second violin is the only instance of microtonality in the quartet, apart from some *glissandi* in the second movement). The second section begins with an imitative idea in the violins, while the third explores numerous possible permutations of a quintuplet rhythmic cell before ending with a short cello solo and a *sff* heptad. The fourth section includes many large leaps and again imitative features and leads without a break into the fifth which uses serially organized dynamic markings (Bodley's sketches contain attempts to construct series of dynamics such as '*ff*, *f*, *mf*, *mp*, *p*, *pp*' or '*sf*, *ff*, *f*, *mf*, *pp*, *p*'). If any composer's influence comes through strongly it is surely that of Pierre Boulez, in particular his serial and pointillistic techniques, which would have been discussed, at least informally, at Darmstadt. Bodley has stated that when writing the Quartet he started with a technical approach which was 'very much concerned with this whole idea of irregularity of rhythm and the question of musical impulse behind it', adding, 'the whole thing did grow … very much from a musical impulse'. [39] Of course, Bodley was open to non-musical influences as well (as he says, 'it was the Sixties after all!').[40] In his sketches he twice noted the word 'Ikebana' — the Japanese traditional art of flower arranging — as he was influenced at the time by the concepts which underlay it and its emphasis on satisfying forms. Ikebana, which purports to bring nature and humanity together, is based on a triangular pattern of three points, which represent Heaven, Man, and Earth, thus allowing for creative expression although governed by certain structural parameters. In 1970, he mentioned that he had 'the greatest respect for much of the Japanese traditional art … . [A] Japanese flower arranger has to learn a very strict discipline and spontaneity tends to come after the discipline has been learnt.[41]

38 Barry, 'Examining the Great Divide', 17
39 Acton, 'Interview', 128
40 Bodley in conversation with the author, 18 June 2001
41 Acton, 'Interview', 124–25

Ex. 16 String Quartet No. 1, I, 1–10

Ex. 17 String Quartet No. 1, II, Opening

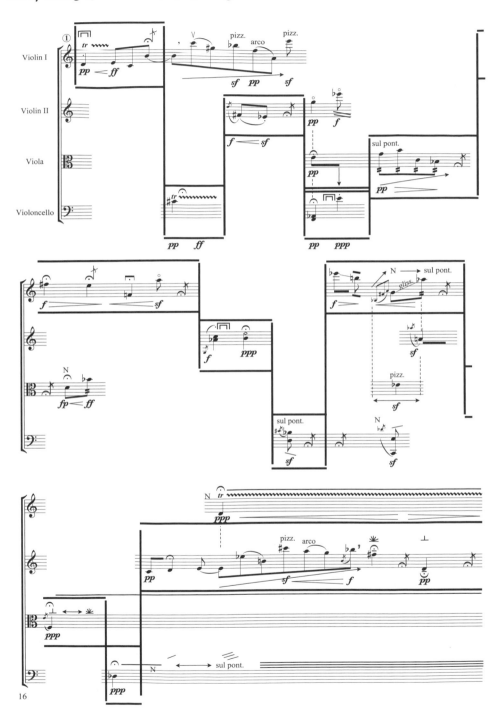

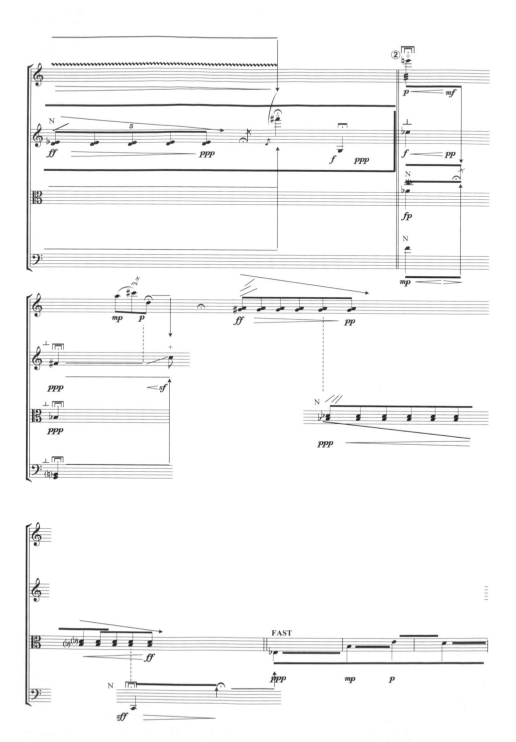

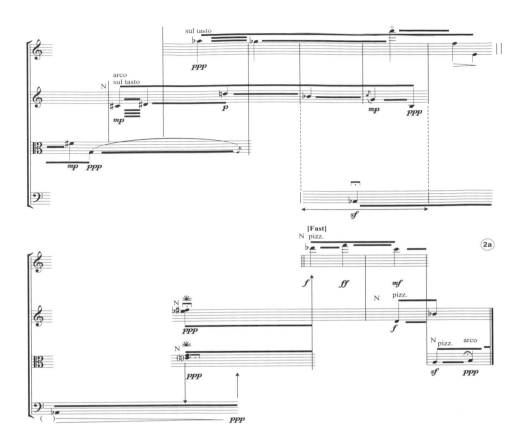

The second movement is considerably more substantial and complex than the first and is divided into eleven metrical and ametrical sections of varying length as noted in his sketches (the shortest lasting 22 seconds and the longest 110). The music in the connecting boxes is to be played consecutively, an idea which was apparently influenced by an account of Critical Path Analysis which Bodley had recently read (Ex. 17).[42] This is an organizational method of prioritizing the planning of a project where certain parts are dependent on others and therefore must be completed in a sequence (i.e. a Critical Path Action and a Non-Critical Path Action). Bodley states that 'the "critical path" moves continuously between the four instruments, while other material is at times related directly to elements that appear in the critical path but is otherwise free in its positioning. The critical path that guides the music is that contained in boxes that are directly consecutive[43] and in many ways it constitutes a method of highlighting main and subsidiary material.

42 Bodley in correspondence with the author, 22 February 1999
43 Bodley, 'The Claims of Conformity', 37

Section 8 contains a prominent passage in the first violin, which Bodley alludes to in his programme note, noting that it reminds him of a seagull he saw flying over the sands as he was cycling along the Howth Road in north Dublin in his teens.[44] Bodley has marked in his sketches for this section 'Bird!!! (flies away)' and notes the word 'Bird' again for the final section. The three exclamation marks indicate perhaps his self-consciousness about using quasi-programmatic elements. This movement also displays some aleatoric elements: hexachords (marked as 'reservoirs of tones') are presented in boxes, mainly for the lower strings as a textural device. They are to be played in random sequence while observing any of the given dynamics. Although he stated in his interview with Acton at the time that he was trying to communicate 'something which is audible to the listener',[45] it might be argued that it sometimes appears as if Bodley had learned too much in Darmstadt and is trying to fit too many techniques into a single work; this can detract from the rhythmic energy which he is clearly striving for and clouds some lyrical moments. The quartet received three more performances that year in Dublin, Belfast and Newcastle-upon-Tyne.[46] It was recorded by the New Irish Recording Company in 1973, but unfortunately the recording was never released.[47] This fine work has since suffered undeserved neglect.

The stimulus for Bodley's next work came from a rather unexpected quarter. In 1968, he was asked to provide an introduction to Robert Bruce Armstrong's seminal study *The Irish and Highland Harps* when it was reprinted.[48] This prompted him to make a study of the Irish harp and explore its expressive possibilities. These studies bore fruit the following year when he was commissioned by the harpists Anne-Marie Farrell and Helen Davies to compose *Scintillae* for two Irish harps. The piece was first performed twenty years later on 24 July 1989 during a summer course organized by Cáirde na Cruite [Friends of the Harp] at Termonfeckin in Co. Louth.[49] In *Scintillae*, Bodley employs serial techniques to generate the pitch material (an 11-note row opens the piece, distributed between both harps) with aleatoric collections being indicated in boxes. A percussive sound world is exploited using *près de la table* (plucking the strings at a point near the soundboard), playing with the fingernails, striking the strings with the palm of the hand, and *glissandi*.[50]

---

44 RTÉ programme booklet, 11 February 1969
45 Acton, 'Interview', 128
46 Anthony Phillips reported that it 'manage[d], in a bleakly cerebral way, to communicate': see *Musical Times*, 110, 1522, December 1969, 1275. A concert programme in Bodley's private collection indicates that it (or maybe a movement) appears to have also been played at a concert on 27 January 1978 in Prague by the Suk Quartet.
47 The tape of this recording is available from the Contemporary Music Centre, Ireland, which is far more faithful to the composer's intentions than the live recording of the premiere.
48 Robert Bruce Armstrong, *The Irish and Highland Harps* (Shannon, 1969 [1904]), v–vii
49 The work was later published in Sheila Larchet Cuthbert, ed., *The Irish Harp Book: A Tutor and Companion* (Dublin, 1975), 211–23.
50 See also Tristan Le Govic, *The Development of the Contemporary Repertoire for the Irish Harp*, unpublished dissertation, University College Cork (2002), 35.

The songs sung by the spirit Ariel in Shakespeare's play, *The Tempest*, have often been set by composers, from the early seventeenth-century lutenist Richard Johnson, to Thomas Arne, to the settings of Michael Tippett in 1962. In September 1969, Bodley set three of these poems, 'Come unto these yellow sands' and 'Full fathom five thy father lies' from Act I, Scene 2, and 'Where the bee sucks, there suck I' from Act V, Scene 1. *Ariel's Songs* were composed for the 1970 Dublin Festival of Twentieth-Century Music, at which they were performed by Marni Nixon (soprano) and John McCabe (piano) on 7 January. In his programme note, Bodley wrote:

> [The] irregularity of rhythm that is often used in music today seems to me particularly suited to the expression of the songs of an unearthly air-spirit, who can flit around in constant motion without the shackles of regular movement in repeated units (as in walking for instance). The character of Ariel is impulsive and spontaneous. The music has therefore been written in a special system of approximate degrees of irregularity, and density, and uses approximate pause-lengths of varying types. The system is used here for the first time as far as I know. The singer and pianist have considerable freedom, but the composer retains a strict control of the basic events. Though the songs are written in a modern idiom the treatment of the test is often illustrative — but in what I hope is a subtle way. Sometimes the illustration refers to the meaning of the words, and sometimes to the strange and wayward character of Ariel.[51]

The freedom ceded to the singer and pianist is intended to facilitate a spontaneous performance in keeping with the character of Ariel. These degrees of density and irregularity are indicated by a box (□) and circle (O), respectively containing numerical values on a scale from 0 to 5. Irregularity refers to the distances between the attacks of the notes and the scale runs from 'regular' to 'medium irregularity' to 'very irregular'. Density refers to the number of attacks relative to the length of time in which they occur (how 'spread-out' the notes are on average), and again on a scale from 0 to 5 rise from 'very low (notes few on average — well spread-out)' to medium (notes are spread in a medium-close way)' to very high (notes are very close together)'. Hazel Farrell has studied Bodley's use of serialism in this work, making detailed references to his preliminary sketches. She explains that the songs are constructed from one row and its various permutations, with the row partitioned into four bars grouped into two tetrachords and two dyads rather than using a linear statement.[52] The interval of a minor third is accorded special importance and Bodley allows himself some freedom in the ordering of the pitches with resultant repetitions and

---

51 Bodley, programme booklet, Dublin Festival of Twentieth-Century Music, 1970
52 Farrell, *Aspects of Pitch Structure and Pitch Selection in Post-War Irish Composition*, 36. For a detailed discussion of Bodley's handling of the row, see Farrell, 37ff.

incomplete statements of the row.[53] Kenneth Loveland of the *Times*, who was present at the premiere, wrote that 'here the composer had gone behind the mercurial impulsiveness of Ariel himself, using an irregular rhythmic pattern and a system of indeterminate pauses to give the singer freedom of performance within a set design.'[54]

The work of the Irish poet and novelist Patrick Kavanagh (1904–67), well-known for his depictions of rural life in Ireland, provided the inspiration for Bodley's next work, *Meditations on Lines from Patrick Kavanagh*, which was completed in 1971. This five-movement work is scored for contralto solo and full orchestra with three percussion players. The score contains a four-page list of special symbols denoting performance instructions, which serves as a useful summary of the many extended performance techniques he had employed over the previous seven years. Only one of the movements, the fourth, consists of an actual setting of a Kavanagh poem ('Canal Bank Walk' for contralto);[55] the remaining four movements are purely orchestral, although they were inspired by lines from other Kavanagh poems. Bodley had hoped to discuss his concept with Kavanagh, but the poet died before a meeting could be arranged. In an interview, Bodley stated that the four orchestral movements are 'not really a musical illustration of the lines, but rather the music coming back in the form of an echo of the poem as if you had dropped, say a penny into a well and waited for the sound to come back to you'.[56] His conception was influenced by the seventeenth-century Japanese poet, Matsuo Bashō (1644–94), one of the leading poets of the Edo period in Japan, in particular Bashō's technique of juxtaposing ideas and allowing the reader or listener to make the desired link between these ideas: 'I have let the music echo the words ... . Some of the echoes that came back have resulted in ideas which on the ordinary conscious level of thought I find extraordinary — and yet somehow right.'[57] The aphoristic excerpts which Bodley chose from Kavanagh's poems for the headings of each movement become almost Irish-style haikus. The first movement is based on lines from 'I had a Future' ('And then the pathos of the blind soul, how without knowing stands in its own kingdom'), the second is from 'Is' ('To look on is enough, in the business of love'), and the third movement is inspired by the poem 'To Hell with Commonsense' ('Gather no Moss you rolling stones, Nothing thought out atones, for no flight in the light'). In this work, he continues his recent pointillistic style, yet in a more accessible and engaging manner with a whole series of miniature soundscapes presented in a palette of orchestral colours. This can, however, make a narrative musical line running through the work hard to detect, either between or within the many sections.

53 Farrell, *Aspects*, 43
54 *Times*, 13 January 1970
55 Bodley later arranged this movement for mezzo-soprano (or alto) and piano.
56 RTÉ Recording Library: interview 'Music and the Musician', 28 February 1974
57 Composer's programme note in programme booklet, Dublin Festival of Twentieth-Century Music, 1972, 27

Ex. 18 *Meditations on Lines from Patrick Kavanagh*, IV (extract)

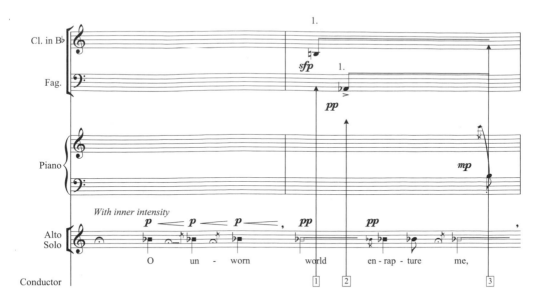

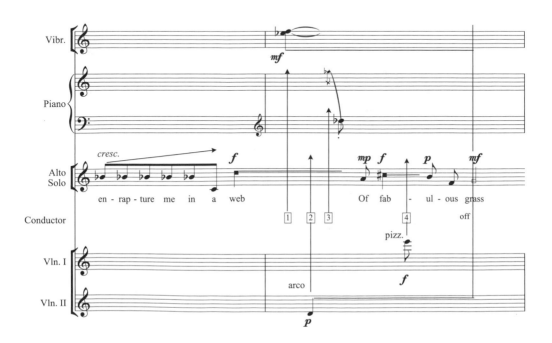

(Notated at concert pitch)

The introduction of the solo voice in the fourth movement furnishes a highly effective dramatic contrast to what has gone before. The orchestral gestures in this movement (from which most of the brass are omitted) are now contextualized more as accompaniment and occasional musical commentary. Bodley's setting of this poem, which gives expression to Kavanagh's religious and pantheistic feelings, is very moving, with its expressive and angular vocal lines. There is considerable use of word-painting: the word 'grow' is set as a dramatic *crescendo* from *ppp* to *f* over string accompaniment; the word 'again' repeats the notes to which the word preceding word 'nature' is set; the phrase 'and a bird gathering materials for the nest for the Word' is accompanied by a solo flute using varying degrees of density and a series of dynamics; while 'abandoned to its delirious beat' is underpinned by rising aleatoric figurations in the strings. The song climaxes on a dramatic pause before the singer declaims, 'O unworn world enrapture me' (Ex. 18), as the poet expresses the wish to become one with nature and be transported into an eternal world. The movement ends with single notes, as softly as it began. The final movement was inspired by the lines 'So be reposed and praise, praise, praise, the way it happened and the way it is' from the poem 'Question to Life'.

The work was first performed on 30 June 1972 by Bernadette Greevy and the RTÉ Symphony Orchestra under Colman Pearce at the Dublin Festival of Twentieth-Century Music. Charles Acton felt that it 'stood well beside two undoubted masterpieces of our century',[58] Shostakovich's Symphony No. 1 and Bartók's Piano Concerto No. 2, and a few days later declared the work's premiere to have been 'one of the climactic events of the whole festival'.[59]

Bodley completed two further works in this style in 1973, both of which were first performed the following year:[60] an orchestral song cycle, Ceathrúintí Mháire Ní Ógáin [Máire Ní Ógáin's Quatrains] for soprano solo and orchestra and September Preludes for flute and piano. Ceathrúintí Mháire Ní Ógáin was commissioned by RTÉ. It sets a group of seven poems by the Irish language poet and scholar, Máire Mhac an tSaoi (b. 1922), Ceathrúintí Mháire Ní Ógáin, which were first published in Margadh na Saoire (Dublin, 1956). Caoimhín Mac Giolla Léith writes that Ceathrúintí Mháire Ní Ógáin is perhaps the best example of Mhac an tSaoi's 'capacity to temper and refine her chosen and given material to produce a richly orchestrated bricolage which projects the changing moods of the eponymous lover's recollections of an affair which has ended (from hostility to nostalgia, from bitterness to pain to resignation to helpless optimism)'.[61] Although this cycle is composed in a modernist idiom with extremely disjunct lines being used to depict the gamut of emotions described by the woman, there are hints of melodic influences from Irish traditional music, such as the considerable amount of melismatic writing for the voice and even the inclusion of a snatch of an Irish-style melody played by the oboe at the end of the second movement. Multiple orchestral textures are distributed across short fragments in this quite sparsely scored work, with individual instruments being given soloistic prominence in certain movements (for instance, the trombone and timpani in the last two movements, respectively).

As the title suggests, September Preludes was inspired by Bodley's fondness for the month of September (see String Quartet No. 1 and News from Donabate) 'with its gradual turning towards autumn and to the serenity of nature as it moves from the brilliant clarity of summer

58 Irish Times, 3 July 1972

59 Irish Times, 7 July 1972. Acton also described it as 'an important, surprisingly accessible, pointillistic work using up-to-date orchestral means but representing another advance by an interesting composer'. Musical Times 113, 1555 (1972), 893

60 September Preludes was first performed on 7 January 1974 by the flautist Patricia Dunkerley (who invited him to write the piece) and John Gibson (piano) at a concert given during the Dublin Festival of Twentieth-Century Music. (The work was later recorded for RTÉ by the London-based contemporary group Lontano). At this concert Bodley conducted the Pulcinella Ensemble in Eight Songs for a Mad King by Peter Maxwell Davies as well as the premiere of Frank Corcoran's Chamber Sonata. Bodley conducted the RTÉ Symphony Orchestra in the first performance of Ceathrúintí Mháire Ní Ógáin with Minnie Clancy (soprano) on 7 June 1974 in the St. Francis Xavier Hall in Dublin.

61 Caoimhín Mac Giolla Léith, 'Contemporary Poetry in Irish: Private Language/Ancestral Voices', Poetry in Contemporary Irish Literature, ed. Michael Kenneally (Lanham, MD, 1995), 89. See also Louis de Paor's reference to the protagonist's 'tension between individual desire and conventional values [which] is central to Máire Mhac an tSaoi's poetic method' in 'Contemporary Poetry in Irish: 1940–2000', 325. See RTÉ programme booklet, 7 June 1974.

in a change which somehow seems to signify acceptance'.[62] He intended this thoughtful and declamatory piece to be merely reflective of the feelings engendered by the month itself rather than programmatic, however. In this work, Bodley uses many of the same techniques from the *Ariel Songs* and the *Meditations on Lines from Patrick Kavanagh*. The duo engages over the five movements in much quizzical dialogue and flexible interplay and 'in many cases the music is governed by the direct reaction of the players to each other rather than by reference to a common musical rhythm'.[63] These preludes display his by now familiar modernist musical language. Although the material of the piece is based on serial techniques, much of the formal focus is on repeated notes. In the first movement for instance, there is a central passage in the flute repeating C sharp almost thirty times with wide-ranging dynamics, and a few bars later, a short passage in which the same instrument oscillates slowly between the notes B and C. Statements of eleven-note rows at the start of the second movement ascend from the bass of the piano to the flute building up into sustained sonorities before the instruments engage in exciting exchanges within multiple changes of tempo, concluding with repeated high trilling F sharps on the flute. These F sharps appear again briefly repeated in a more reflective manner an octave lower in the central part of the short third movement, which lasts a mere eight bars. It opens with a statement by the piano of the first six notes of a row, which is completed by a statement of the remaining six in the flute. The fourth movement (Ex. 19) opens and closes with full twelve-tone statements which frame repeated-note gestures in both instruments which die away rapidly (these also appear in the outer movements). The E flat–G dyad (the major third which Bodley likes to place within dissonant contexts) occurs over twenty times in the fifth and final movement in the piano (already anticipated in the flute and piano in the previous movement) and confers arguably certain tonal references at strategic moments (although being in the highest register they have more of a percussive function). Robert Henderson in the *Daily Telegraph* described the *September Preludes* as 'introspective, yet highly articulate [and which allowed] considerable freedom to the players within a cogent, expressive and tautly integrated structure'.[64]

Throughout this period, Bodley engaged with many of the diverse musical languages of the Darmstadt school and deployed them with considerable success. He did not share the general antipathy of the post-1945 avant-garde to nationalist idioms, however, and did not see why they should necessarily be incompatible with contemporary techniques in any future works. In August 1969, Acton gave a short series of lectures at the Language Centre of Ireland on topics such as 'The Irish Musical Tradition' and 'A Search for Celtic Music', exhorting more musicological research into aspects of Irish music. Around this time, Bodley embarked on a quest for a new musical language which would draw both on the folk music of Ireland and on what he had learned in Darmstadt.

---

62 Bodley, programme note, Dublin Festival of Twentieth-Century Music, 1974, 20
63 Bodley, programme note, Dublin Festival of Twentieth-Century Music, 1974, 20
64 *Daily Telegraph*, 14 January 1974

Ex. 19 *September Preludes*, IV, Opening

3. Engaging with Irish Traditional Music

From the very beginning of his career, Bodley has been deeply engaged with Ireland's Gaelic cultural heritage, especially with the Irish language and Irish folk music, to an extent which is unusual amongst most other Irish composers of his generation. The effects of this engagement on his compositional output, especially from the early 1970s onwards, were profound and far-reaching. Over a period of twenty-five years, Bodley attempted to achieve a synthesis of Irish folk music and European modernism in a style uniquely and very recognizably his own. This aspiration was not new in the history of Irish music in the twentieth century. In an interview in 1958, Bodley's teacher John F. Larchet expressed the hope that a great Irish composer of international stature would yet emerge, who would create 'his own school or style which will influence his contemporaries and the composers who will follow him'. Were such a figure to possess

> a thorough knowledge and a keen appreciation of the folk-music and the literature of Ireland, Gaelic and English ... [together with] ... knowledge of great music [and] unusual technical skill ... after years of incessant and conscientious study, and experience of original composition, he will speak with his own voice [and] from the depths of his Irish soul will be born the music that to us, Irish people, will seem evocative of the spirit of our country.[1]

As Pine comments, Larchet's remarks suggested that Irish music 'had a destiny which would be fulfilled when a "Sibelius" or a "Dvořák" or a "Bartók" would emerge, capable of reconciling "national ideas and ideals" with the techniques of classical

---

1   Radio Éireann 'Composers at Work' series, 1958, cited in Pine, *Music and Broadcasting in Ireland*, 218–19

composition.'² It would certainly appear as if Bodley consciously set out to realize this ambition and become a figure of comparable stature. In an interview with Acton in 1970, he indicated that he had begun to explore the possibility of evolving a compositional idiom influenced by Irish folk music and even expressed the wish that he would like to see 'our national composers writing in a national idiom'.³

Around this time, Bodley embarked on a close study of Irish music, particularly the tradition of unaccompanied solo vocal music known as *sean nós* [old style]. In some styles of *sean nós* singing, the airs are ornamented quite considerably in performance and sung with a rhythmic freedom that makes it difficult for collectors to transcribe the renditions of individual performers into conventional musical notation. Bodley had become keenly interested in this problem through teaching courses on Irish folk music at UCD as well as through his involvement with the Folk Music Society of Ireland (Cumann Cheoil Tíre Éireann), which he had founded jointly with Brendán Breathnach, Hugh Shields and Tom Munnelly in 1970. His work in this area led him to evolve a notational system which he described in an article published in the journal *Éigse Ceol Tíre* [Folk Music Studies] in 1973.⁴ Here he outlined his method of notating ornamentation and interpolated vowels in the more complex melodies and included various examples, such as the rendition of the well-known tune *Dónal Óg* by the traditional singer Máire Áine Ní Dhonnchadha. He cites it first in its basic melodic form and then with ornamentation indicated by single or more dots before and after, and above and below, the notes to be decorated.⁵ He also stressed the importance of the tone quality and texture of the singer's voice in any discussion of traditional singing, making the point that 'the type of voice production used in traditional Irish singing is closely related to the style of ornamentation'.⁶ Bodley highlighted the importance of the structural *rubato* inherent in the slow air and ended his short article with the exhortation that 'no effort should be spared to record all the singers now living'.⁷

Bodley was also well-versed in the history of Irish 'classical' music and the compositions of his contemporaries in Ireland. He wrote an introduction to a 1970 reprint of Grattan Flood's well-known 1905 book, *A History of Irish Music*,⁸ which was praised by Stanley Sadie in the *Musical Times* for summarising 'most sanely the book's value and its failings: its breadth ... and its fierce patriotism' and he noted that 'Bodley maps out some of the areas where Flood has done little more than whet the appetite for future research (particularly

2   Pine, *Music and Broadcasting in Ireland*, 272. See also Edmund Hunt, 'Where is the Irish Bartók?' *The Question of Art Music and Its Relation to the Traditional Music Genre: A Study of Some Approaches and Contemporary Developments*, unpublished dissertation, University of Newcastle-upon-Tyne (2006).
3   Acton, 'Interview', 129
4   Seóirse Bodley, 'Technique and structure in "sean-nós" singing', *Éigse Ceol Tíre*, 1 (1973), 44–54
5   Bodley, 'Technique and structure', 44
6   Bodley, 'Technique and structure', 47. See also Seán Williams, 'Melodic Ornamentation in the Connemara Sean Nós Singing of Joe Heaney', *New Hibernia Review* 8, 1 (2004), 122–45.
7   Bodley, 'Technique and structure', 54
8   William Henry Grattan Flood, *A History of Irish Music* (Shannon, 1970 [1905])

the early 18th century)'.[9] Sadie subsequently invited him to contribute articles on Irish composers to the first edition of the *New Grove Dictionary of Music and Musicians*.[10]

Bodley's increasing engagement with Irish folk music had undoubtedly been stimulated by the activities of his close contemporary, the composer and performer, Seán Ó Riada (1931–71). Ó Riada was generally regarded during his lifetime as one of the most important Irish composers of his generation, but his promise was only partially realized during his relatively short life in a small body of original compositions which are uneven in quality. He enjoyed considerable popular success with his atmospheric scores for two Irish language documentary films, *Mise Éire* [I am Ireland] (1959) and *Saoirse* [Freedom] (1960). He was also instrumental in reviving interest in Irish folk music through the formation in 1961 of the traditional music ensemble Ceoltóirí Cualann [The Musicians from Cualann], which performed his own arrangements of Irish folk music. Bodley respected Ó Riada's abilities and admired what he had accomplished for traditional music. The two men did not come into frequent professional contact, but in the early summer of 1970, Bodley had an opportunity to work closely with him when they both taught on a two-week course on Irish traditional music which was organized by the Music Department at University College Cork. Bodley gave daily lectures on 'Arrangements and Recordings of Irish Traditional Music'.[11] He recalled that one night after he had finished working, he was chatting with Ó Riada about music and its development: Ó Riada had

> become very interested in the individual statement — the musical statement made by a single person rather than as a group. How this line of thought might have been expanded by him we will never know. I doubt if either of us realised that he was so soon to make the ultimate statement.[12]

9   *Musical Times*, 112, 1536 (February 1971), 140
10 Bodley Private Collection. Bodley had already corresponded with Sadie on 4 October 1971 suggesting that the following composers would, in his opinion, merit inclusion: Bodley, Boydell, Fleischmann, Larchet, May, Ó Gallchobháir, Ó Riada, Potter, Victory and two English-born composers working in Ireland, Raymond Warren and James Wilson. Bodley wrote the entries on Boydell, Ó Gallchobháir, Ó Riada, Potter, and submitted the section on art music for the 'Ireland' entry; perhaps for reasons of space, this only comprised two pages (as opposed to the eight-and-a-half pages for folk music by Brendán Breathnach), and forty years of contemporary Irish music were covered in two sentences.
11 Aloys Fleischmann gave two lectures during this course on a research project to compile a thematic index to the published collections of Irish folk music, which was being carried out in the Department of Music in University College Cork. This ambitious project, which had been initiated in the 1950s, was eventually published in 1998 as *Sources of Irish Traditional Music c. 1600 – 1855: An Annotated Catalogue of Prints and Manuscripts 1583–1855* by Garland Press in New York, six years after Fleischmann's death.
12 Seóirse Bodley, 'Remembering Seán Ó Riada', *The Capuchin Annual*, 39 (1972), 304

After Ó Riada's death the following year, Bodley composed a piece for flute and piano entitled In Memory of Seán Ó Riada, which he described as 'a slow sean nós air ... interspersed with sections of a jig tune and interpolations of a questioning and ironic quality'.[13]

In an article 'Remembering Seán Ó Riada', which Bodley wrote for The Capuchin Annual in 1972, he emphasized the importance of Ó Riada's dual contribution to Irish musical life:

> The world of symphonic music knew him through his orchestral music. The traditional musicians were familiar with his activities in Irish music. And the in-between audience that has an interest in both without being directly involved in either could find an approach to him through [his folk music] arrangements [and] the film music, especially that of Mise Éire. ... He brought to all of his activities ... a profound ability to question the values of both music and society that will be sorely missed. In a sense it is these questions and their resolution that provide a continuing activity of his, now that his work as composer and musician is ended. Not alone his music — but also his life-style forms a question mark in Irish life. Even if all the questions his life raises are never fully answered, they will provide a source that cannot be ignored, of thought and consideration for any sensitive Irish person.[14]

Nearly a decade later in 1981, Bodley published an article assessing Ó Riada's original compositions, some of which reflect a variety of modernist influences including serialism.[15] Bodley evidently had reservations: he professed his sincere admiration for Ó Riada's musicianship while acknowledging his technical limitations as a composer, and concluded:

> The variety and fecundity of ideas in Ó Riada's original compositions is striking. Those of us who knew him recall his sense of humour and his interest in new ideas. Flexibility, humour and a sense of play are useful attributes in discovering new ideas and new combinations thereof. Development or consistent application of a style or method, on the contrary, requires a certain seriousness or even a sense of rigidity. Perhaps it is for this reason that one looks to Ó Riada's works for their ideas, interesting juxtapositions of elements and feeling for the unexpected, rather than searching for perfectly balanced and stylistically logical music. Most of all, however, Ó Riada's original compositions are a reminder that there was another side to his character than the light-hearted persona so often adopted by him in conversation. These works show a concern for the development of music, a serious questioning of the purpose of life and a sense of the tragedy of the human

13 Bodley, programme note, 21 October 1971
14 Bodley, 'Remembering Seán Ó Riada', 303
15 Bodley, 'The Original Compositions: An Assessment' in Fryer, Grattan and Harris, Bernard, eds., Integrating Tradition: The Achievement of Seán Ó Riada (Ballina, 1981), 28–40

condition that belies any impression of him as a lightweight or frivolous person. Perhaps the humorous impression he so often liked to create was in part an attempt to conceal an underlying sense of anguish at the human condition and the forms its musical expression had taken in the twentieth century. The evidence of the original compositions would certainly point towards such a conclusion.[16]

Ó Riada's work raised at least the possibility of a style which would constitute a synthesis of folk music and art music. Indeed, Axel Klein suggests that Bodley's compositions from 1972 onwards represent the kind of successful bridging between the two which had always been expected of Ó Riada and that, while accepting that Bodley might well have written these works anyway, it is not unreasonable to point to the influence of Ó Riada.[17] Around this time Bodley's artistic outlook and compositional aesthetic underwent considerable change and the question of trying to evolve a distinctively Irish mode of musical utterance assumed fresh urgency for him. It is clear that he was ambitious to accomplish what Ó Riada had failed to realize in his own work. In June 1974, Bodley sent Acton a copy of his 1973 article on *sean nós*, commenting that 'all I have to do now is to use this to write the "great Irish music" that everybody keeps talking about, and I will have filled another gap in Irish life!'[18]

The first important score in which Bodley's change of stylistic direction became manifest was a short work for two pianos entitled *The Narrow Road to the Deep North*, which was written in 1972. The title of this score is taken from a chronicle of the same name by Matsuo Bashō (whose work also influenced his *Meditations on Lines from Patrick Kavanagh* the previous year), which describes his journey to the north of his native country in 1689–91. Bodley, however, intended the title as an allusion to Northern Ireland and the work represents his personal and artistic response to the political and social events which had recently culminated in violence there.[19] *The Narrow Road to the Deep North* was first performed in Belfast on 17 February 1972 by Raymond Warren and Evan John in the Whitla Hall of Queen's University, Belfast. Bodley subsequently made a version of the score for solo piano, which was first performed by the Irish pianist John O'Conor in 1977 and recorded by him in 1980. There are virtually no alterations in the solo version although Réamonn Keary has argued persuasively that 'the antiphonal effect used widely throughout the piece would obviously be more effective on two instruments'.[20] The work has been widely performed, mostly in its solo version, and it remains one of Bodley's best-known compositions.

---

16 Bodley, 'The Original Compositions: An Assessment', 40. See also a review of Bodley's article by Brendán
    Ó Madagáin in the *Connacht Tribune*, 4 December 1981.
17 Klein, *Die Musik Irlands im 20. Jahrhundert*, 453
18 Bodley to Acton, 21 June 1974, cited in Pine, *Music and Broadcasting in Ireland*, 272
19 Bodley, programme note, 17 February 1972
20 Réamonn Keary, *A Survey of Irish Piano Music from 1970 to 1995*, unpublished dissertation, National
    University of Ireland, Maynooth (1995), 12

Ex. 20 *The Narrow Road to the Deep North* [solo version], 37–43

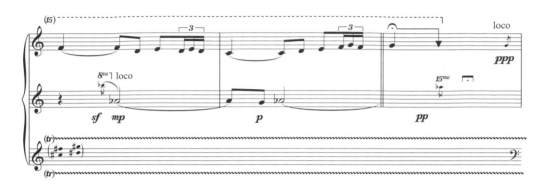

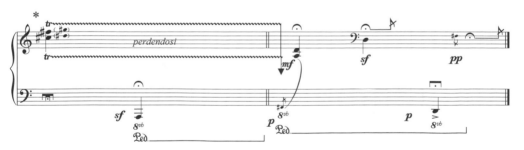

* No break in trills

In this sombre score, Bodley juxtaposes a slow melody (suggesting a stylized evocation of the *sean nós* tradition) with dissonant material, which he devised 'by applying certain constructional principles of Irish music in an atonal manner [although] there are also a number of straightforward tonal elements that appear as "blocks"'.[21] The atonal material appears both in episodes between the various statements of the air and as an accompaniment to it. The melody which opens the piece recurs later two octaves higher (Ex. 20), then in more extended form in the bass, and once again in a truncated version at the opening pitch. In the final bars, Bodley quotes a fragment of the well-known Irish tune, 'A Spailpín, a Rúin' [My darling spalpeen] (spalpeen being an old term for a migratory labourer), 'suggesting that

21 Bodley, programme note, 17 February 1972

the melody represents in a way the wanderings of a working journeyman through a strange landscape'[22] and the piece closes as it began, by affirming C major.

Axel Klein considers this score to be one of the most important contributions to the twentieth-century Irish literature for the piano and notes its key position as a milestone in what he has characterized as the 'creative conflict' between folk music and art music.[23] For Bodley, the work represented a particularly significant achievement in its mediation between the seeming irreconcilables of folk music and an avant-garde idiom. This was largely made possible by his realization that 'that continuous irregularity is regular in its continuity', which prompted him to explore what might happen were he to 'insert an Irish style melody into an avant-garde background and by this means make the irregular even more irregular. (Not regularly irregular, but irregularly irregular, to use terms loosely based on medical descriptions of the human heart-beat).'[24] The result, in many ways, was like hearing Irish music with ears attuned to the avant-garde idioms he had heard at Darmstadt.

Bodley now began to develop this complex stylistic duality, in which tonal elements deriving from folk music were embedded in an atonal context. In an RTÉ radio broadcast in 1976, he declared that he did not see tonality and atonality as opposites,

> but rather as a continuum stretching from the type of music in which you can recognise very easily an obvious tonality, to one in which the tonality is obviously shifting. There is no absolute point at which you can say tonality has actually ceased. It is curious how things cannot exist without their own opposites all the time.[25]

His next composition in this style brought him closer to attaining the kind of distinctively Irish mode of musical utterance to which he aspired. This was the orchestral work *A Small White Cloud Drifts Over Ireland*, which was completed in 1975 and first performed on 5 January 1976 by the RTÉ Symphony Orchestra under Proinnsías Ó Duinn during the Dublin Festival of Twentieth-Century Music. In the composer's words, the piece is 'a musical picture of the ethos of Ireland formed at a viewpoint from which a new synthesis can be discerned'.[26] It has become one of Bodley's best-known compositions and has been performed with some frequency both in Ireland and abroad.

---

22 Ó Cuinneagáin, *The Piano Music of Seóirse Bodley*, 47, quoting Bodley's introductory remarks prior to a performance of the two-piano version of *The Narrow Road to the Deep North* given by himself and Kathleen Gallagher on RTÉ radio, 28 January 1975.

23 Axel Klein, 'Bodley, Seóirse', *New Grove* 2. Klein also uses the metaphor of Bodley dropping dissonant bombs on an Irish melodic landscape but without destroying it. See Klein, *Die Musik Irlands im 20. Jahrhundert*, 269–70, and also Bodley's comment in an interview in the *Irish Times* in 2002: 'I thought about putting something in the middle of this that would totally conflict with it.' 'A Note of Change', *Irish Times*, 25 March 2002.

24 Bodley, 'The Claims of Conformity', 40

25 Transcribed from the RTÉ radio programme 'It is not a music that will live alone', 26 September 1976.

26 Bodley, RTÉ programme booklet, 5 January 1976

In his programme note for the premiere, Bodley explained that in writing the work, he approached 'Irish traditional music from the viewpoint of irregular musical structure, derived from my experience in avant-garde music':

> It combines bits of newly-composed jig, reel and slow air tunes with highly contrasted elements: clusters, simple tonal chords (in irregular lay-out), lyrical passages in thirds on two solo violins and some vigorous dramatic ideas ... . Here Ireland is viewed as if from the vantage-point of a small white cloud drifting over the country. From below, the spirit and feeling of both people and landscape float upwards [and] can be experienced as a totality in which song, dance, gaiety and human feeling are intermingled — a totality in which the conflicts are integrated into a larger picture.[27]

The work (which lasts about fifteen minutes) opens on a sustained D major chord in the strings played *pianissimo* with dramatic *crescendo* and *molto vibrato* fluctuations, but by bar 4 this is interrupted by dissonant piano and percussion interjections which set the scene for the juxtaposition of traditional-style melodies and a more contemporary language throughout the work. A jig in D major for the solo violin begins in bar 20 (having been outlined briefly a few bars previously) accompanied by trills in the upper strings, a tremolo ninth in the xylophone, and fragments from the harp and piano (Ex. 21). This material and the jig are developed in this first section and reach a brief climax (bars 118–22) which cadences unambiguously in D major. Fragments of the jig are used to lead into the slower second section, which begins at bar 203. It opens with a sustained C major chord (which shifts occasionally to F major) in the lower strings, which underpins two solo violins leaping in thirds and a seventeen-bar flute melody (marked *intenso, rubato*) reminiscent of a traditional slow air. This haunting theme is also juxtaposed with some fragmentary dissonant ideas, but these remain unobtrusively in the background. A muted horn call, remnants of the air on the oboes, and *ppp* tremolo strings *sul ponticello* form a link to the third section, *Allegro*, at bar 251, which opens with a lively reel in G major given to a solo violin. This section is perhaps evocative of what Bodley describes in his programme note as 'the darker elements in the Irish scene' with the 'kaleidoscopic effect' of the contrasts being realized,[28] as tonal passages are juxtaposed with atonal ones. The opening of the middle section is recalled for 13 bars from bar 389 and the jig tune in D major interpolated with C major block chords brings the piece to a close with an emphatic *tutti* D major chord.

---

27 Bodley, RTÉ programme booklet, 5 January 1976. See also Fanny Feehan, 'Living Irish Composers', *Ireland Today*, 886, 7 (May 1976), 7.
28 Bodley, RTÉ programme booklet, 5 January 1976

Ex. 21 *A Small White Cloud Drifts Over Ireland, 20–28*

The work met with an enthusiastic reception from music critics on the occasion of its premiere. Acton hailed it as representing the synthesis of contemporary art music and folk music which he had hoped Ó Riada might have achieved, 'an Irish music that was far from those foreign-sounding and derivative Irish rhapsodies' written by an earlier generation of composers.[29] Another Dublin critic, Fanny Feehan, wrote in the magazine *Hibernia* that she considered it to be 'one of the most gifted works to come from an Irish composer'.[30] Kenneth Loveland, reporting on the Dublin Festival of Twentieth-Century Music for the *Times*, described the score as 'sensitively composed' and noted that 'in a quietly contemplative spirit of distant observation, it mixes fragments which appear to have a traditional Irish flavour with cluster chords and abstract shapes to a subtly evocative effect'.[31] The response of subsequent commentators has been more ambivalent, however. When the piece was played by the National Symphony Orchestra of Ireland in 1997, Douglas Sealy opined that the composer had not succeeded in integrating the disparate musical material into a persuasive unity and that their juxtaposition seemed to him incongruous.[32]

In the spring of 1976 after the premiere of *A Small White Cloud Drifts Over Ireland*, Bodley attended the Salzburg Seminar on American Music as a Salzburg Seminar Fellow (with fellow Irish composers, Frank Corcoran and Roger Doyle) from 28 March to 16 April. In the course of the Seminar, he had the opportunity to attend analytical talks by the American electro-acoustic composers John Eaton and Paul Lansky. Bodley's ongoing interest in this area of electro-acoustic and computer music would lead to the establishment of a Studio for Electronic Music in 1993 in UCD.

Bodley's exploration of the expressive possibilities of musical material deriving from Irish folk music was continued in two works for piano, *The Tightrope Walker Presents a Rose* and *Aislingí*, which date from 1976 and 1977 respectively. The first of these is a simple miniature lasting a mere 40 bars and was written as a present for the composer's first wife.[33] Its title, as Bodley explained in a newspaper interview, alludes to one of his favoured metaphors for the act of composing: 'my image of the composer is that of a tightrope walker. You can lean over a long way in one direction if you counter-balance in the other direction. The

---

29 *Irish Times*, 6 January 1976
30 Fanny Feehan, 'Seóirse Bodley: Astride Two Traditions', *Hibernia*, 13 February 1976. See also Feehan's comments in a letter to the editor of *Hibernia*, 27 February 1976.
31 *Times*, 14 January 1976. Later that month he suggested that a style could emerge which would 'use Irish colours as successfully as Bartók used Hungarian ones', *South Wales Argus*, 30 January 1976.
32 Douglas Sealy, reviewing a performance of *A Small White Cloud Drifts Over Ireland* in the National Concert Hall by the National Symphony Orchestra under Kasper de Roo, *Irish Times*, 7 May 1997. He also suggested that 'the music lurches from one traditional cliché to another in a way that sounds like a mixture of Hindemith and The Chieftains, a marriage never made in heaven'.
33 *The Tightrope Walker Presents a Rose* was not performed in public until 11 September 1983 by Patricia Kavanagh at the National Concert Hall. It was also played by John O'Conor, a former student of Bodley's at UCD, at a concert to mark the end of UCD's occupancy of Earlsfort Terrace on 17 May 2007 and has been included on the Royal Irish Academy of Music's Grade VII syllabus for 2009–11.

important thing is not to fall off; which will happen if you lean too far in one direction.'[34] This seems an apt description of the creative balancing act in which Bodley was engaged at the time, in his efforts to synthesise folk music elements with an avant-garde idiom. In his preface to the score, he writes that the work's material is based 'on aspects of traditional Irish music both slow and quick [which are] contrasted with other musical thoughts [that] frame and contrast with the Irish elements.'[35] Four dramatic *fff* bars in the right hand are contrasted against gentle *mp* thirds in the bass in the opening *Adagio* section which consists of a slow air in C major. Three *ff* bars act as a link to the 13 bars of an *Allegro* jig-like passage in G major before the piece ends with a reprise of five bars of the slow air (Ex. 22).

The compositional techniques employed in this bagatelle also feature extensively in *Aislingí*, which is a substantial work in five movements lasting about twenty-five minutes. The Irish title, which can be loosely translated as 'Dream-visions', alludes to the poetic genre of the *aisling* cultivated by eighteenth-century Gaelic poets. These poems often expressed the desire for the emancipation of their native country from foreign domination and typically described a vision of a beautiful woman who personified Ireland. This genre prompted Bodley to attempt to devise a new type of musical form which would be distinctively Irish — an ambition which was inspired by his countryman John Field's invention of a new type of keyboard miniature, the nocturne. Bodley characterized his concept of the *aisling* as 'a visionary Irish musical piece ... with a musical style ... based to a large extent on Irish music — the Irish music of the living tradition [with] extensive use of varying types of Irish traditional melody and ornamentation ... re-interpreted in terms of the piano'.[36] The work is dedicated to the memory of Amhlaoibh Ó Súilleabháin (Humphrey O'Sullivan), a diarist who left an important and wide-ranging record of rural life in Co. Kilkenny between 1827 and 1835. According to Bodley, Ó Súilleabháin's writings 'provided much of the inspiration for the music':[37] the fourth *Aisling*, for example, was prompted by his diary entry for 18 April 1827, which consists of a lyrical description of a day in the countryside that he enjoyed in the company of a woman of whom he was fond:

> We walked through the dark evergreen pine woods ... . We could hear the lark's song in the nearby meadows, the shorter call of the blackbird, the thrush and all the smaller birds which seemed to be in harmony with Maread de Barra's gentle lively

---

34 *Sunday Independent*, 15 May 1977
35 Bodley, prefatory note to the facsimile score, Contemporary Music Centre, Ireland
36 Bodley, programme note in 'Contemporary German and Irish Music' series booklet, November 1989. Acton attempted a dictionary style definition: 'A piece, quick or slow or both, in which both post-Viennese modern international piano techniques and also melodic lines and ornaments in the idioms of Irish traditional music are used, but the elements are in juxtaposition rather than combination or integration.' *Irish Times*, 16 January 1979.
37 Bodley, prefatory note to the facsimile score, Contemporary Music Centre, Ireland

melodious speech ... . We reached Cluain Lachan with its ponds, pools, lakelets, streams and murmuring waterfalls ... . I never remember a more pleasant day. [38]

Ex. 22 *The Tightrope Walker Presents a Rose, 29–40*

Dublin 1976 (for Olive)

This *Aisling* evokes the mood of this text rather than being literally descriptive, conjuring up the sensuous atmosphere of a warm spring day. Fragments of a jig tune (harmonized

38 *The Diary of Humphrey O'Sullivan 1827–1835*, translated from *Cín Lae Amhlaoibh*, a selection from the diaries edited by Tomás de Bhaldraithe (Dublin and Cork, 1979), 20–21

in perfect fourths) intrude briefly on a long and highly ornamented slow air played over a drone-like pedal B flat (Ex. 23). The opening chords return in the final bars to round off the movement, but cadence this time in B major.

The fifth *Aisling* provides 'a grand finale to the set'[39] and concludes in rousing fashion with a very lengthy fermata, during which the pianist is required to sustain as much of the final nine bars of *fff* D major chords for as long as possible. *Aislingí* is undoubtedly one of Bodley's most overtly 'Irish' scores. Extensive use is made of musical material deriving from stylized evocations of folk music, which is juxtaposed with avant-garde pianistic sonorities of various kinds to change the meaning of the basic Irish material. In his study of Bodley's piano music, Pádhraic Ó Cuinneagáin has detailed the ways in which folk influences are perceptible in the work, such as in the use of improvisatory runs evocative of a style of ornamentation known as the *sruth mór* [great stream], which was employed by the ancient Irish harpers, or of the deployment of grace notes in a way that recalls the piping technique known as 'cranning'.[40] Earlier that year, Bodley had noted the 'problems of translating elements of Irish music into a 20th century setting', on account of the fact that 'even Irish-born classical musicians are by no means familiar with the traditional Irish musical style of phrasing and ornamentation'.[41] This prompted him to supply the work with a preface describing the style of performance he had in mind. *Aislingí* was first performed on 29 August 1977 by the Irish pianist John O'Conor in St. Canice's Cathedral during Kilkenny Arts Week.

In 1977, Bodley embarked on a series of collaborations with one of Ireland's most distinguished literary figures, the poet Brendan Kennelly (b. 1936). A native of Co. Kerry and a fluent Irish speaker, Kennelly is a highly prolific writer who had by then already published over twenty volumes of poetry, as well as novels and plays. Kennelly's work, like Bodley's, is frequently based on Irish subject matter and musical imagery features extensively in his work. It is not surprising, therefore, that he has allowed a number of composers to set his poetry, including Jane O'Leary, Nicola LeFanu and Michael Alcorn. Bodley's engagement with Kennelly's writings occurred at an important juncture in this phase of his career, as he seemed to be temporarily unsure how to solve the technical problems inherent in structuring large-scale compositions in his new idiom. For the time being, he overcame this difficulty by having recourse to texts, as some early twentieth-century atonal composers had done before him.

---

39 See Keary, *A Survey of Irish Piano Music from 1970 to 1995*, 11: 'This appears by its diversity to not only summate the previous four movements, but also to be a compendium of the entire music literature.'
40 Ó Cuinneagáin, *The Piano Music of Seóirse Bodley*, 118–19
41 *Irish Times*, 7 April 1977

Ex. 23 *Aislingí*, IV, 71–112

The first work to result from this encounter was *A Chill Wind* for mixed choir of 1977, which sets Kennelly's translations of five Irish poems from his collection *A Drinking Cup* (1970). It was commissioned for performance at the Dublin Festival of Twentieth-Century Music and was premiered on 12 January 1978 by the RTÉ Singers conducted by Proinnsías Ó Duinn. In his programme note, Bodley explained that his chosen texts all explore the experience of 'a chill [striking] at the heart' and emphasized the contemporary relevance of the original poems, despite their antiquity. He continued:

To give expression to Irish emotional states (at once traditional and contemporary) seems to me to add to our human understanding of ourselves — especially when the emotions are those whose existence we often deny. ... The aim here is a new directness of expression.[42]

The first poem, 'On the murder of David Gleeson, Bailiff', rejoices maliciously in the murder of a much-hated official. The choir demands that there be 'no words of pity' for him and raucously jeers his name over eight bars, before ending with the vengeful hope 'half-whispered, with utmost venom', that his suffering may never end. The second, 'Etain', which lasts a mere 20 bars, evokes an Irish mythological heroine of legendary beauty. Bodley's setting uses traditional Irish nonsense syllables which, according to the composer's directions, are to be sung 'suggestively' and with 'gleeful malice' in the tempo of a reel. The certainty that 'Etain won't sleep tonight' is stated on a repeated sonority superimposing triads of D minor and A major in seven parts. Bodley uses the A major chord as a link to the much longer third piece, 'Hate goes just as far as love', which portrays the experience of a lover's rejection. This A major triad is now superimposed with a G major chord, and the resultant sonority is repeated throughout to represent the protagonist's emotional numbness, eventually dying away *perdendosi* at the close. Hatred is also the theme of the fourth poem, *Knockmealdown* (Ex. 24). Named after the highest peak in the Knockmealdown mountain range, which is located on the border of counties Waterford and Tipperary, it employs a musical language which adumbrates the idiom of many of Bodley's subsequent Kennelly settings. The desolate winter landscape described in the poem is evoked with very simple musical means, with two sopranos intoning ornamented passages reminiscent of Irish folk music over sustained C major chords sung by the rest of the choir.

The final movement, 'The Old Woman of Beare', is the most substantial of the set. The text here is a translation of a celebrated Old Irish poem dating from the tenth century, the interpretation of which has been the subject of extensive conjecture. The nineteenth-century Gaelic scholar Kuno Meyer suggested that it was 'the lament of an old hetaira who contrasts the privations and sufferings of her old age with the pleasures of her youth, when she had been the delight of kings'.[43] Other scholars have suggested that the old woman of the title is the Cailleach Beara [The Hag of Beara], an ancient mythological being associated with winter. Here, Bodley again makes extensive use of the sonority of two superimposed triads (this time with an augmented triad in the bass), to evoke the old woman's forgiving recollection of past lovers: 'I don't hate the men who swore the truth was in their lies.' Driving passages of sustained superimposed triads follow ('and still the sea rears and plunges into me, shoving, rolling through my head, images of the drifting dead'), and after unison declamations, the song ends with the following words (with the word 'farther' echoing in strongly rhythmic exchanges between the parts):

42 Bodley, programme booklet, Dublin Festival of Twentieth-Century Music, 1978, 26–27
43 Kuno Meyer, 'Songs and stories from Irish MSS', *Otia Merseiana*, 1 (1899), 119–28, 119

Ex. 24 *A Chill Wind: Knockmealdown*, 1–19

The sea grows smaller, smaller now.
Farther, farther it goes
Leaving me here where the foam dries
On the deserted land,
Dry as my shrunken thighs,
As the tongue that presses my lips,
As the veins that break through my hands.

A Chill Wind met with a very favourable critical reception on its first performance (Acton considered it to be 'Bodley's greatest achievement to date') and is undoubtedly one of the most persuasive works from this phase of Bodley's career.[44] It is an effective and unified cycle, and the drama of the final song is particularly impressive. As Malcolm Barry has pointed out, the attempt to integrate two very different types of musical material is notably more successful here than in some of the composer's instrumental works from this period and it brought Bodley a step closer to achieving his stylistic aims.[45]

The following year Bodley was commissioned by RTÉ to compose a song cycle, for which Kennelly agreed to write new texts. He initially proposed a dramatic work with a similar theme to his poem Islandman which had been published earlier that year. Bodley pressed him to devise a text with a female protagonist, however, as the possibility had arisen of writing a work for the distinguished Irish mezzo-soprano Bernadette Greevy.[46] Over the course of many meetings, Kennelly provided Bodley with ninety pages of poetry from which they eventually selected twenty-two poems. The cycle, which Bodley has described as 'a large-scale dramatic cantata for solo voice and piano', was entitled A Girl.[47]

A Girl narrates the story of an unmarried young woman who becomes pregnant, and eventually drowns herself on account of the humiliation to which she is subjected. In his programme note for the first performance, the composer wrote that the songs 'trace her emotions and thoughts as she moves towards the only logical solution she can see' and are a sympathetic portrayal of someone who is 'pushed to extremes'.[48] Kennelly has described how his poems were inspired by a vivid childhood memory of a teenage girl from his village who committed suicide under similar circumstances:

44 Irish Times, 14 January 1978
45 See Barry, 'Examining the Great Divide', 19.
46 See Bodley interview with John Holohan, Sunday Independent, 22 October 1978.
47 Bodley's programme note from premiere reprinted in the programme booklet for the 1980 Dublin Festival of Twentieth-Century Music, 12. The sequence of poems comprising A Girl was published in Kennelly's Familiar Strangers: New and Selected Poems 1960–2004 (Newcastle-upon-Tyne, 2004), 98–108. Kennelly explained in the foreword that the more familiar things become, the stranger they are. As Feehan writes, the girl 'first takes us into her simple country routine [and] we travel the land with her, take in the familiar landscape'. Feehan, 'The Importance of Being Seóirse'.
48 Bodley, programme booklet, Dublin Festival of Twentieth-Century Music, 1980, 11

What I remember about the girl in this poem is the way she replied, simply, 'Yes, sir' and 'yes, ma'am' to adults who were going to considerable lengths to advise her, praise her or chastise her over some matter. She refused to be drawn in to what they said; she remained deferentially apart. I also recall the quick, dark way she had of throwing a glance over her shoulder at you as she moved away from you. A quick, shy glance, at once searching and fugitive. She always seemed to be moving away into herself and always quickly scrutinising whoever she was leaving behind. This girl worked for different people in the village where I was born and grew up. One day when she was sixteen or so she walked out of the village and into the river that we all knew so well. I was eight or nine then. I remember the men bringing her body through the streets. A couple of days passed before anyone recognised her. Almost forty years later her phrases and her (to my child's eye) fascinating way of looking back over her shoulder returned to me. I began to write poems about her, through her. Or she wrote them through me. Who knows?[49]

The Kennelly scholar, John McDonagh notes that A Girl is 'an excellent early example of two of Kennelly's favoured poetic techniques: the adoption of a female voice and the extended poem sequence'.[50] In a joint paper with the author on A Girl in May 2007, McDonagh also explained that metaphors of water recur throughout Kennelly's early work and that the poems follow a characteristic pattern with an emphasis on movement, both physical and spiritual.

The harmonic language of the cycle might be described as neo-tonal. It begins and ends firmly in C major (as do many of Bodley's pieces at this time), and tonal passages are juxtaposed with a judicious and expressive use of dissonance. The melodic lines display extensive ornamentation in an Irish style. The work as a whole is quite understated and Bodley has considerable recourse to devices such as sustained sonorities, repeated notes and frequent singing on a monotone. In the opening 'November Cloud,' the left hand

49 Brendan Kennelly, *Breathing Spaces: Early Poems* (Newcastle-upon-Tyne, 1992), 140. In a separate note for *Transitions*, Bodley and Kennelly's radio adaptation of the cycle for two speakers, piano and prepared piano as an RTÉ entry for the *Prix Italia*, Kennelly writes that 'these songs are an attempt to trace, even to celebrate, the emotional logic leading to a girl's suicide. They constitute an act of inquiry which develops into an act of homage. Though her life is shown as being hard, perplexing, painful, even squalid at times, her death is not merely a matter of sadness but is also a climactic moment of deliverance from various forms of bondage, a climax of freedom from a drama involving hardship and indignity as well as moments of happiness and beauty, vividly apprehended. What is insisted on is the passionate logic of her final decision. Her death is a matter not of self-deception, but of honesty. That is why the work, dealing with a sad theme, is really a celebration of the agonized growth of a moral consciousness, a hymn to the painfully achieved independence of one human being,' Bodley Private Collection.

50 John McDonagh, *Brendan Kennelly: A Host of Ghosts* (Dublin, 2004), 32. He notes further the 'nice and perhaps unintended irony' of the Vermeer painting *Girl with a Pearl Earring* on the cover of the 2001 collection *Glimpses* 'an image that uncannily matches Kennelly's description of the girl who inspired his earlier extended poem'.

sustains a C–G fifth in the bass for the entire 30 bars under the soloist's ornamented lines beginning 'November cloud is the colour of my mind, my body is music'. A rising accented motif which is first heard in the accompaniment in bars 8–9 returns in the last song, as do the open fifths in the bass. There are other unifying factors in the cycle, such as the insistent minor thirds in the upper piano part which recur throughout No. 3 ('Familiar Things') and appear again at 'the water laps in my head deeper than ever, moonlight glints like a million blades in my favourite river' for the last fifteen bars of No. 18 ('The Slaughterer'). Bodley has commented in this connection: 'The dramatic implications of equating the "familiar" with the thoughts of the river in which she will eventually drown emphasise the continuity of the girl's emotional logic.'[51] Often the piano accompaniment is restricted to the absolute minimum: No. 20 ('Strength') is only 11 bars long and employs a static chordal texture which allows the vocal protagonist the freedom of an Irish slow air. The accompaniment to No. 20 consists of two major triads, while that of No. 21 ('Emptiness') is based on a single chord of D major repeated in different registers to support a recitative. But even more minimal is the accompaniment to an earlier song in the cycle, No. 12 ('Summer') which consists of 26 bars of repeated added ninth chord in crotchets which the pianist must 'continue repeating steadily, independent of the voice's rhythm, pauses, tempo-changes etc.' Repetitive sonorities are also a feature of No. 5 ('Polka'), No. 15 ('All things move towards peace'), and No. 17 ('Possession'). The final song (Ex. 25) opens with the dramatic statement 'I am going out, not down' in a resolute C major. Bodley superimposes G flat major on this C major in bars 27–30 to produce a clashing sonority reminiscent of Stravinsky's celebrated 'Petrushka chord'. This is sustained to intense emotional effect under the words 'smell of cruelty to the end, hitting my heart' and recurs during bars 33–36. An Allegro molto section follows, which recalls the same accompaniment from the middle section of No. 17 ('Possession'). At the climax, the girl cries for her parents and 'drowns' on a pianissimo C major chord in bar 85. The opening fifths motif in the following bar at the Andante prepare for the final statement, 'the water a long shroud, my livingness drifting for ever into a November cloud', and the cycle closes tragically with the motif repeated three times as a sonority over the open C–G fifths in the bass.

A Girl was first performed on 17 October 1978 by Bernadette Greevy and John O'Conor in a concert devoted to Bodley's music in the National Gallery of Ireland.[52] Greevy and O'Conor performed the cycle again during the Dublin Festival of Twentieth-Century Music on 6 January

---

51 Bodley, programme booklet, Dublin Festival of Twentieth-Century Music, 1980, 11. Bodley describes the various types of emotional statement which are represented: 'lyric recitation; dramatic statement; dramatic questioning; dramatic monologue; expressive monologue, etc. The cycle also deals with the mixed emotions: positive/negative elegiac mood; joy and horror combined; peace and rhapsodic joy; emptiness and joy.'

52 The concert also included performances of A Narrow Road to the Deep North and Aislingí. For an account of this concert, see Fanny Feehan, 'The Importance of Being Seóirse', Hibernia, 4 January 1979.

1980, and also included it in their recital at the Wigmore Hall in London the following month on 19 February. They subsequently recorded the work on the Gael Linn label.[53]

This cycle was very well received. Fanny Feehan reported after the premiere that 'this was the first occasion when I have seen an audience at a first hearing of a new work shocked into momentarily stepping outside their normal placidity and goodwill towards a new work, and becoming really emotionally involved'.[54] After his second hearing in January 1980, Acton suggested that

> the total synthesis of Bodley's music and Brendan Kennelly's words was as complete as in any of the great cycles of history. [Bodley's] music … truly added to and illuminated Kennelly's words making a totality that, as far as I was concerned, amounted to a major work of our century and a commanding assertion of Irish creativity.[55]

In his review of the recording, Acton also recommended it to his readers as 'a complete fusion of words and music that will take your heart away'.[56] Elsewhere, he commented that Bodley had been notably more successful here in his attempts to integrate Irish folk music with avant-garde idioms than in other recent works such as *The Narrow Road to the Deep North*, in which 'there was little or no fusion — the two elements were as oil and water unemulsified'.[57] The Irish composer Jane O'Leary (b. 1946) declared it to be 'a landmark in the history of Irish music', noting the indigenous appeal of 'its "Irishness" (in the sense of direct use of traditional tunes, whether originally composed or otherwise)', although for O'Leary this aspect created a 'disturbing juxtaposition'.[58] Ronald Crichton in the *Financial Times* was less enthusiastic, suggesting that 'the cycle does not bite very deep, there is too much in words and music about rain'.[59] However, Alan Blyth writing in the *Daily Telegraph* after the first London performance stated that 'Bodley's writing for the voice convincingly combines the lyrical and the declamatory with a strong and understandable leaning towards the melodic cut of his homeland.'[60]

---

53 Bodley himself performed the cycle on numerous occasions, both in Europe and during a tour of China in 1987.

54 Feehan, 'The Importance of Being Seóirse'

55 *Irish Times*, 8 January 1980

56 For reviews of the recording, see *Irish Times*, 26 January 1981 and *Classical Music*, 2 May 1981.

57 *Irish Times*, 9 January 1981. See also Honor O'Connor who noted 'the tension between the vocal and piano parts [which] creates a virtual third part: the spirit of the girl caught in the tensions of love and hate on the one hand, and between herself and the realities of the world on the other.' 'Sounds and Voices: Aspects of Contemporary Irish Music and Poetry', *Anglo-Irish and Irish Literature: Aspects of Language and Culture*, 2 (1988), 212

58 Jane O'Leary, 'Dublin Festival of Twentieth Century Music', *Perspectives of New Music*, 17, 2 (Spring–Summer, 1979), 266

59 *Financial Times*, 21 February 1980

60 *Daily Telegraph*, 20 February 1980. Blyth added that Greevy realized 'its inner tensions in her direct, unaffected, interpretation'.

For his next work, a choral song cycle entitled *The Radiant Moment*, Bodley turned to writings by the poet, critic, and one-time Director of the National Gallery of Ireland, Thomas MacGreevy (1893–1967). This was commissioned by the 1979 Cork International Choral Festival for the Seminar on Contemporary Choral Music. The premiere was given on 26 April of that year in the City Hall, Cork by the RTÉ Singers under Eric Sweeney. The six songs comprising the cycle divide into two groups: four 'Songs of Love and Farewell' and 'Two Songs: of time Present and time Past'. The text of the first song, 'Ten Thousand Leaping Swords' (Ex. 26) refers to a celebrated phrase from Edmund Burke's speech on the death of Marie Antoinette: 'I thought ten thousand swords must have leaped from their scabbards, to avenge even a look that threatened her with insult.' MacGreevy's poem has been described by Norman Vance as evoking 'a sudden vision of beauty and love'.[61] Bodley sets the opening sixteen bars in D major, coming to rest on a flattened seventh. This C serves as the link to the following four bars of F major in unison with groups of ornamented grace notes 'in the Irish style', which lead (again with a C) to a very serene *subito pianissimo* sonority of A flat major superimposed onto G flat major on the word 'beauty'. Bodley's setting employs a tonal harmonic language (except for an F–F sharp clash on the word 'absurdities') and is predominantly triadic in texture, with much divisi writing. (The work requires a minimum of ten singers — three sopranos and altos, two tenors and basses.) The song ends with a five-fold cry in ten parts on the Greek word for 'sea', *thalassa* — an allusion to the shout of joy, '*thalassa, thalassa!*', given by ten thousand Greek soldiers when they eventually caught sight of the Black Sea on their homeward journey after an unsuccessful campaign against the Persians in 401 BC (this episode is recounted in a celebrated passage in Xenophon's *Anabasis*).[62]

'Arrangement in Gray and Black',[63] subtitled 'To the memory of a student of François de Sales' (the sixteenth-century philosopher, cleric and saint), depicts the delicate form of the dying girl with an ornamented melody over sustained major seconds. The contrasting middle section in C sharp minor refers to her unhappy life and after the questioning words 'her faith?' (sung to C major thirds), the material of the opening returns to express her unrequited hope of 'unfailing life in unfailing love'. The third movement, 'Dechtire' (who was the mother of Cúchulainn) has a stumbling syncopated accompaniment with the men repeating 'I do not love you' — Dechtire as a girl's name also being used here by MacGreevy to personify Ireland. 'Did Tosti Raise His Bowler Hat?' incorporates references to the Italian composer Francesco Tosti and the American and Australian sopranos Geraldine Farrar and Dame Nellie Melba. Bodley dwells on the word 'Ireland' which is repeated a dozen times and he quotes a fragment of Tosti's famous song 'Goodbye', which

---

61 Norman Vance, *Irish Literature since 1800* (Harlow, 2002), 161
62 This and the other poems in the cycle are discussed in Susan Schreibman, *Collected Poems of Thomas MacGreevy: An Annotated Edition* (Dublin, 1991).
63 It is also a reference to James McNeill Whistler's painting, 'Arrangement in Grey and Black No. 1 (better known as *Whistler's Mother*).

he requires to 'be sung with sincerity — or at any rate, not parodied'. The second part of the work opens with a setting of 'Nocturne of the Self-Evident Presence', a poem inspired by MacGreevy's first visit to Switzerland. The final movement of the cycle, 'Hommage to Marcel Proust', is the longest, and recalls a sleepy Sunday afternoon of MacGreevy's childhood in Tarbert at the mouth of the Shannon estuary. This returns to the ornamented style of the second movement. It incorporates quotations from various Victorian parlour songs alluded to by MacGreevy, such as the Thomas Moore melody, 'Believe me, if all those endearing young charms' and Michael Balfe's setting of Byron's poem, 'Maid of Athens, ere we part', but juxtaposes them with material evocative of Irish folk music. The composer describes the result as an attempt 'to do musically what Joyce did in *Ulysses* when he juxtaposed popular songs with highly intellectual elements.'[64]

In 1979, Bodley was commissioned by the Irish government to write a symphony to commemorate the centenary of the birth of the Irish poet and educator, Pádraig Pearse (1879–1916). Pearse was one of the leaders of the ill-fated Easter Rising in April 1916, for which he was executed the following month. Pearse had been an ardent propagandist for the Irish language and Gaelic culture, and Bodley sought to honour his memory by incorporating a range of allusions to Gaelic mythology and early Irish literature into the symphony. In his programme note for this, his second symphony for full orchestra, he remarked that Pearse 'understood the position of the language itself at the heart of the Irish tradition, and its importance as a tool for helping the Irish people to a deeper understanding of themselves'.[65] The symphony, which is scored for large orchestra, is entitled 'I Have Loved the Lands of Ireland', a translation of a phrase from the writings of the Irish monk and saint, Colum Cille (521–97). In his programme note, Bodley explained that he called it a symphony 'in the sense of being a musical statement of depth and size' rather than because of any formal considerations. He deliberately placed the word symphony in brackets *after* the title, wishing to indicate thereby his adoption of a more contemporary approach to the genre. He described the result as 'a post-modern Irish symphony'.[66] One should not conclude from this designation that modernism had lost its appeal for Bodley. And, although he accorded the work (and indeed perhaps validated it with) the sub-title 'symphony', he did not feel bound to observe conventions or established precedents.

64 *Sunday Independent*, 25 March 1979. Geraldine Neeson noted that Bodley was 'resurrecting the idiom of two Irelands — the Anglo-Irish of the 1900s and the traditional mode of expression [but] both visions were suggested rather than emphasised'. *Cork Examiner*, 27 April 1979

65 Bodley, RTÉ programme booklet, 9 January, 1981. The composer's notes are reprinted in the score published by the Contemporary Music Centre, Ireland.

66 Bodley, RTÉ programme booklet, 9 January, 1981. Barry in 'Examining the Great Divide', 20, questioned Bodley's appellation of 'post-modern' which 'must have negative connotations in respect of "modern" as if he had had consciously rejected "modernism". If there is a positive theoretical underpinning to his recent music it can only be on the purely narrative level of "Irishness": his own civic consciousness dictating his musical procedures. ... Since the means he uses to achieve "Post-modernism" are so obviously situated in the vestiges of his musical-historical consciousness, however, and since the incompatibilities are merely exposed, there is a contradiction here, too.'

Ex. 25 *A Girl*, No. 22, 'I am going out', 1–30

Ex. 26 *The Radiant Moment:* 'Ten Thousand Leaping Swords', 17–32

* The 1st Bass part in this bar may be sung by 2nd Tenors

Each of the work's seven movements is inspired by a quotation from early Irish sources, although these are not used as actual titles. John Page has remarked upon the significance of 'the combination of symphonic thought and Irish identity' in Bodley's second and third symphonies and notes that the importance of the text in these symphonies 'signifies the close relationship that pertains between a literary and mythical tradition and perception of an Irish identity'.[67] Bodley explained that he understood the 'lands' of the title in a metaphorical sense as a 'sense of territories of the Irish mind and spirit' and that the work is an attempt 'to delineate the essence of the emotional and psychological history of the Irish people':

> In doing so it evokes three aspects of Ireland: reality, experience and myth. The expressions of reality and experience in the Early Irish poems are as alive as ever. In a similar manner the mythical figures embody essential psychological realities. The myths are Irish — but also universal. The meaning of heroism, or the relationship of the individual to his surroundings and tradition are matters that are everywhere dangerous to brush aside.[68]

These three concepts — reality, experience and myth — are addressed in the seven movements as follows: Reality (movements 1 and 6), Experience (2 and 4), and Myth (3, 5 and 7). The subtitle of the first movement, 'The sun shines through the window', alludes to a phrase penned by an unknown scribe in the margin of a medieval Irish manuscript: 'Is séim linn indiu bloscadh inna gréne frisna marganu le thrati' [Pleasant is the glinting of the sun today on these margins because it flickers so]. It begins serenely in C major with the sonority of horns and then trumpets in thirds, and the movement evokes the 'glinting' and 'flickering' of the sun with a lengthy and ornamented celesta solo interpolated with pizzicato string textures. Three *sforzando* tutti interjections followed by shimmering string and vibraphone figurations lead into a brass chorale section. Passages in thirds in the oboes and clarinets appear only to be interrupted by the three *sforzando* chords again at the end of the movement. The second movement, which is perhaps the most impressive of the seven, engages with the theme of exile. It takes its motto from lines by Colum Cille: 'Fil súil nglais fégbas Érinn dar a hais noco n-aceba íarmothá firu Érenn nách a mná' [There is a grey eye which will look back on Ireland, no more shall it see the men of Ireland or its women]. Here Bodley wishes to depict the 'grinding harshness of exile; recollections of home in brief flashes of memory [and] and feelings of longing',[69] which was so much part of the Irish experience in the past. The harmonic language of the movement is, for the most part, tonal with modal inflexions. The movement has a clear tonal centre of E minor, though there is a brief passage featuring string clusters to support an oboe solo

67 John Page, 'A post-war "Irish" Symphony: Frank Corcoran's Symphony No. 2', *Irish Music in the Twentieth Century: Irish Musical Studies 7*, ed. Gareth Cox & Axel Klein (Dublin, 2003), 138
68 Bodley, RTÉ programme booklet, 9 January, 1981
69 Bodley, RTÉ programme booklet, 9 January, 1981

as well as a short turbulent middle section (*Allegro*) which is rather more dissonant. This leads to an expansive *Andantino* with piccolo interjections which will be heard again in the sixth movement, 'The Blackbird'. This is followed by a warm and majestic *Adagio* theme in C major (Ex. 27), which presumably evokes the nostalgia of exile. It is repeated a semitone higher before the movement ends firmly in E minor with six sharply emphatic chords.

The third movement, 'Aisling I: Morrígan', employs the musical form that Bodley had invented for his piano cycle *Aislingí*. The title alludes to the formidable Celtic goddess Morrígan, who was spurned by the mythological hero Cúchulainn and exacted her revenge by hindering him in battle. The movement, which proceeds in a brisk *Allegro*, can thus be heard as loosely programmatic. At its climax, a noble trumpet solo which presumably represents Cúchulainn is answered by mocking clarinet figurations suggestive of Morrígan, which are punctuated by insistent bass drum interjections. This movement is perhaps less successful than its predecessor, as it is somewhat fragmented and lacks the drive to convey the sense of the demonic, which Bodley presumably intended. The fourth movement evokes the legendary Gaelic princess Gráinne, who was torn between her passionate love for the hero Diarmaid Ua Duibhne and loyalty to her intended husband, the aging warrior Fionn MacCumhaill. It is based on the lines of Gráinne speaking to Fionn about Diarmaid: 'Fil duine frismad buide lemm díuderc, ara tibrinn in mbith mbuide, huile, huile, cid díupert' [There is one on whom I would love to gaze, for whom I would give the whole bright world, all of it, all of it, though great were the sacrifice]. Scored for strings, wind and horns only, there are clear programmatic elements. From letter A the strings build up in clusters to introduce a short solo violin recitative suggestive of Gráinne, which is followed by another idea given to solo horn in unison with the cellos that almost certainly depicts Diarmaid. The rest of the movement consists of elaborately ornamented cor anglais and clarinet solos, punctuated twice by a gentle 'love-duet' for two solo violins. Bodley gives detailed instructions regarding the style of performance: the cor anglais solo 'to be played in Irish style' without *rallentandi* at phrase endings, while the pastoral clarinet solo 'must at all costs flow effortlessly'. The movement, which began in B flat major, ends serenely in C major with *pianissimo* sustained chords on strings and horns.

The warrior Cúchulainn is portrayed again in the energetic fifth movement, which is also cast as an *Aisling*. Here, Bodley evokes parallels between the ancient hero Cúchulainn who died bravely on the battlefield and the self-sacrifice of the modern-day nationalist Pearse who fought for his country's independence. Three timpani are required, one of which is placed offstage, to produce frenzied antiphonal effects from rehearsal letters B to C to symbolize conflict and courage. The mighty hero is also depicted by brass sonorities, though his gentler side is evoked in the middle section by a noble Irish-style melody in the first violins from letter E. This is repeated in slightly modified form by unison strings before a reprise of the opening material, which brings the movement to a dramatic close. The sixth movement, 'The Blackbird', is scored for strings, flutes and clarinets, with a prominent part for solo piccolo. It draws inspiration from lines by Colum

Cille, 'Int én gaires ansin tsail álainn guilbnén as glan gair; rinn binn buide fir druib druin; cas cor cuirther, guth ind luin' [The bird that calls from the willow, beautiful is its little beak with its pure song; sweet yellow bill of a sturdy dark lad; skilful the tune that is played, the voice of the blackbird]. The principal theme on the piccolo, which is heard over *pianissimo* C major chords in the strings, derives from the song of a blackbird that Bodley had notated many years previously. Other woodwind respond with trills evocative of bird-song, and the movement dies away on a sustained C major chord. The concluding movement is also an *Aisling* entitled 'Banba', Celtic goddess whose name is a poetic epithet for Ireland. The expansive Banba theme appears twice in the strings, first after a plaintive solo bassoon melody introduced by a gentle timpani roll, and again after a lively and energetic middle section. A brief reflective passage ensues of quiet solo violin tremolo over gently sustained strings, before the symphony is brought to a rousing close.

Symphony No. 2 was first performed in Dublin on 9 January 1981 by the RTÉ Symphony Orchestra under Colman Pearce, a conductor who is a notable interpreter of Bodley's work.[70] Despite its enthusiastic reception from the audience, the response of the Dublin critics was somewhat ambivalent. Charles Acton wrote in the *Irish Times* that the work 'came across with a fine sense of occasion', but was concerned by the failure of the musical material to develop in the first two movements. However, he found that the remaining five movements 'formed a fascinating and integrated whole on their own terms. Interestingly enough, the fast movements had the most immediate appeal. They showed a marked individuality and a great sense of drive and purpose.'[71] The critic for the *Evening Press* felt that the score was weakened by 'the excessive deployment of elements of our own traditional music and occasional lapses into fragmentary abruptness', continuing, '[Bodley's] own personality seems crushed and overcome [and the main ingredient] actually becomes a major distraction and its principal inhibition'.[72] The music critic, Ian Fox, writing in the *Irish Tatler*, suggested that the work would be better entitled a 'Divertimento' and remarked that it would 'make a superb ballet score'.[73] Reflecting on the symphony a couple of years later, Malcolm Barry considered it to be 'curiously dated'. He expressed regret that Bodley had 'abandoned what he called "modernism" in favour of extra-musical impulses', adding that 'with the bathwater of avant-garde devices has gone the baby of Bodley's own acute musical perception'.[74]

70 The Symphony was subsequently broadcast on BBC Radio 3 on 28 October 1983 by the BBC Philharmonic Orchestra under Bryden Thomas.
71 *Irish Times*, 10 January 1981
72 *Evening Press*, 10 January 1980. Fanny Feehan considered that the work held 'up a mirror to the Irish soul'. 'Seóirse's Second', *Hibernia*, 4 September 1980, 25
73 Ian Fox, 'Irish Music in the Classical Field', *Irish Tatler*, March 1981, 15
74 Barry, 'Examining the Great Divide', 20

Ex. 27 Symphony no. 2: *I Have Loved the Lands of Ireland*, II, 93–102

The composition of Bodley's second symphony was followed closely by his third, which was commissioned by RTÉ for the inauguration of the National Concert Hall in Dublin on 9 September 1981. For many decades, Dublin concert-goers had lamented the lack of a dedicated concert hall worthy of a European capital, which meant that the RTÉ Symphony Orchestra and visiting orchestras were forced to perform in venues such as the Phoenix Hall, the Francis Xavier Hall, the Gaiety Theatre, or the much larger Theatre Royal or Adelphi Cinema, all of which, for a variety of reasons, were unsuitable. In the years leading up to the First World War, the Italian composer and pianist Michele Esposito, one of the central figures in Dublin's musical life of the period, had campaigned for the construction of concert hall, but his efforts were unsuccessful.[75] This campaign was reinvigorated in the late 1950s. Plans were mooted to build a concert hall on Haddington Road to be named after the recently assassinated John F. Kennedy, but these too came to nothing. Eventually, it was decided to convert the Great Hall in Earlsfort Terrace, which had belonged to UCD.[76] The inauguration of the National Concert Hall was understandably an event of considerable moment in Dublin's musical life, and the decision to commission Bodley to compose a new work for the occasion indicated that he was now regarded as a major creative figure. *Ceol: Symphony No. 3* was performed together with Beethoven's Ninth Symphony before an invited audience at the official state opening of the hall and was repeated the following evening at a gala concert for the general public. The soloists were Violet Twomey (soprano), Bernadette Greevy (mezzo-soprano), Louis Browne (tenor), William Young (bass) and Aindreas Ó Gallchoir (speaker). These were joined by the combined forces of the RTÉ Symphony Orchestra, the RTÉ Singers and RTÉ Chorus, Our Lady's Choral Society, and the boys of St. Patrick's Cathedral Choir, Dublin, under the baton of Colman Pearce.[77]

Symphony No. 3 bears the descriptive title 'Ceol', the Irish word for music. The work, which is about twenty-five minutes long, is scored for substantial vocal and choral forces that include SATB soli, SATB choir, semi-chorus, children's choir and speaker in addition to a large orchestra; in the final section, the participation of the audience is also required. Bodley once again turned to Brendan Kennelly who provided a set of new poems for the occasion which 'examine the nature of music.'[78] The symphony is in

75 See Jeremy Dibble, *Michele Esposito* (Dublin, 2010).

76 For a summary of the developments leading to the conversion of the Earlsfort Terrace premises into the National Concert Hall, see Patricia Butler and Pat O'Kelly, *The National Concert Hall at Earlsfort Terrace, Dublin: A History* (Dublin, 2000). See also Gareth Cox (ed.), *Acton's Music: Reviews of Dublin's Musical Life 1955–1985* (Bray, 1996), 151–61, and Pine, *Music and Broadcasting in Ireland*, 506–14. Bodley was appointed to the first board of directors of the National Concert Hall.

77 The performance on 9 September was broadcast live on television to the BBC and to the USSR and recorded on LP together with A. J. Potter's *Sinfonia de Profundis*, but the disc was issued by RTÉ only in a limited and private release — apparently, because members of the RTÉSO were unhappy with the quality of their playing in the Potter symphony. This was a pity because Bodley's symphony has not been performed since. For an account of the circumstances, see Charles Acton's article in the *Irish Times*, 12 July 1982.

78 Bodley, RTÉ programme booklet, 9 September 1981

ten numbered sections which are grouped into three movements, the first movement comprising sections I–IV, the second sections V–VII and the third sections VIII–X. Each section is introduced by a motto in Irish, which is declaimed by the speaker. While there are pauses between each of the three movements, the constituent sections of each movement are played without breaks.

Ceol begins with eighteen introductory bars of C major rising from ppp in the basses to tutti fff in a manner reminiscent of Richard Strauss's tone-poem Also Sprach Zarathustra, dropping in dynamic at one point to allow the speaker to announce the motto at the start of the first section 'Níl fearann, níl tíos agam, Níl fíonta ná ceol …' [I have neither land nor house, wine nor music …]. Bodley intended that C major should 'symbolise the inner core of music itself'.[79] this symbolic sonority reappears at strategic junctures, most notably in the symphony's final section. The poem invites listeners to participate in 'the music of life'.[80] Here, as elsewhere in the work, Bodley employs choral textures that feature Irish-style ornamentation, ascending overlaying clusters and rich homophonic passages, such as at the line 'Hearts are beating in the house of music', which is accompanied by softly pulsating timpani (Ex. 28). Starting at a very soft dynamic, the harmony moves from C major through neighbouring keys before C major returns fortississimo — a gesture which is repeated in a varied form towards the end of the work. This section links to the next by means of a held C in the cellos, which almost imperceptibly becomes a sustained D (the reverse move links sections IX and X). The motto for the second section is 'Níl clagar is binne ná ceol a' mhála' [No sound is sweeter than the music of the pipes]. In this Andante, which is lightly scored for flute, clarinet, horn, choir and strings, Bodley celebrates 'music's curious ability to "sound on" long after it has ceased'.[81] However, the mood is rather darker than the motto might suggest, with dissonant superimpositions of thirds used to evoke a somewhat disturbed atmosphere at the line 'dead words were lying around the place like the broken glass ungathered on the floor'. This section opens with a theme marked 'quasi hornpipe', which recurs on the clarinet towards the close, preceded by an eleven-bar descent in thirds played by two solo violins. The third section — a love song for solo tenor, who is accompanied by the choir — is introduced by the words 'Mo Cheol Thú' [You are my music]. The five bars of high As in the soprano line are answered by the tenor in the final two bars of the section, settling gently on an F major chord. According to Bodley's programme note, the fourth and final section of the first movement, which bears the motto 'An Ceol agus an Náire' [Music and Shame], is a description of 'the terrible fate that awaits those ashamed of their own internal music, condemned as they are to a "very respectable corner of hell"'.

79 Bodley, RTÉ programme booklet, 9 September 1981
80 Bodley, RTÉ programme booklet, 9 September 1981
81 Bodley, RTÉ programme booklet, 9 September 1981

The second movement opens with a section featuring the solo baritone, '... ag ceartú ceoil is ag cumadh rann' [... shaping song and composing verse]. The soloist complains about poor singing, while the chorus observes ironically that 'Any fool can make music now!' After this phrase is repeated in a *glissando* shout, the mood changes abruptly and a *pianissimo* tremolo links to the sixth section, 'Laoithe Dóchais' [Lays of hope], which constitutes the symphony's emotional centre of gravity. The mezzo-soprano soloist, accompanied by humming in the main choir and vocalizations of a simple D major melody by the children's choir, describes a 'wonderful teacher' of songs (Ex. 29), who is contrasted with the teacher's brother — a drunkard who defiantly declares, 'I will live out what the songs say while you teach the children to sing'. As the narrative unfolds, the brothers become reconciled — a turn of events depicted in music of pastoral serenity. The final section of this movement, 'Ceol na mBréag' [Music of Lies], is a surreal depiction of such fantastic events as two mountains walking into a room, Dublin city rowing out to sea in a boat, and seals and frogs making hay in Grafton Street. As Bodley points out, 'each statement in the poem is more outrageous than the last, yet they lead to a final sentence that has a peculiar logic of its own: "Dead and living darlings keep their living and dead laws / smoke from all our chimneys signal happiness is the cause."' The final line is set to forceful music that is overtly reminiscent of Orff's *Carmina Burana*. Earlier the symbolic C major sonority makes what seems to be an ironic appearance at the words 'the eagle was born clutching happiness in its claws'.

The opening section of the third movement, 'Níl sa cheoil uile ach gaoth' [There is nothing in music but wind] lasts barely a minute. The text pays homage to the orchestral instrumentalists as producers of music and the choir lists the instruments as they appear. The closing eight bars are given to choir and soloists alone and reflect on 'the ephemeral nature of music and man', the solo soprano holding a high A which recalls the solo tenor's sustained A at the end of section III. The following section, 'Ceol na Farraige' [The music of the sea] establishes links with the opening section of the symphony, the word 'listen' featuring prominently in both. Bodley comments that 'the sea here represents the depths of the unconscious beyond the conscious mind. The music of the sea is the music of those depths from which come both treasure and treachery'. The closing bass D quietly slips to C for the final section, 'Ceol an Cheoil' [The music of music]. Here, the audience members become participants in the performance, being required to join in a choral refrain — an idea which Bodley acknowledges was inspired by Aloys Fleischmann's choral work *Song of the Provinces* (1963).[82] After ten bars of C major, the tonality shifts abruptly up a semitone to

---

82 Bodley emphasized this influence during his speech to launch the first two volumes in the new Field Day Music series, *Aloys Fleischmann* (2006) by Séamas de Barra and *Raymond Deane* (2006) by Patrick Zuk at the Contemporary Music Centre in Dublin on 21 September 2007. *Amhrán na gCúigí* or *Song of the Provinces* of 1963 was intended for a gala choral event at the Cork International Choral Festival in 1964 but was actually first performed on 29 June 1965 in Dublin by Radio Éireann forces conducted by Fleischmann himself. Fleischmann, however, demanded more from his audience than Bodley did, requiring a rehearsal beforehand. See de Barra, *Aloys Fleischmann*, 117–19, and on a later work of Fleischmann's requiring audience participation, *Clonmacnoise* (1989), see 151–52.

D flat major for the first of four appearances of this refrain, 'Is ceol tú féin, Is ceol tú féin, Is ceol tú féin i gcónaí', which the singing translation in the score renders as 'Your song is you, Your song is you, Your song is you for all your days'. Bodley provided this translation but 'only for use when the work is performed solely in English'. His intention was that the Irish language itself should be perceived as bursting into song at this point. Acton remarked about this passage that 'for the opening of our Concert Hall it was entirely proper that [it] should have music herself as a persona and audience taking part in a refrain'.[83] The refrain is preceded each time by brass triads, a harp *glissando* and cymbals as a clear cue for the audience. Each subsequent statement is sung another semitone higher in D major, E flat major, and E major respectively (Ex. 30). A unison E serves as a pivot to return to C major for a passage recalling the very opening of the symphony, which depicts music returning 'to that mysterious silent region where it has its origins'.

The symphony was greeted with a standing ovation from the audience at the premiere, but received mixed reviews in the press. Acton suggested that the work had features in common with Vaughan Williams's *Sea Symphony* and felt that Bodley had 'written music as old-fashioned or as individual or as strange as Ó Riada's Hölderlin songs seemed when they appeared', which he stressed he meant as a compliment.[84] Mary MacGoris called it 'a finely-wrought work which without being calculatedly "Irish" gently reveals its native inspiration'.[85] However, for Bernard Harris, the work

> was evidently aimed at meeting the formal needs of a great occasion. It never became taxing or demanding for even the simplest of musical tastes [and one] was occasionally reminded of those arrangements of Irish traditional tunes which the RTÉSO. so often performed and recorded in the fifties and sixties ... in their approach to this work Brendan Kennelly and Seóirse Bodley responded to that call for an aesthetic statement to which we might respond authentically — fully aware of our situation individually and communally in time and place. It would seem, however, that their over-conscious preoccupation with the outer accidentals of our cultural heritage runs the risk of obscuring its very essence. *Ceol* may point the direction but it is not the way.[86]

The problem of how Irish folk music and avant-garde techniques could be convincingly integrated was to occupy Bodley for over another decade.

83 *Irish Times*, 12 September 1981
84 *Irish Times*, 10 September 1981
85 *Irish Independent*, 10 September 1981
86 Bernard Harris, 'On the Way to Ceol', *Soundpost*, 4 (October/November, 1981), 27. 'The general idiom, however', Harris said, 'reflected the composer's highly personal approach to problems of contemporary composition as well as his preoccupation with integrating an Irish traditional note into his works.'

Ex. 28 *Ceol*: Symphony No. 3, I, 54–59

(Notated at concert pitch)

Ex. 29 *Ceol*: Symphony No. 3, VI, bars 2–25

(Notated at concert pitch)

Ex. 30 *Ceol*: Symphony no. 3, x, bars 49–55

(Notated at concert pitch)

4. Growing Recognition

By the early 1980s, Bodley had come to be regarded as one of the most significant Irish composers of his generation. The steady growth of his reputation was accompanied by signs of wider recognition. In 1980, his portrait was painted by the distinguished Irish artist Paul Funge (b. 1944). The fine likeness that resulted was displayed at a Funge exhibition in the Project Theatre in Dublin in March 1980 and subsequently hung in the National Concert Hall. The following year, Bodley was invited to become a founder member of Aosdána, an association set up by the Irish Arts Council in 1981 to honour creative artists considered to have made an outstanding contribution to the country's cultural life. In 1982, Bodley received the prestigious Marten Toonder award, and in 1984 he was promoted by UCD to Associate Professor.

From the late 1970s onwards, Bodley's energies were increasingly directed towards two very different types of creative activity. The first of these grew out of his association with RTÉ, which led to invitations to compose incidental music for a number of television documentaries. These were mostly historical or biographical in nature, one of the most notable being a portrait of James Joyce, *Is there one who understands me?* made in 1982 by Seán Ó Mórdha, a director who produced a number of programmes on Irish writers for RTÉ.[1] This documentary includes interviews with friends, relatives and Joyce scholars, and was shot on locations where Joyce lived and worked. The reviewer for the *Sunday Tribune* described Bodley's score as 'haunting elegiac music [which] echoes around the stronger visual images and underscored an evocation of remembering tinged with regret'.[2] The documentary won an Emmy award in New York in November 1982 and was subsequently re-mastered and broadcast again ten years later during the Joyce centenary

---

1 The documentary's title is a quotation from the closing pages of *Finnegans Wake*.
2 *Sunday Tribune*, 7 February 1982

in 1992.[3] Bodley's score, which also can be performed as a concert work, consists of nine sections lasting about sixteen minutes. Another documentary, *Between the Canals* (1983), evoked Dublin in the 1950s and included reminiscences of distinguished literary figures such as Patrick Kavanagh, Brendan Behan and Flann O'Brien. Bodley's scores for these documentaries were composed for small chamber ensembles, which he conducted for the recording sessions. In 1983, he and A. J. Potter provided the music for a four-part series, *Caught in a Free State*, which was subsequently broadcast on the British station Channel 4. Directed by Peter Ormrod and written by Brian Lynch, this portrayed the experiences of Luftwaffe pilots interned in Ireland during World War II and the activities of German agents who infiltrated the neutral Free State of Ireland to liaise with the IRA.

The second type of creative activity centred on amateur musicians. Bodley welcomed the opportunity to write music specially tailored to the needs of non-professional performers, remarking in an interview: 'It gives you an opportunity to create something in terms of everyday life. Artists shouldn't cut themselves off from society.'[4] This desire to fulfil what he evidently regards as a composer's social obligation led him to accept a commission in 1984 to write an anthem for the Gaelic Athletic Association (GAA) — an amateur Irish sporting organization that promotes traditional Gaelic games — for a concert in celebration of the organization's centenary held in the Opera House in Cork on 7 October 1984.[5] The text for this work, *Amhrán an Chéid*, was written by the composer. It is not clear whether it was intended to be sung at GAA matches, but if so, there is no record that it was ever performed again. Bodley has also composed and arranged music suitable for children. His most substantial contribution in this vein was a workshop piece for schoolchildren entitled *The Fiddler*, which was commissioned by the Music Association of Ireland and first performed on 6 October 1987 by students of St. Louis Convent School in Monaghan and the Cork-based Jupiter Ensemble. This charming and highly effective score is based on an Irish folk tale about a fiddler who becomes the finest player in the country, thanks to supernatural assistance. It is written for speaker and professional string trio, with optional parts for chorus, percussion and other instrumentalists, depending on the resources available. The work is well worth the attention of music teachers, as it is designed to allow the participation of student performers at varying levels of ability and effectively combines a contemporary idiom with Irish-style material.

Bodley's most extensive engagement with amateur performers, however, has been in the field of liturgical music. Between 1976 and 1980, he composed three settings of the Mass for congregational use, responding to the demand for English-language settings

---

3   The film was also released in the United States in June 1983, but this version used music from the period instead of Bodley's score.
4   *Sunday Independent*, 23 September 1984
5   It is scored for baritone, unison chorus (audience participation) and orchestra and was performed by Martin Dempsey (baritone) and the RTÉ Concert Orchestra under Proinnsías Ó Duinn: see *Irish Times*, 15 October 1984.

of the liturgy after the Second Vatican Council. The first of these, *Mass of Peace* (1976) was written for the National Commission for Sacred Music. It is scored for celebrant (or cantor), choir (unison/SATB), congregation and organ and was first performed in 1977 at the Carmelite Conference Centre in the Dublin suburb of Ballinteer.[6] Later that year, it was recorded for commercial release by the Clonliffe College Choir with Bodley conducting. This work has been particularly successful: 1,000 full scores and 10,000 congregational copies were issued, all of which sold out within two months.[7] Sections of Bodley's setting were performed during an open-air Mass in the Phoenix Park on the occasion of Pope John Paul II's visit to Dublin on 29 September 1979, which was attended by one and a half million people. Bodley was present to hear this vast crowd singing his music, surely a unique experience for any composer.

Reflecting on the challenges involved in writing music of this nature, Bodley has remarked:

> Liturgical masses are not easy to write if you attempt to reach a high musical standard. ... [The composer] is expected to be very concise, so as not to hold up the liturgical movement. The texts of the mass that he has to set are irregularly shaped yet they must be made singable by an average congregation. He must write music that a congregation can not only understand but perform. There are strict limitations as to vocal style and range. For example a melody for a mixed adult congregation must be written within that vocal range that is common to both the high and low voice. Unquestionably it is a challenge to attempt to write in a very restricted and limited style. ... However, extreme confines can mean that one has to try to rise above the limitations. With the use of optional descants and different performance options it is possible to create a musical style that is suitable for many different types of congregation. The liturgical mass ... is in some ways both more demanding ... [than] the Latin Mass of the past.[8]

Mass for Peace undoubtedly owes something to the example of Seán Ó Riada, who composed two settings of the Mass towards the end of his life for the choir in his local parish church of Coolea, a village located in an Irish-speaking district of Co. Cork. In Bodley's view, Ó Riada's settings successfully accomplished the difficult task of writing music that was not only appropriate for liturgical use, but was also completely suited to the community

---

6 Charles Acton, who was present at the performance of the mass in a liturgical context, described it as 'singable, beautiful and beyond all doubt Irish in feeling ... about the first fully successful setting for genuine congregational use (in accordance with the Vatican Instruction) of the English text of the Mass'. Acton, *Irish Music and Musicians* (Dublin, 1978), 29
7 *Irish Times*, 7 April 1977
8 Bodley, 'A Special Category', *Music Ireland*, May 1990, 10

for which it was composed, being stylistically rooted in Irish folk music.[9] The influence of Irish folk music is equally pronounced on his *Mass for Peace* (Ex. 31), as it is on the masses which Bodley composed subsequently. This increases its stylistic accessibility for Irish congregations, for, as Bodley points out, folk music is 'in their psyche, barely below the surface and it comes out when they sing'.[10]

Ex. 31 *Mass of Peace, Gloria,* 1–14

9   Bodley, 'Remembering Seán Ó Riada', 303
10   *Sunday Independent,* 25 March 1979

Two further settings of the Mass, *Mass of Joy* and *Mass of Glory* followed in 1978 and 1980, respectively. *Mass of Joy* was first performed by the choirs of Clonliffe College and Mater Dei Institute of Education on 8 March 1979 under Bodley's direction before a congregation of over one thousand.[11] The work is subtitled 'In Honour of St. John of God' and was commissioned by the Brothers of St. John of God to commemorate their founder and patron during the centenary of their Irish province. Scored for cantor, unison/SATB, congregation and organ, much of it is designed to be sung by a leading group which can also be a section of the congregation rather than the choir. Optional descants are provided which may be performed either by singers or instrumentalists. Three trumpet parts can be added to the Gospel Acclamation and percussion to the recurrences of the refrain in the *Gloria*. The more ceremonial *Mass of Glory* (*Aifreann na Glóire*) was commissioned by the Sisters of Loreto Abbey in Dublin to mark the closing of their chapter and was first performed by them on 15 August 1980. The Mass is written for six-part SSATBB (or optionally SSA) chorus or soloists and congregational participation. The accompaniment is written for harmonium or organ, but may also be performed by a string ensemble. Various optional instruments can be added, and it is possible to sing the text either in English or Irish. In 2005, all three Masses were published by Carysfort Press in a one-volume edition which has proved to be extremely successful commercially in Ireland and North America.[12]

Bodley has also made arrangements of traditional Irish and German carols and Irish religious folksongs. Amongst the most notable of these are a set of four Kilmore Carols for solo voice and piano which he arranged in 1986. Some time before, Bodley had transcribed performances of these carols by Jack Devereux, a traditional singer from Kilmore in Co. Wexford, for inclusion in an edition of the Wexford Carols by Diarmaid Ó Muirithe. They are traditionally sung from Christmas Eve until Epiphany by a choir of six men in unison and are freely ornamented. Bodley supplied the edition with a commentary in which he describes the nature of the ornamentation and the manner of performance.[13]

11   *Irish Times*, 12 January 1980 and 18 March 1980
12   *Seóirse Bodley: Three Congregational Masses*, ed. Lorraine Byrne (Dublin, 2005)
13   Diarmaid Ó Muirithe, ed., *The Wexford Carols* (Mountrath, 1982). See also *Irish Times*, 22 December 1998.

Ex. 32 Chamber Symphony No. 2, II, 40–50

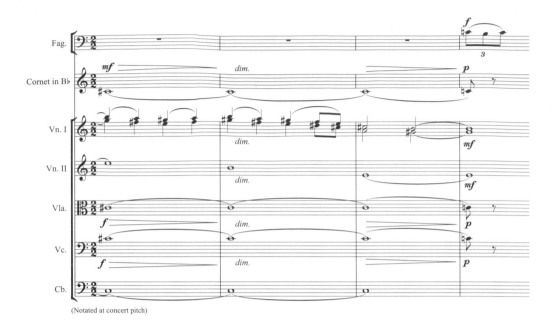

(Notated at concert pitch)

In addition to these works for amateurs, Bodley steadily continued to produced works for professional performers. His first substantial score of this nature after the Second and Third Symphonies was the second Chamber Symphony, which was written for the Ulysses Ensemble, a chamber group founded by the conductor Colman Pearce and the oboist Peter Healy. The work was commissioned with financial assistance from the Irish tobacco firm of P. J. Carroll & Co., which sponsored regular series of summer concerts held initially at their Dublin headquarters at Grand Parade on the Grand Canal from the mid 1970s to the late 1980s. Bodley conducted the premiere at one of these concerts on 17 June 1982. The Second Chamber Symphony is scored for wind quintet, cornet, trombone, glockenspiel and a small string section (a minimum of 4.3.2.2.1) — larger forces than his Chamber Symphony No. 1 eighteen years earlier, but without the extensive percussion section required in that work. The musical language of the two scores is quite different. In the second chamber symphony, Bodley continues to explore the creative possibilities of Irish folk music within a mildly dissonant harmonic language, and much of the thematic material is pervaded by folk influences. Bodley uses the cornet prominently in the slow second movement (Ex. 32), where it plays a melody very similar to the 'Dublin City' theme from his incidental music to the James Joyce documentary 'Is There One Who Understands Me?', composed earlier that year. This movement, as well as the *Adagio* fourth movement, which is scored for wind quintet and strings alone, is serene in mood. The two fast outer and middle movements of this five-movement symphony share similar triadic material, and the piece closes in an animated fashion, its momentum only briefly interrupted for two recitative-like passages for the strings and lower winds accompanied by a *fortissimo* glockenspiel tremolo and answered by trills in the upper winds.

The work met with a somewhat muted critical response. The *Irish Times* observed that the symphony seemed 'overextended' — a not unreasonable comment, given the extensive repetition to which the melodic fragments comprising the work's musical material are subjected.[14]

Bodley's next chamber work, *Celebration Music*, was an occasional piece commissioned by the National Institute of Higher Education for performance at its graduation ceremonies. The piece has been performed regularly since, and is still played at the graduation ceremonies of Dublin City University, as the Institute was renamed when it acquired university status in 1989. In writing the work, Bodley aimed to impart a distinctively Irish atmosphere to the event. It is scored for three trumpets and string quartet and is in five movements (the trumpets are omitted from movements II and IV). At the suggestion of Acton, Bodley prepared an alternative version scored for string orchestra rather than string quartet, and the work was first performed in this guise on 21 September 1984 in the National Concert Hall, Dublin by the RTÉSO under Colman Pearce.[15] The transcription differs only in small details from the original. In his programme notes, Bodley described the structure of the work as follows:

> The two irregularly-shaped allegros frame a sustained 'Song Without Words'; this last is based on a freely-developed 'Irish-style' melody. The Scherzo is irregular, like the allegros, but with hints of elements of circus music. The Processional which ends the work is related to the opening movement (also called 'Processional')[16]

and is constructed in a manner which allows it to be brought to a conclusion at a number of different points depending on the amount of music required for the academic procession, though it is obviously intended to be played in full at a concert performance.

Bodley continued his use of material deriving from Irish folk song in his *Trio for Flute, Violin and Piano* (1986), which was commissioned and first performed by the Irish new music ensemble, Concorde.[17] The work's six movements are all linked by the melodic and harmonic use of sixths. This sonority features in the opening nine bars of the *Moderato* introduction to the substantial first movement (*Allegro*), which then features lively ornamented Irish-style dance tunes and lyrical melodies played within dissonant contexts. A slow-moving *Andante* follows, with long lyrical lines in the flute and violin over static piano chords. The third movement, a dramatic *Allegro moderato* features snatches of traditional melodies in the flute and violin and repeated double-dotted figures. It closes with a short recitative for violin, which settles on a sonorous F sharp major chord five

---

14   *Irish Times*, 6 January 1992
15   Acton made this suggestion in a review in the *Irish Times*, 18 November 1983.
16   Bodley, RTÉ programme booklet, 21 September 1984
17   See the composer's prefatory remarks to the facsimile score issued by the Contemporary Music Centre, Ireland.

bars before the end — a sonority that is compromised by the addition of an E–B fifth in the bass in the last bar. The violin holds a succession of low sixths in the opening of the fourth movement (*Moderato*), while the piano takes on the role of upper voice over the flute part in the outer sections. The structure of the fifth movement (*Andante*) was inspired by an odd personal experience — hearing a friend play reels on a tin whistle while a burial was taking place in a nearby graveyard. This macabre contrast made a considerable impression on the composer.[18] The movement can be regarded as programmatic in that it opens with a lugubrious melody played an octave apart in the flute and the right hand of the piano part accompanied by soft, funereal chords in the lower register of the piano. Over a sustained piano chord the flute descends from a high F with the violin imitating the line, but its entries are staggered at an ever-increasing distance. In the middle section the flute plays parts of a reel to the accompaniment of piano textures that grow denser (Ex. 33), before being joined by the violin in a descent in sixths. The movement ends with a snatch of an air in the flute accompanied by softly chiming chords and muffled thuds in the bass of the piano. The short introduction to the final movement features prominent rising sixths in the piano. During the lively *Allegro* that follows, long melodic passages given to the violin and flute are driven along by an energetic piano part. This *Allegro* is interrupted twice by an *Adagio* section. The first of these is only five bars long, and the second opens with a transposition of the material of the first *Adagio* up a semitone, which is then extended over twenty-seven bars. After the first *Adagio*, the material of the *Allegro* is restated a semitone lower, and after the second, a semitone higher. Bodley's technique of transposing and rearranging earlier material rather than developing it harks back as far as the final movement of his Violin Sonata of 1959. Some listeners may find these repetitions unpersuasive: in a review of the premiere in 1986, Barra Boydell suggested that 'despite many sections of great beauty, there was a sameness about much of the music [and it lacked] the strength of expression associated with so much of [Bodley's] output'.[19]

It is interesting to note that Bodley's work continued to provoke a certain amount of controversy during this period, particularly with regard to his ongoing attempt to incorporate folk influences in his work. While Acton hailed the Chamber Symphony No. 2 as 'perhaps the loveliest work [Bodley] has ever written and certainly a milestone in his oeuvre',[20] Bernard Harris responded more equivocally: although he acknowledged the work's 'many moments of real beauty', he admitted to finding Bodley's use of material deriving from folk music 'increasingly hard to accept'.[21] Writing about *I have Loved the Lands of Ireland: Symphony No. 2*, the composer Frank Corcoran also expressed similar ambivalence — on the one hand declaring the work to be 'very much Irish music', but questioning whether it was 'trying too hard, too self-consciously, to be so':

18   Bodley, prefatory remarks to the facsimile score, Contemporary Music Centre, Ireland.
19   *Irish Times*, 8 July 1986
20   *Irish Times*, 18 June 1982
21   *Soundpost*, 9 (1982), 25

Ex. 33 Trio for Flute, Violin and Piano, V, 31–33

Is the national voice too strident? — and this question comes directly from the *technical* aesthetic one, namely is the folk-derived element handled with sufficient artistic distance?[22]

The following year, Corcoran admitted to unease that 'we in Ireland are desperately worried about our identity' and suggested that, in his opinion, 'no Irish composer yet has really used Irish material effectively'.[23] Particularly intense controversy was provoked by a composition for a quartet of solo voices and electronics entitled *The Banshee*, which was commissioned by BBC Northern Ireland and first performed on 25 April 1983 at the Sonorities Festival in Belfast by the London ensemble Electric Phoenix. This score, for which Bodley wrote his own text, seeks to evoke a supernatural harbinger of death ('banshee' derives from the Irish *bean sí* or 'fairy woman') that features in Irish folklore.[24] Much use is made of extended vocal techniques in conjunction with musical contours and ornamentation derived from Irish folk music (Ex. 34). These sonorities are synthesized by a ring modulator, band-pass filter and digital reverberation (with the frequency and balance being operated by the singers themselves), all contrasted with passages of *a cappella* singing. The work features some effective freely atonal homophonic writing with clusters

22 Frank Corcoran, 'New Irish Music', *Interface*, 12 (1983), 43
23 Bernard Harris, 'From a Conversation with Frank Corcoran', *Soundpost*, 18 (1984), 18
24 While composing the score, Bodley drew on the work of UCD colleague Patricia Lysaght, who had carried out extensive research on Banshee lore. Lysaght subsequently wrote a book on the subject, *The Banshee: The Irish Supernatural Death-Messenger* (Dublin, 1986), which included four short excerpts from Bodley's text on the dust jacket.

interspersed with unison passages, as well as some overtly tonal and modal passages. It also includes wailing *glissandi* and multiphonic effects which need to be performed with complete conviction if the work is to make its point. The piece ends with similar material to that of the beginning and dies out *perdendosi* on the final word, 'whist' [or 'whisht'], the word used to command a Banshee to stop circling the house.

The Banshee provoked a scathing review from Bodley's fellow composer, Raymond Deane, who argued that 'the [folk] idioms themselves, while fresh and alive within a traditional context, here degenerate into the merest clichés'.[25] A few months previously, Deane stated bluntly that, in general, 'attempts to wed traditional Irish music to an "avant-garde" idiom can only lead to a kind of Bord Fáilte aesthetic' — an ironic reference to the images of Ireland promoted by the Irish tourist board at the period, which some people found rather cloying.[26] Clearly, some commentators inclined to the view that Bodley's aims were impossible to realize, feeling that folk music was fundamentally irreconcilable with modernist techniques. Writing after a performance of the *Trio for Flute, Violin and Piano* in 1997, Douglas Sealy concluded that Bodley's attempt 'to bring Irish traditional music into the classical realm' was 'laudable', but ultimately 'misguided'.[27] Malcolm Barry similarly suggested that Bodley had failed to 'resolve the contradictions that he exposes (between traditional music and modernism)'.[28] It is arguable that these criticisms miss the point, however, and that Bodley did not find it necessary or desirable to effect a resolution of this nature — assuming that it is even possible in the first place. As Klein has trenchantly observed, Bodley has never sought 'to fuse the traditional with the sophisticated', but was instead bringing the different musical materials into open confrontation, as 'traditional melodies [clash] with modern discords, triads with clusters.'[29] For Klein, Bodley's music from this period represents 'the most challenging encounter of the two Irish musical traditions so far', as it constitutes 'the only instance of a cultural encounter of the two musical traditions in which both remained uncompromisingly intact, a unique achievement.'[30]

25 Raymond Deane, *Soundpost*, 14 (June/July, 1983), 25
26 Raymond Deane, *Soundpost*, 13 (April/May, 1983), 40
27 *Irish Times*, 7 May 1997
28 Barry, 'Examining the Great Divide', 20
29 Axel Klein, 'Roots and Directions in Twentieth-Century Music', *Irish Musical Studies 7: Irish Music in the Twentieth Century*, Gareth Cox and Axel Klein, eds. (Dublin, 2003), 178
30 Klein, 'Roots and Directions in Twentieth-Century Music', 178. See also Fanny Feehan's remarks in her article 'The Importance of Being Seóirse': '[Bodley] uses such idioms as are normal from the native archive, and the fact that they fit so superbly and individually into his music makes him almost unique because as yet no other composer in this country has made such good use of our heritage'.

Ex. 34 *The Banshee, 97–129*

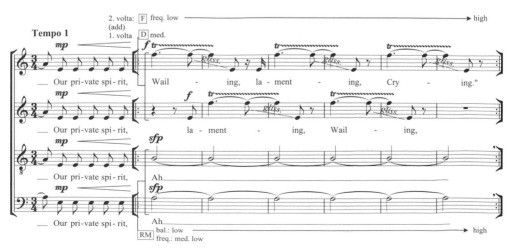

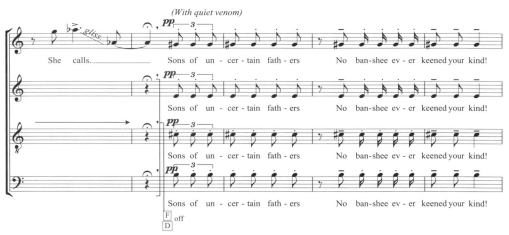

In the late 1980s Bodley separated from his first wife and he met Jennifer Laski, a Canadian doctor living in Dublin. Tragically, their first child Dara was born suffering from Patau's syndrome, a rare disorder resulting from chromosomal abnormality, and only survived for a month.[31] In gratitude for the remarkable care provided by the staff at the National Maternity Hospital, Holles Street, where Dara was born, his parents organized a concert in aid of the institution's Special Care Baby Unit. This took place on 4 May 1990 at the National Concert Hall with the RTÉ Chamber Choir, and the Irish Chamber Orchestra under Bodley's direction. Many of Bodley's friends and colleagues participated, including the singers Virginia Kerr, Aylish Kerrigan, Frank Dunne and Conor Biggs, as well as the pianist Philip Martin. Bodley conducted the first public performance of A Concert Mass, which had been commissioned by the artist Paul Funge for the Gorey Arts Week in Co. Wexford in 1984, but had never been performed publicly, as this festival was discontinued.[32] The Mass is in eight movements and is scored for SATB soli, SATB, and strings. The text, which Bodley wrote himself, takes the form of 'reflections or meditations on the principal sections of the mass as it exists in its modern liturgical form'.[33]

Ten years after his second and third symphonies, Bodley produced another two symphonies in close succession in 1990–91, both of which were paired subsequently on a Marco Polo recording with the National Symphony Orchestra of Ireland (NSOI) conducted by Colman Pearce. Symphony No. 4 was commissioned by the Orchestra Sinfonica dell'Emilia-Romagna 'Arturo Toscanini' and was performed on 21 June 1991 under José Ramon Encinar in the Teatro Farnese, Parma, Italy. This concert formed part of the European Exhibition of Contemporary Music, which was held from 18–22 June 1991 and featured the work of fourteen composers from member states of the European Economic Community. The Irish premiere was given by the NSOI under Colman Pearce on 22 February 1994. Bodley noted that in this symphony he combines

> elements of Irish music, both in more obvious form and also as an influence in shaping the melodic style; sharp dissonance; irregular forming; developing variation ... . Unusually for me, I have made my first references to classical form in an orchestral work in many years. Clearly the movements are not in any of the classical forms as such, but the style of the third movement could be related to the classical scherzo and the finale to the rondo, in a very general way in each case.[34]

---

31 Born 15 October 1989. They had two more children: Ruairi (b. Dublin, 21 December 1991) and Deirdre (b. Toronto, 10 September 1995), who live in Canada.

32 The work had previously received a broadcast performance on RTÉ Radio on 30 June 1989. Also in 1989, Bodley collaborated with Lily Van Oost (1932 – 97), an artist working with fabric, for a performance of his Phantasms for flute, clarinet, harp and cello at the Douglas Hyde Gallery at Trinity College Dublin.

33 Seóirse Bodley, 'A Special Category', 10

34 Seóirse Bodley, Orchestra Sinfonica Dell'Emilia-Romagna 'Arturo Toscanini' programme booklet, June 1991, 20

Of particular significance across the first two movements are the two motifs introduced in the very quiet opening 11 bars: The first, x, begins with a scotch snap in bar 1 in the basses doubled in the bass clarinet. The second motif, y, a menacing F–G–F–A flat–B flat, is played by the same instruments in bar 6, and both followed by *sul ponticello* textures. This short *Andante* introduction leads swiftly to a folk-like theme, which is interrupted by *sfzorzandi* tutti interjections (bars 47–53). This tension subsides and another lyrical idea is introduced on solo violin, but this too is disrupted, albeit less forcefully, by chords in the horns and strings (bars 111–14) before being restated to the accompaniment of a clashing countermelody in a second solo violin (from bar 120). Motif x is used to open the second movement with solo muted trumpet in bar 2. Bodley develops the motif y imitatively, but a somewhat ominous atmosphere is created by irregularly spaced *fortissimo* timpani strokes in bars 55–59 and the *pianissimo* timpani roll which accompanies the plaintive violin solo in bars 85–91. This solo leads to an effective passage in which a clarinet solo is accompanied by a striking string texture featuring alterations of solo instruments and each section as a whole (bars 91–97). This movement closes with allusions to motifs x and y as the clarinet solo dies away to nothing. The predominantly lively third movement (which Bodley describes as a 'quasi-scherzo'), contains a muted brass passage which is played in *staccato* crotchets in bars 117–23, which is replicated at the opening of the final movement before the upper strings and woodwind recall a semiquaver flourish from the third movement. The first violins and flute introduce a jaunty 6/8 idea in bars 33–34, which is developed and contrasted with versions of the above-mentioned brass passage, the last appearance in bars 97–102 being played without mutes. The movement settles on a sustained low D in the cellos in bar 143 for nine bars while a solo flute plays a slow Irish air *Andantino ma rubato* (Ex. 35). These few moments of nostalgic serenity are dramatically interrupted by four bars of raucous *glissandi* in the strings and brass, an allusion to Bartók's parodic quotation of the 'invasion' theme from the first movement of Shostakovich's Seventh Symphony in the fourth movement of his *Concerto for Orchestra*. One wonders if this gesture has a wider symbolic resonance, representing the beginning of a rejection by Bodley of his Irish-influenced style, although Bodley himself saw it as his personal rejection of those who criticized his inclusion of Irish music in his works.[35] Whatever the reason, only fragments of the 6/8 theme remain, with fleeting reminiscences of previous material being reintroduced before the symphony ends with 13 bars of emphatic *tutti* chords.

35 Bodley in conversation with the author, January 2009

Ex. 35 Symphony No. 4, IV, 143–155

(Notated at concert pitch)

After completing his fourth symphony, Bodley continued work on his fifth, which was commissioned to commemorate the signing of the Treaty of Limerick on 3 October 1691. This was an event of considerable importance in the history of seventeenth-century Ireland, as it brought the Williamite Wars to a close. Conflict had raged between the opposing forces for two years, culminating in a series of defeats for the Jacobite side, and a final heroic defence of the besieged city of Limerick. The treaty concluded after its surrender promised toleration for Catholicism, though this agreement was subsequently not honoured. Bodley's Symphony No. 5 is subtitled 'The Limerick Symphony' and was first performed in Limerick on 4 October 1991 by the RTÉ Concert Orchestra conducted by Proinnsías Ó Duinn during a four-day Tercentenary Commemoration. The work is not programmatic in any obvious sense, though it is pervaded by sharp contrasts of peacefulness and turbulence. While the composer could not but be aware of the political and cultural consequences of this turbulent episode in Irish history, he envisioned his symphony more as a reflection on 'human feeling rather than on that of historical fact or political complexity' and as a meditation on the themes of 'conflict, desire for peace, the sorrow of loss of life, bravery, the hope for the future'.[36]

The symphony is cast in five movements, and interestingly, though it is permeated by musical references to the folk tradition, this influence is noticeably less pronounced than in other recent works. At times, the musical language recalls the work of Stravinsky and Shostakovich, aligning the work with the European mainstream whilst still retaining Bodley's clear stylistic fingerprints. A *Grave* section opens the work with tutti scotch snaps in the first bar which are repeated in bars 14–15 after a flourish in the flute. A sequential motif (bars 16–19), a falling minor ninth motif (bars 20–22), and an expansive theme in the violins and clarinets over tolling bells (bars 33–38) provide much of the material for the following *Allegro*, which begins in bar 54. Bodley uses the technique of developing variation to unify and contrast this material, much of which is found across all the movements.

The first of the two slow movements (*Andantino*) begins with a crotchet passage and then features flute, oboe and clarinet solos, mostly supported by sustained string chords. In the second half, the opening six bars are repeated twice slightly varied, and the movement ends very quietly with muted strings and bell-like sounds in the vibraphone and harp. Contrast is provided in the energetic central movement (*Allegro*) with much use being made of the opening semiquaver figures. Although this *Allegro* is intended to depict conflict and is punctuated by dramatic string, brass and percussive interjections, it is not without its more reflective moments. The fourth movement (*Andante*) is, like the second, tranquil in nature and consists of a long meditative first violin line, again featuring large leaps, and tinged with a certain piquancy by the semitonal clashes with the second violins. This melody is taken up by the flute (bar 91) over a syncopated string accompaniment and is gradually joined by the first violins in unison (bars 175–200). The peacefulness is, however, interspersed with short *agitato*, *tremolo*, and animated

---

36 Bodley, RTÉ programme booklet, 4 October 1991. Given the importance of the civic occasion, it is surprising that the first performance received so little coverage in the press.

dotted-rhythm passages, but they do not intrude significantly on the predominantly gentle mood of the movement. The final movement opens (Ex. 36) with a syncopated motif featuring the leaps of minor ninths which appeared prominently in bars 20–22 of the first movement. Thereafter large intervallic jumps in sequential passages (including octaves in more tonal passages contrasted in places with clashing minor seconds) provide most of the material. As in the final movement of Symphony No. 4, contrast is provided by a reflective episode featuring flute solo before the movement's energetic conclusion, during which the principal thematic ideas are heard over rolling triplet figurations in the lower strings. Unfortunately, this attractive work has not been revived since its first performance, which is puzzling, as it is far more than a mere *pièce d'occasion*: it transcends the location and historical event which occasioned its composition and would amply repay the attention of conductors.

This period of intense productivity continued with the composition of String Quartet No. 2, which is separated by the elapse of almost a quarter of a century from its predecessor. In 1992, Bodley was commissioned by RTÉ together with four other Irish composers to write string quartets. All five works (the others were contributed by Paul Hayes, Colman Pearce, Rhona Clarke and Eibhlís Farrell) were premiered on 21 May 1993 in the National Gallery of Ireland, Dublin, on which occasion Bodley's quartet was played by the Degani String Quartet. Bodley noted that despite the extreme difference in texture and style between his two string quartets, 'both share a common emphasis on melody'.[37] Obviously the concept of melody here is a more conventionally lyrical one as opposed to the very angular and dissonant writing of the first quartet, prompting Ian Lawrence to suggest that Bodley had become more at ease with his Irish environment in the intervening years.[38] Bodley has commented that, in this work, he chose not to employ 'deliberate conflicts of style', the musical influences being 'integrated into the texture rather than left in contention.'[39] In these three movements (*Allegro–Andante con moto–Allegro*) he again uses developing variation as a structural device. The final movement has much in common with the third and final movements of Symphony No. 5: the bustling semiquaver figurations, the sequential passages, and the same pulsating and driving rhythm of the triplets in the bass towards the end. The movement's musical material is mostly generated by the interplay of three contrasting intervallic contours which are announced shortly after the opening: the minor thirds (E–G and G–B flat) traced in the opening two unison semiquaver bars, the tritones in the first violin in bars 5 and 7 and the sevenths in bars 17–18 (Ex. 37). Much use is made of static passages moving in semibreves (for instance in bars 45–52, where a quasi-medieval mood is evoked using non-vibrato). Ian Fox considered the quartet to be 'music of real power and originality and a valuable addition to Irish chamber music', though it has to be said that it suffers occasionally from the overuse of sequential constructions.[40]

37 Bodley, CD liner notes, *Contemporary Music from Ireland 2*, CMC CD02, 1997
38 Ian Lawrence, *Transformations: The String Quartet in Britain and Ireland since 1885* (Dorset, 2004), 60
39 Bodley, *Contemporary Music from Ireland 2*
40 *Sunday Tribune*, 30 May 1993. See also *Irish Times*, 22 May 1993, which, in contrast, noted 'empty melodic gestures' and a 'permeating greyness'.

Ex. 36 Symphony No. 5, V, 1–6

(Notated at concert pitch)

Ex. 37 String Quartet No. 2, III, 1–25

During this phase of his career, Bodley composed several important song cycles, many of them for the mezzo-soprano Aylish Kerrigan, with whom Bodley came into contact in the early 1980s. Born of Irish parents in San Francisco, Kerrigan studied vocal performance at the University of Oregon and was based for many years in Germany. Over the next fifteen years, she and Bodley gave numerous recitals together, making regular appearances in Ireland and Germany, as well as performing in Spain, Macedonia and China. In addition to standard repertoire such as lieder by Schubert, Brahms, Wolf and Richard Strauss, their programmes regularly included twentieth-century works and music by Irish composers such as Frederick May, Aloys Fleischmann and James Wilson. These concerts would often feature Bodley's own songs and arrangements and, on occasion, piano pieces such as *Aislingí* or *The Tightrope Walker Presents a Rose*.

The first work that Bodley composed for Kerrigan was a group of three songs entitled *A Passionate Love*, for which he wrote his own texts. These songs, which can also be performed by a baritone, were first performed by the duo at a concert given on 5 May 1985 in the Hugh Lane Municipal Gallery of Modern Art, Dublin. The second phrase of the vocal line in the first song 'Aflame' ('The killing chill of love assuages') presents the musical material on which the cycle is based: a chromatic line in bar 9 and a four-note motif (x) in bar 10. This motif makes a significant appearance in a brief *Andante* passage at the words 'No more we'll go a-roving' — a quotation of a line from a well-known poem by Byron, which is itself an allusion to a Scottish song 'The Jolly Beggar'. 'Aflame' ends with the soprano affirming that the lovers' passionate feelings for one another will lead them to 'rove again' — at which point the A major chord reappears. The opening phrase of the second song 'A Quiet Evening' (*Andante*) also features motif x, which is then restated twice, descending a semitone at each repetition. This song also makes extensive use of the chromatic line and it ends, like the first song, on an A major chord in the right hand. The vocal lines in this and the following song are extensively ornamented in a manner recalling Irish traditional music and Bodley supplies detailed directions about how the mordents and turns are to be performed. The final song, 'A Human Voice' (*Moderato*) uses motif x in bars 6–7 on the words, 'sing for joy', and Bodley employs numerous sequential patterns in the interpolated *Allegro* sections. The song ends with eleven bars of recitative featuring superimposed major/minor sonorities (which are derived from motif x) and the cycle ends as it began on C. The premiere was reviewed by Barra Boydell, who described it as a 'moving cycle' of 'considerable power and intensity'.[41]

In August 1987, Bodley and Kerrigan travelled to China for a two-week cultural visit, which was assisted financially by the Irish Department of Foreign Affairs. They left on 17 August and were met the next day in Beijing by Brendan Ward, Secretary of the Irish Embassy. They remained in the Chinese capital for four days, which allowed them some time for sight-seeing (visits to the Great Wall and the Forbidden City), in addition to giving a recital at the Hai Dian Theatre. They next flew to Changsha (where Mao Zedong studied and taught) in south-central China, where they performed in the Dong Feng Theatre and Bodley gave a seminar on Irish traditional music at the Changsha Music Teacher Training College. The next stop on their itinerary was Guangzhou (Canton) in the south, just west of Hong Kong, where they arrived on 25 August and took the opportunity to visit various temples (including the famous Temple of the Six Banyan Trees) before their concert in the Beilei Theatre two days later. They moved to nearby Zhaoqing City for a night to visit Dinghu Mountain and the Seven Star Crags before returning to Ireland. The programmes for their recitals, which were attended by large audiences of between 1,000 and 1,500 people, included A Girl and some of the Aislingí. Bodley reported that 'while it might be assumed that the arrangements [of Irish airs] would be more accessible … it was in fact the original works that most gripped the audience, though the reception for all the performances was most gratifying'.[42] Before leaving for China, Bodley had arranged a Chinese flower-drum song as an encore and Kerrigan had learned the pronunciation of the Chinese text with the help of staff at the Chinese Embassy in Dublin.[43]

In 1987, Bodley collaborated for the first time with the distinguished Irish poet Micheal O'Siadhail (b. 1947), composing a song-cycle entitled The Naked Flame based on his texts.[44] The work is written for mezzo-soprano (or baritone) and piano and was commissioned by RTÉ. It is dedicated to Bernadette Greevy, who gave the premiere on 15 November 1988 with the Irish pianist Mìceal O'Rourke in the National Concert Hall, Dublin. Greevy and Bodley subsequently performed the cycle in UCD on 27 April 1989 and in 1996, the composer and Aylish Kerrigan recorded it for the Echo Classics Digital label. The cycle comprises twelve songs and lasts for approximately forty minutes. In the programme booklet, O'Siadhail supplied the following comments on his texts: 'The poems focus on our human vulnerability to the joys and falls of living; by laying ourselves open to life's flame we grow and deepen. The overall sequence of the poems suggests a life-cycle with patterns of change and recurrence, hurt and healing, loss and renewal.[45] Bodley supplemented the poet's remarks by explaining that 'this idea is reflected in all of the poems in one way or another, lending them an underlying unity, though the subject matter is quite diverse'.[46] The cycle's basic musical material is presented in the opening bar of the first song 'Tuning in' — two hexachords, which between them comprise eleven notes of the chromatic scale (the pitch A is omitted and G is repeated). These hexachords have a complex symbolic import: the upper three pitches of each symbolise the future and the lower three the past. In addition, 'various sections of the twelve-note chord are connected to the recurring ideas of impermanence, the balance of opposites, hovering, hurt and the moment'.[47]

42 Bodley, Report to Department of Foreign Affairs, 28 September 1987. Bodley Private Collection. Bodley recorded the details of his visit in a diary.
43 Irish Times, 12 September 1987
44 O'Siadhail has also worked with other Irish composers supplying texts for song cycles by James Wilson (Dublin Spring, 2001) and Colman Pearce (Summerfest, 1993).
45 Bodley, programme booklet for the first performance, 15 November 1988
46 Bodley, programme booklet
47 Bodley, programme booklet

Ex. 38 *The Naked Flame*, 'Hurt', 1-7

Bodley has emphasized the thematic linkages between O'Siadhail's poems by means of recurring musical ideas: the second and tenth songs share some musical material, for example, as do the fifth and the eleventh.[48] The sixth song in the cycle, 'Hurt' (Ex. 38) opens with repeated hexachords (marked 'desolate'), but although the upper three pitches in the first bar replicate those in the opening bar of the cycle, here they all constitute superimposed major and minor triads. These triads, which also feature melodically in the vocal line, subsequently reappear as chromatically descending minor root position triads in the bass. The hexachord changes character to incorporate quartal sonorities six bars from the end, now using only five individual tones, one of which is duplicated: this significant and very audible alteration is presumably intended to emphasise the line 'All that is certain is change'. This new sonority then slips chromatically from D in the bass to B flat. The sustained pitch C sharp plays a very important structural role in bars 12, 29 and 30 where it underpins the singer's bitter and ultimately resigned comments, also on repeated C sharps: 'You of all people to doublecross!' (see Ex. 38); 'Intimacy cuts both ways'; '(that way you'd have called the tune)'; 'But I know that I know nothing.' Most of the

48 Seóirse Bodley, programme booklet for the first performance, 15 November 1988

writing stays within a restricted compass; there is little word painting but some imitation of preceding vocal gestures in the accompaniment. The next song builds on the triadic ideas as a linking device just as the superimposed triads ended the preceding song.

This cycle has been very well-received. When it was performed by the composer and the Irish soprano Sylvia O'Brien at a concert held in the Hugh Lane Gallery in Dublin on 20 April 2008 to mark Bodley's seventy-fifth birthday, it met with a rapturous reception from the audience. The reviewer for the *Irish Times* on that occasion described the songs as

> respectful, insightful and unerringly apposite settings ... spontaneously responsive to an individual line or word .... Bodley matches every image, bringing the débutante [of the fifth song] to joyous life with a busy, carefree piano part, or exploding from the gentle dream-world of a pastoral metaphor into O'Siadhail's final outburst.[49]

To mark the 400th anniversary of the disastrous expedition sent by King Philip II of Spain to invade England in 1588, the Spanish Armada Commemoration Society under its President, the marine historian John de Courcy Ireland, organized a Spanish Armada International Symposium in Sligo from 4 to 9 September 1988. This location was chosen because of the numerous Spanish wrecks strewn along the west coast of Ireland and in particular because it was eight miles from Streedagh Strand, an important site of Armada wreckage. The Society commissioned Bodley to set a new poem *Carta Irlandesa* [Letter from Ireland][50] by the Spanish poet, Antonio González-Guerrero, which resulted in a cycle of four songs for mezzo-soprano or baritone and piano. Bodley and Aylish Kerrigan performed the cycle at the opening of the symposium on 4 September 1988. In the poem, a Spanish sailor Francisco de Cuéllar, who was aboard the shipwrecked galleon *San Pedro*, describes in a letter of 1589 from Antwerp the great misery that the crew had endured, hoping that his story would reach his king. Bodley opens the piece by immediately establishing a Spanish atmosphere with rolling arpeggiated chords in the piano ('measured, but like an improvisation') to sound like a guitar being strummed, and repeatedly notes in triplets in Spanish-Cuban *habañera* style for the voice (Ex. 39). De Cuéllar goes on to relate that he would not have survived the great suffering in Ireland had God not 'placed him in the company of savages who are of good faith and also Christians'. The natives' simple, devout and patriotic way of life is described in

---

49 *Irish Times*, 22 April 2008. At the premiere twenty years earlier, Michael Dervan had noted the generally spare musical language which approached 'at times in its simplicity some of the effects of songs by Ives', *Irish Times*, 16 November 1988. This influence is not surprising given that Bodley often included songs by Ives in his recitals with Kerrigan. Four songs from the set were performed at a Bank of Ireland 'Mostly Modern' series in 1998 where the reviewer, Martin Adams, noted that their 'free chromaticism has its roots in twentieth-century pastoralism', *Irish Times*, 16 February 1998.

50 The poem is published in an English translation as 'News from Ireland' by Patrick Gallagher in *God's Obvious Design: Spanish Armada Symposium, Sligo 1988*, Patrick Gallagher and Don William Cruickshank, eds. (London, 1990), 249–75.

the second song. Hexachords similar to those heard at the beginning of the first song reappear in the first half of the third, where they assume a different mood, this time repeated forcefully to underscore the hazardous nature of the sailors' journey across Ireland and Scotland before the mood relaxes to depict their safe arrival in Flanders. These chords are used again in both arpeggiated and sustained forms in the final bars of the short fourth song, *Postdata* ('Postscript').

Bodley had retained many personal and professional contacts in Germany over the years, in particular through his many tours with Aylish Kerrigan. The singer participated in the first performances of a number of new works which were first performed in the mid 1990s in Bochum, Stuttgart and Torgau respectively. One of these, *By the Margins of the Great Deep* (1995) is a very gentle, sonorous and slow-moving setting of George Russell's ('Æ') mystical poem depicted with much use of repeated diatonic chords. A song with similar syllabic and disjunct handling of the text is *Look to this Day!* (1997), a translation of an ancient Sanskrit salutation to the dawn. When Bodley employs rare melismatic writing in these two songs it is all the more effective for its infrequent use.

 The most substantial of these new works resulted from a commission from a choir in the German town of Torgau, which is situated on the river Elbe, some thirty miles northeast of Leipzig. During the Reformation, Torgau was notable for its support of Martin Luther who was a frequent visitor, and the first Lutheran church was established in the *Schlosskirche* there. (Today it is better known perhaps for the historic and symbolic meeting of American and Soviet troops on the ruins of the bridge over the river in April 1945.) Luther's close friend, the Kantor and composer Johann Walter (1496–1570) lived and worked in the town for much of his life and the two men collaborated on collecting and writing hymns. To commemorate both the 450th anniversary of Luther's death and the 500th anniversary of Walter's birth, Bodley was approached by the Johann-Walter-Kantorei Torgau to write a choral work based on texts by both men, which Bodley left in their original *Frühneuhochdeutsch*, or Early New High German. The result was an attractive half-hour piece, *Fraw Musica* (which can be translated as 'Lady Music') for mezzo-soprano, SATB, string orchestra, flute, optional bassoon, and organ (Bodley subsequently made a version with piano accompaniment of two of the movements). The work's title is taken from a poem which was written by Luther as a rhymed preface to Walters's poem *Lob und Preis der löblichen Kunst Musica* [In Praise of the Laudable Art of Music] of 1538, and which employs the traditional poetic conceit of personifying music as a revered and beautiful maiden.[51] Magnar Breivik writes that this conceit is 'rooted in the medieval tradition that

---

51   In this connection, see Robin A. Leaver, *Luther's Liturgical Music* (Cambridge, 2007), 78ff.

connects female personifications with the disciplines of the *septem artes liberales*. Luther's poem praises both the joys of music and its humanising powers.'[52]

Fraw Musica was first performed in Torgau's *Schlosskirche* on 5 October 1996 by Aylish Kerrigan, the Johann-Walter-Kantorei and Musica Juventa Orchestra under Ekkehard Saretz as part of the programme of a festival devoted to 'Ireland and its Diaspora'. There were two subsequent performances in Germany and an Irish premiere took place later that year on 11 December 1996 in the National Concert Hall with Kerrigan, the Goethe Institut Choir and the Hibernian Chamber Orchestra under the direction of John Finucane. The Irish choirs were joined by 36 members of the Torgau Choir, who came to Dublin to participate in the premiere.

Fraw Musica is in nine movements. Luther and Walter's texts, as Bodley has remarked, 'concern music and its relationship to human feelings and spirituality', adding, however, that they are 'not without humour and colour'.[53] The opening movement celebrates the power of song and displays the moderately modern musical language of the whole work. The choral writing is well conceived: much use is made of passages in unison and thirds, and care is taken to ensure that such dissonant sonorities as occur can be sung with relative ease. The second movement is the first of two solo songs for mezzo-soprano[54] and is scored for strings and a flute. Its text describes a nightingale whose song brings happiness. The poem set in the third movement (*Allegro moderato*) stresses the fact that God sent us music and exhorts all to use it to praise Him. In the course of this, there is, unusually for Bodley, a unison *crescendo* on a complete statement of the octatonic scale (bars 33–37). In the fourth movement, a peaceful *Adagio*, the mezzo-soprano ponders on the heavenly craft of music accompanied by wordless vocalizations in the choir, and in the fifth, the choir and soloist are accompanied by pizzicato strings and strumming triple-stopping to reflect the lighter mood of the text, which depicts King David dancing for joy. The style of the lilting sixth movement (*Andante*) praising God in the highest at times recalls the music of John Rutter, while the seventh depicts the contrasting effects of music on man and the animal kingdom. The eighth movement is a gentle *Adagio* for mezzo-soprano with organ accompaniment, which functions as a reflective interlude before the

---

52 Magnar Breivik, 'A Twentieth-Century musica instrumentalis: Boethius and Augustine in the Musical Thought of Paul Hindemith', in Nils Holger Petersen et al., eds., *Signs of Change: Transformation of Christian Traditions and their Representations in the Arts, 1000–2000* (Amsterdam and New York, 2004), 223–24. Hindemith wrote a *Gebrauchsmusik* cantata entitled *Frau Musica: Musik zum Singen und Spielen auf Instrumenten nach einem Text von Luther*, Op. 45, No. 1 (1928, revised in English in 1943), a work which Breivik has also studied in some detail: Magnar Breivik, 'Contexts of Hindemith's *Frau Musica*', Eyolf Østrem et al., eds., *The Arts and the Cultural Heritage of Martin Luther* (Copenhagen, 2003), 171–85. It is interesting to note that Bodley took the simple architectural style and proportions of the Schlosskirche into account when composing the piece. See 'Seóirse Bodley: Michael Dungan talks to the composer', 9.

53 Bodley, programme booklet, University College Dublin, 4 March 1998

54 Bodley's arrangement of the second and eighth movements for mezzo-soprano with piano accompaniment are perhaps less successful as the texture in the original relies too much on the solo flute in No. 2, and the long sustained passages in the strings and organ in no. 8.

Ex. 39 *Carta Irlandesa*, I, 1–10[55]

* Roll as marked

55 'I tell you they were days of great suffering. In the hills of Ireland our men were dying (shivering and naked as the day that they were born) of cold and hunger and much misery.' [Translation by Patrick Gallagher, *God's Obvious Design*, 253]

Ex. 40 *Pax Bellumque, 96–103*

(Notated at concert pitch)

celebratory finale. In the last movement Luther's chorale, *Ein' feste Burg ist unser Gott* ('A Mighty Fortress is Our God') based on the 46th Psalm is played augmented by the bass instruments from letter C to F as 'the joyous music, singing "a new song", continues over it'.[56] The work concludes joyfully with a statement of the final phrase of the chorale. It is surprising that this appealing work has not been performed more frequently, as it is effectively written and is well within the capabilities of a good amateur choir.

The last major vocal work from this period sets poems by Wilfred Owen and Thomas MacGreevy. Both men were both born in 1893 and both fought in the British Army during the First World War. MacGreevy served at Ypres and the Somme, and though wounded, survived, living until 1967. Owen also served on the Somme, but was less fortunate, being shot and killed on the Sambre-Oise Canal to the east just a week before the Armistice. Owen's many anti-war poems written during the wretched final year of his life gained worldwide fame; MacGreevy, by contrast, produced only one on this theme, *De civitate Hominum* [Of the city of free men], which was written after the war in the 1920s. In his preface to the score, Bodley has described how his pacifist convictions led him to set MacGreevy's poem together with Owen's well-known *Dulce et decorum est* in 1997, entitling the combination *Pax Bellumque* [Peace and War] — a title chosen in part because the poets had both used Latin titles for their poems. The work, which is in one continuous movement, is scored for soprano, flute, clarinet, piano, and violin. It was first performed on 2 May 1997 in the National Concert Hall, Dublin by the soprano Tine Verbeke and Irish chamber ensemble Concorde, which had been responsible for commissioning it.

Horace's ode, *Dulce et decorum est pro patria mori* [It is sweet and right to die for your country] was used as British propaganda during the First World War. This prompted Owen to allude to it in the title of his vivid and harrowing poem, which depicts a gas attack taking place as soldiers limp back from the front to the rest camp behind the lines. The title of MacGreevy's *De Civitate Hominum* is a punning allusion to the title of St. Augustine's *De civitate Dei* [The City of God]. Bodley chose this text specifically because of the contrast it afforded 'with the earthbound claustrophobia of Owen's poem': it describes a First World War pilot crashing ('streams down into the white, a delicate flame, a stroke of orange in the morning's dress'), but is also, as Lee Jenkins points out, a 'meditation on the poet's art in a time of war'.[57] Bodley deliberately chose to use a female voice in order to produce what he describes as an effect of 'intentional distancing': '[as] a consequence the singer

56 Bodley, programme booklet, UCD, 4 March 1998

57 Lee M. Jenkins, *Wallace Stevens: Rage for Order* (Eastbourne, 2006), 99. See also Jenkins, 'Thomas MacGreevy and the Pressure of Reality', *The Wallace Stevens Journal*, 18:2 (1994), 157–69. The poem is dedicated 'To A. S. F. R.', A. S. Frere, his friend and editor at the London publishing house Heinemann. See also Susan Schreibman, *Collected Poems of Thomas MacGreevy: An Annotated Edition* (Dublin, 1991), xxiii: 'MacGreevy defamiliarizes the horror and transforms it into the vividly surreal.'

does not, indeed cannot, adopt the persona of the protagonist(s) of the poems. Rather the settings endeavour to approach directly the poetic voice expressing itself in each poem'.[58]

The two poems are structurally framed by a prelude (bars 1–30) and a postlude (bars 255–85) with an interlude (bars 104–34). The two songs, which are very similar in texture, are integrated musically through the employment of recurring melodic cells and sonorities derived from quartal and quintal material in the piano part. The music does not intrude on the text, but rather provides a very sensitive and contemplative accompaniment to reflect on the anguish of war. There are occasional moments of tension, for instance during the passages evoking the panic induced by the gas attack in the first poem and the imminent crash of the plane in the second. The relatively understated soprano line is punctuated by *forte* or *fortissimo* high notes at many crucial moments, such as when the text alludes to 'Five-Nines' (explosive shells) in bar 56. The last line of Owen's poem, 'the old lie' *Dulce et decorum est pro patria mori*, is sung 'woodenly' on repeated Ds (Ex. 40). The final sonority of the piece as it dies away, after a questioning pause, superimposes triads of A and E major, but with an added G natural, reflecting perhaps the final line of MacGreevy's poem which depicts the death of an airman: 'Holy God makes no reply, Yet'. This ambiguous ending seemed to Bodley to be 'particularly suited to the overall feeling of the piece'.[59]

From the late 1980s onwards, Bodley's musical language had begun to undergo further change. The influence of Irish traditional music became far less pronounced, and he gradually reverted to a more atonal idiom from which explicit tonal references were not excluded. In the next phase of his career, Bodley would re-engage with the stylistic and technical explorations of his serial compositions of the 1960s and reconsider his employment of tonality.

---

58 Bodley, programme booklet for the first performance, 2 May 1997
59 Bodley, programme booklet for the first performance, 2 May 1997

5. Changing Direction

In the late 1990s, the style of Bodley's work once again underwent considerable change. His creative engagement with Irish traditional music appears to have run its course, and after thirty years he resumed the stylistic explorations of his serial and post-serial phase of the 1960s. Although some were perplexed by this abrupt change of direction through a new reflection on his earlier style, others welcomed it.[1] This new tendency became manifest in three piano works, *News from Donabate*, *Chiaroscuro* and *An Exchange of Letters*, which were completed between 1999 and 2002. Although these works re-engage with the avant-garde idioms which he had encountered on his visits to Darmstadt, they differ from his earlier works in one crucial respect: Bodley now allows himself to include tonal elements within his freely atonal language and to use serially generated material based on rows of more than twelve notes. All three works are extremely challenging and require a virtuoso technique, in contrast to the piano music he had composed previously, which is generally more modest in its demands.

According to Bodley, the change of style manifest in *News from Donabate* came about because

> the experiences that gave rise to [the work] could not be encompassed using stylistic musical references from Irish traditional music. By definition it had to be more abstract and consequently more oblique in expression. For different reasons the same is also true of *Chiaroscuro* [and] *An Exchange of Letters*.[2]

1 For comments on Bodley's stylistic change, see Michael Dervan (*Irish Times*, 25 March 2002) and Eric Sweeney, 'Will the real composer please stand up?', *Journal of Music in Ireland*, 2, 5 (July/August, 2002), 17.
2 Bodley, programme booklet, RTÉ Living Music Festival, 27 October 2002, 38

Ideas for a large-scale solo piano work had begun to take shape as early as 1996, but he made desultory progress due to the necessity of completing various commissions.³ The title for the work seeks to evoke both a place and a state of mind. Bodley had actually intended to call it, *From the Other Side* and also considered giving it the sub-title *September Music No. 2*,⁴ an appellation which harks back to another work that took shape around the same time, his first String Quartet of 1968, which, as has been noted, was originally conceived as the first movement of *September Music No. 1*. Donabate is a small seaside village north of Dublin where Bodley used to stay every September during the mid-1960s. In 1967, during one of these visits, he experienced what he describes as

> a startling and quite unexpected change of consciousness ... . It was as if I viewed the ordinary quotidian world from a perspective quite dissimilar to that of my usual perceptions. Everything was quite different (while on another level remaining the same). Seeing the normal world from another viewpoint, everything had a different meaning. Even ordinary human relationships were changed and priorities were altered. It was not a fleeting experience. With varying degrees of intensity it lasted some 2.5 weeks. At its height it became quite overwhelming in its immediacy. All was suffused with a radiance within itself —something that is always there but unseen. Shortly after I left Donabate the altered perception faded ... .⁵

For a number of years subsequently, Bodley had thought of composing a work that would attempt to evoke this experience.⁶ However, as he explained in an interview given in 2003, his folk-music derived compositional idiom of the 1970s and 1980s with its tonal references seemed unsatisfactory for this purpose:

> I wanted to write a work that would somehow be illuminated from inside. But in order to do the sort of work I had in mind, I wanted to avoid any kind of a) sentimentality and b) any too direct expression. So I deliberately wanted to put myself in a sort of indirect mode of expression.⁷

3   See 'Seóirse Bodley: Michael Dungan talks to the composer', 11. The following discussion of *News from Donabate* draws on the present writer's article 'Darmstadt Revisited: Seóirse Bodley's *News from Donabate* (1999)', in Barra Boydell, ed., *Proceedings of the 1st Annual Conference of the Society for Musicology in Ireland: NUI Maynooth, 2–3 May 2003* (Maynooth, 2004), 137–42.
4   E-mail correspondence between Bodley and Micheal O'Siadhail, 10 March 1999
5   CD liner notes, *News from Donabate* (Contemporary Music Centre, Ireland)
6   'Seóirse Bodley: Michael Dungan talks to the composer', 11
7   Michael Dungan, 'An Interview with Seóirse Bodley', 2003, www.cmc.ie. Accessed 21 April 2003.

As a result, he found himself returning to his musical language of the 1960s, as the piece 'needed the sense of distance and elliptical expression that could only be achieved in a dissonant and irregularly shaped atonal idiom'.[8]

The piece comprises ten movements, which are given the following titles:

1. Night-scene with electric light and starlight
2. Such a morning
3. Six inches above the ground
4. The breath
5. Red flagpole in sunlight
6. A walk to the post-office
7. Through the narrow gate on a fine morning with dew
8. Twelve noon — but why bother going?
9. The wheel turns by itself
10. The Sea

According to the composer, these titles are not intended to suggest a programmatic content, but he decided to provide them in the hope that they might help 'to make his thought processes a little more transparent.'[9] The piece is based on a twenty-one note series which repeats seven of the notes twice and one note (D) three times. Bodley records that when 'using the larger tone rows beyond twelve notes, like fifteen- or sixteen-note rows [he was less] concerned with the question of tonality or atonality, but just more with using it as a sort of distancing device so that, in a way, it's like holding yourself back a bit. And somehow the expression becomes more intense.'[10] In the first piece, *Night Scene with electric light and starlight*, the prime form of the row can be traced through bars 1–4 and its retrograde inversion in bars 9–10 (Ex. 41). However, such formal constructions do not preclude elements of quasi-programmatic depiction, such as the flickering demisemiquaver figurations which are presumably meant to be heard as evocative of the different types of light alluded to in the title. The second movement, 'Such a morning', was originally to be called 'Vormittag am Strand' [Morning on the beach] after a poem by Christian Morgenstern (1871–1914). This is richly varied in texture, alternating between rippling arpeggiated chords, resonating thirds, outbursts of rapid figurations and subtle echo effects, before ending slowly with very soft semibreve chords. After a third movement featuring hammered repeated notes interpolated with soft chords and more linear passages, the fourth opens with tremolos (which return again briefly at the end) and trills, and, after a more dramatic middle section,

---

8   Bodley, 'The Claims of Conformity', 56
9   Bodley, CD liner notes, *News from Donabate* (Contemporary Music Centre, Ireland)
10 Dungan, 'An Interview with Seóirse Bodley'. He added that he had done this before in *Meditations on Lines from Patrick Kavanagh* of 1971 by using the phrases from the poem 'as a stimulus ... as a starting point but not attempting a direct expression'.

settles on sustained chords highlighting a minor third, B–D over nine bars in the closing two pages. The fifth movement revels in the sound of a series of minim chords (separated by whole bar rests in the central part). There is a prominent scotch snap motif in bars 20–27 (with a perfect fifth F–C repeated four times from bars 24–27), which appears to be derived rhythmically from the grace notes which precede many of the minim chords. The exhilarating sixth movement, 'A walk to the Post Office', features brilliant passages of repeated chords and individual notes (in particular, an insistently reiterated top A), with contrast being provided by some more reflective moments towards the end. This lengthy movement is followed by the shortest of the set, the luxuriant 'Through the narrow gate on a fine morning with dew', which lasts a mere twenty-one bars. It is not difficult to hear traditional clock chimes in the eighth movement, which alludes to midday in its title. The ninth movement builds up small clusters with accented notes and features thirds prominently, as does the final movement which surveys the whole range of elements from the previous movements: irregular rhythms, rapid flourishes, repeated notes and rich sonorities. This expansive fifty-minute piece makes great demands on both the performer and the listener and, although it is possible to perform individual movements separately, the composer feels that they make a greater impact when played in the context of the entire cycle. *News from Donabate* was first performed by Andrei Roudenko on 21 February 2001 at the Musicailt Festival in the Aula Maxima at the National University of Ireland, Galway. It was performed again in October of the same year in Yokohama by the Korean pianist Kyung-Ok Kim at the World Music Days festival organized by the International Society for Contemporary Music. Bodley attended this event and took the opportunity to visit the Zen gardens in Kyoto. His long-standing interest in Japanese culture was stimulated by a lecture given by Bruno Maderna at Darmstadt in the early 1960s, in which the latter spoke about 'Zen Buddhism and the idea of the instinct as a legitimate part of the approach to musical composition — and this at a time when structure, rigid compositional techniques and total serialism were predominant'.[11]

The second composition in the sequence of piano works from this period is *Chiaroscuro*, which was commissioned as a test piece for the Dublin International Piano Competition in 2000.[12] This short piece was inspired by a painting by Michelangelo Caravaggio (1571–1610), *The Taking of Christ* (c. 1602), which had been presumed lost for over two hundred years but was rediscovered in the dining room of a Jesuit house in Dublin and put on display in the National Gallery of Ireland in the early 1990s.[13] The picture vividly portrays

11 Bodley, 'October 2001: A Journey to Japan', *aicnews*, November 2001. Bodley also referred to the art of Zen in Acton, 'Interview', 124.
12 Three other test pieces were commissioned from the Irish composers Kevin O'Connell, Marian Ingoldsby and James Wilson. *Chiaroscuro* was performed by six contestants including two in the final round of the competition, Lidija Bizjak and Kirill Gerstein. Bizjak won the prize for the best performance of a commissioned test piece with *Chiaroscuro*: see *Irish Times*, 19 May 2000.
13 See Sergio Benedetti, *Caravaggio: The Master Revealed* (Dublin, 1993). The authenticity of the painting continues to be debated.

Jesus' betrayal by Judas. As the Caravaggio scholar Helen Langdon remarks, 'everything heightens the scene's dramatic intensity: Christ, aware that he has been betrayed, suffers with humility. In the brutal face of Judas, who has kissed him, there is nascent horror.'[14] Langdon has also drawn attention to the artist's subtle employment of light and shade to heighten the emotional effect.

Chiaroscuro is subtitled 'The Taking of Christ', and the composer has stated that 'the subject of the painting also underlies the musical content'.[15] The title itself is a term used in the visual arts to denote a technique of defining three-dimensional figures or objects by means of extreme contrasts of light and shade (it being derived from a compound of two Italian adjectives, *chiaro*, meaning 'bright' or 'clear' and *oscuro*, 'dark'). Although this exciting and virtuosic piece is not obviously programmatic, it is clear that Bodley sought to convey the drama inherent in Caravaggio's visual depiction of the betrayal of Christ. However, his conception appears to have been influenced more by the painter's technique than the actual content of the picture. Bodley explains that it is 'based on a fifteen note tone-row [and] requires of the pianist a wide range of colouristic techniques and the ability to suggest the different contrasting musical colours that often appear in quick succession or indeed together'.[16] These contrasting shades are intimated by arpeggiated and chordal sonorities played at differing dynamics ranges, encompassed by rapid bursts of demisemiquaver quintuplets which drive the music forward (Ex. 42). These are overlaid with single notes and some brief intervallic ideas (the composer's preference for intervals suggesting tonal references, thirds especially, which was also significant in his late-1960s phase, is again apparent here). He also employs repeated single pitches, mostly for textural reasons, but sometimes to accentuate a particular pitch such as the B flat in bars 31–34, or the G sharp repeated eight times in bars 38–40 with dynamic markings ranging from *fff* to *p*. It might be suggested that the sinister foreboding of Judas's betrayal is conveyed by passages featuring trills and tremolos, such as bars 52–59. Nothing could be further from the style of *The Tightrope Walker Presents a Rose* of 1976 than *Chiaroscuro*; they could have been written by two different composers. In its employment of dramatic extremes of dynamics and register, *Chiaroscuro* has much in common with the post-war piano music of Boulez and Stockhausen, yet retains certain quasi-tonal references as Bodley avoids a rigid application of the series. This fine piece undoubtedly deserves to be more widely known.

14 Helen Langdon, *Caravaggio: A Life* (London, 1998), 233
15 Seóirse Bodley, 'Notes', *Piano Album III* (Dublin, 2000)
16 Bodley, 'Notes', *Piano Album III*

Ex. 41 *News from Donabate*, 'Night-scene with electric light and starlight', 1–15

Ex. 42 Chiaroscuro, 85–91

The third piano work from this period, *An Exchange of Letters*, was written in 2002. In that year, Bodley was featured in the 'Composer's Choice Series' of concerts, which was organized by the National Concert Hall in Dublin to showcase the work of living Irish composers. Bodley was invited to devise a recital programme for the pianist Rolf Hind, which was to include contemporary repertoire as well as a new work of his own specially commissioned by the National Concert Hall for the occasion. *An Exchange of Letters* was first performed on 25 March 2002, together with a selection of Études by Ligeti and *Nomos Alpha* by Xenakis.[17] The work comprises seven movements, all of which have descriptive but non-programmatic titles. Bodley uses a fifteen-note row, which is presented in the right hand at the very opening of the first movement, 'Moon Dreams over Greenland' (G sharp, C sharp and D are repeated after all twelve chromatic notes have been stated). This opening movement, which features Bodley's favoured interval of the third, intersperses rich sonorities with thinner textures that almost seem to vanish in the ethereal uppermost regions of the piano during the closing bars. *Inner Sea* opens with a four-note motif in the bass, a motif that becomes very prominent in bars 7, 16 and 85 particularly. The fifteen-note row is crushed into the right hand of the first bar of 'Immortal', a movement characterized by rapidly repeated notes. The last three bars of this piece are repeated exactly at the start of the final piece, in which they are subjected to more extensive development. The fourth piece, 'Via Negativa' [The negative path], alludes to a way of understanding God through negation which is common to a number of religious traditions including Christianity, Judaism and Islam, and which attempts to convey a sense of God's ineffability by describing what he is not. Bodley writes that 'a wonderful experience is felt through negative forces, just as a photograph might be experienced by looking through the negative. This is emphasized in the low, violent opening, although there is a resolution of sorts in the ending.'[18] The opening fifteen-note row appears in retrograde in the first two bars of the right hand and twelve-tone aggregates are presented in tetrachords in bars 6, 11 and 12, followed immediately by the 'missing' three pitches (Ex. 43). As in the other pieces from this period, rhythmic irregularity is also much in evidence (ratios such as 7:4 in bar 3 or 11:8 in bar 8 for instance) and the descending chords are reminiscent of the first movement of *News from Donabate*. 'Unchosen Bond', with its reiterated sonorities, is followed by the short 'Peaceful Nature of Desire', which concludes with thin pointillistic textures. The final piece 'Flames of Uncounted Candles' opens with the last three bars of 'Immortal', and with what Bodley calls 'a flickering figure' which generates most of the movement's *tremolo* textures. The title of this last piece appears in a short love poem by the American Imagist poet, Amy Lowell (1874–1925), *The Bungler*, which begins 'You glow in my heart like the flames of uncounted candles'. The piece builds to a climax (via what appears to be a snatch of a *fugato*

17   Bodley chose the Études because Ligeti 'has assimilated the music of the nineteen-sixties avant-garde, yet produced original, absorbing piano music indirectly connected to the Romantic tradition'. Bodley, programme booklet, Composer's Choice, National Concert Hall, 25 March 2002
18   Bodley, programme booklet, Composer's Choice, National Concert Hall, 25 March 2002

opening in bars 50–53) with *crescendi* from *pianississimo* to *fortississimo*, culminating in a highly rhetorical presentation of the fifteen-note row with a final and extra D added for good measure.

Ex. 43 *An Exchange of Letters*, 'Via Negativa', 1–12

This new phase of creativity also saw the production of several significant orchestral and vocal compositions in addition to these solo keyboard works. In 2000, the National Youth Orchestra of Ireland (NYOI) and the Arts Council of Ireland commissioned an orchestral work to be performed during the millennium celebrations. Bodley found this commission particularly rewarding, as he had spent much of his career working with young musicians and welcomed the opportunity to write something especially for them. The work is dedicated to 'the many who, no longer my students, have become my friends'.[19] Sinfonietta was first performed by the NYOI under En Shao on 24 July of that year at the University Concert Hall, Limerick, and subsequently in Dublin, and it was included in the programmes given by the orchestra during its tour of Germany later that summer. The work is scored for large forces with triple woodwind, and every section of the orchestra is brought into prominence at some point during its course. Unlike the two piano works just discussed above, this work harks back stylistically, structurally and harmonically to his Symphony No. 5 and String Quartet No. 2 of 1991 and 1992 respectively, featuring sequences, scotch snaps and some melodic contours reminiscent of Irish folk music.

In the introductory Adagio, a short motif is announced by the woodwind in bars 2–3 which is characterized melodically by thirds and sevenths. This idea (which is also heard at the opening of the last movement) is later developed considerably, particularly in lyrical passages in the strings. The Allegro, which constitutes the main body of the movement proper, commences in bar 11 with a repeated-note brass statement that is later heard on other instruments. This bright and lively movement brings all the sections of the orchestra into prominence at some point. The slow second movement (Adagio) features numerous solos with long, extremely angular lines, especially for the solo tuba and violin, which combine in dialogue at the beginning, middle (with the flute) and end. There are substantial solos for the woodwind but with occasional eerie interjections from the tuba, which contrast incongruously with the lyrical and mellifluous music given to the strings. The final movement (Allegro moderato) opens with the two-bar motif presented at the outset of the first movement, now given to flutes and violins (Ex. 44). This is developed in conjunction with a contrasting idea featuring rapid demisemiquaver repeated-note outbursts that alternate antiphonally between trumpets and trombones (from bar 73). This rhythmic motif, which first appears as rapid upward flourishes in the woodwind from bar 3, recurs frequently throughout the movement. It subsequently generates a subsidiary semitonal idea which is first heard on solo cello in bar 88, and an accompanying figure in the violins under a triplet figure introduced in bar 129. The Sinfonietta concludes in a rousing fashion with three closing bars of B flat major.[20]

19 Bodley, programme booklet, National Youth Orchestra of Ireland, 24 July 2000
20 The Irish Times critic Michael Dervan noted the Sinfonietta's 'curious restriction of temperature': 'Bodley retains something of the fragmentation and gestural thrust of the avant-garde style, but now, dressed in the intervals of a different harmonic world, the actual notes seem almost too tame, inadequate to their task.' Irish Times, 27 July 2000

Ex. 44 *Sinfonietta*, III, 1–2

In the same year, Bodley completed a short song cycle *The Earlsfort Suite* for mezzo-soprano and orchestra to new texts by Micheal O'Siadhail. This work featured in a series of concerts organized by Dúchas, the Heritage Service for Ireland, which was given the Irish title of *Ceol Reoite* — 'Frozen Music', an allusion to Goethe's famous dictum 'Architecture is frozen music'. Dúchas commissioned fifteen composers to write works to commemorate important buildings and significant heritage sites in Ireland, in this case inviting Bodley to celebrate in music the history of the National Concert Hall building in Earlsfort Terrace. The work was first performed on 17 September 2000 in the National Concert Hall by Bernadette Greevy (to whom it was dedicated) and the RTÉ Concert Orchestra under Proinnsías Ó Duinn. The composer subsequently made a version for voice and piano, which was published in 2008. Bodley wrote that 'the music is concerned with the underlying features of the poetry, gentle celebration in the first song, nervous anticipation in the second, inward and outward celebration in the third'.[21] Lorraine Byrne Bodley, who edited the piano version and who has also published on the poetry of O'Siadhail, sums up the three poems concisely as spanning 'a gap between intimate losses and more public, shared experiences of history's passing, touching upon music's intimacy with our long developing and changing culture'.[22] 'Delivery' (Ex. 45) celebrates the birth of a baby in the local Stella Maris Home on Earlsfort Terrace in 1947 (the year of O'Siadhail's own birth) and refers to notable events of that year such as the discovery of the Dead Sea Scrolls and the composition of Prokofiev's Sixth Symphony and Tennessee Williams's play *A Streetcar Named Desire*, ideas which are then interwoven. An opening motif based on thirds provides most of the musical material for Bodley's setting, whether in building lush and nostalgic sevenths and ninths over descending basses, superimposed in isolated sonorities (such as occur in bars 22 and 29 after the words 'fire' and 'desire', respectively), in a descriptive melismatic passage (bars 19–20) depicting the 1947 eruption of the Icelandic volcano, Hekla, or ubiquitously in the accompaniment and interlude. 'Rite of Passage' alludes to the fact that the National Concert Hall was formerly the Examination Hall of the National University. The text mentions nervous students and a Latin paper as well as anticipating its future use in the line, 'a tuned-in orchestra hushed under the baton'. The third song, 'Streetscape', describes the concert hall vestibule where now 'listeners hush to the raised baton' and outside in a changed streetscape where we find 'our shells and selves shaped by what we shape'.

---

21 Bodley, RTÉ programme booklet, 17 September 2000
22 Byrne Bodley, *A Hazardous Melody of Being*, xxix

Ex. 45 *The Earlsfort Suite, 'Delivery', bars 1–29*

After the premiere, Martin Adams wrote that 'the music's harmonic and melodic styles, and its feel for declamatory vocal lines, deftly capture the poetry's evocations of the Nation Concert Hall's past and present. The piece avoids superficial depiction, yet is accessible.'[23] *In Quiet Celebration...*, a short solo piano piece composed earlier that year and dedicated to his future wife Lorraine Byrne, has much in common stylistically with *The Earlsfort Suite*.

23 *Irish Times*, 19 September 2000

Bodley honoured the memory of those who died in the New York attack on the Twin Towers on 11 September 2001 with another song cycle, *After Great Pain*, commissioned by the James F. Byrnes Institute for a commemorative concert organized by the state of Baden-Württemberg, Germany. Bodley selected four texts by Emily Dickinson and one by Walt Whitman, and the first performance took place at the Landesbank, Königstrasse in Stuttgart on 11 September 2002, exactly a year after the tragedy, with Aylish Kerrigan (mezzo-soprano) and Gabriele Schinnerling (piano). The poems all deal with the experience of pain, grief and death. However, the final song, a setting of Dickinson's poem *Tie the strings to my life, My Lord*, ends in a mood of acceptance as the poet bids farewell to the world. Shortly afterwards, he was commissioned by RTÉ to compose an orchestral work for inclusion in a series of concerts featuring the music of Robert Schumann which was scheduled for 2004. *Metamorphoses on the name Schumann* was first performed on 23 April of that year by the National Symphony Orchestra of Ireland under Gerhard Markson at the National Concert Hall, Dublin. As the title suggests, in this score Bodley employed a favourite compositional device of Schumann's — devising musical themes from the names of various personages by translating some or all of their constituent letters into musical notation (a good example being his *Variations on the name 'Abegg'*, Op. 1). The musical material of the work is based on four notes which can be derived from Schumann's surname using German note names — E flat (Es) C B (H) and A — which are used in combination with all twelve notes of the chromatic scale to form a sixteen-note row. The four 'Schumann' notes form a mobile unit within this row, and can appear in the middle or at either end of it. These four notes are presented in the opening bar by full orchestra (Ex. 46) and are then integrated into the piece before appearing again prominently just before the end of the piece in a *fff* statement with the upper wind in the extreme high register on the pitch A (bars 274–77). Bodley writes that 'the piece itself is a musical statement that is vigorous and irregular in its rhythmic shaping [and] the sections are delineated with very clear and definite colours'.[24] There is much solo writing in the piece, giving it also a *concertante* character with a long sinuous oboe melody at the beginning (bars 2–20), a violin solo (bars 50–67), and the polar opposites of the tuba and piccolo engaging in dialogue against string *glissandi* (bars 24–35). Bodley notes the importance of this idea which 'is reflected later on in a melodic foreground of strings, woodwind and xylophone over soft trombone slides' (bars 215–23).[25] In many ways the soloistic features of the *Sinfonietta* are combined with aspects of the musical language of the three solo piano pieces of 1999–2002. On the occasion of the first performance of this exciting and absorbing piece, the critic for the *Irish Times* offered what might strike many listeners as an apt description of the work: 'weird, without obvious homage to Schumann, and highly engaging'.[26]

24 Bodley, RTÉ programme booklet, 23 April 2004, 4
25 Bodley, RTÉ programme booklet, 23 April 2004, 4
26 *Irish Times*, 26 April 2004

Ex. 46 Metamorphoses on the name Schumann, I

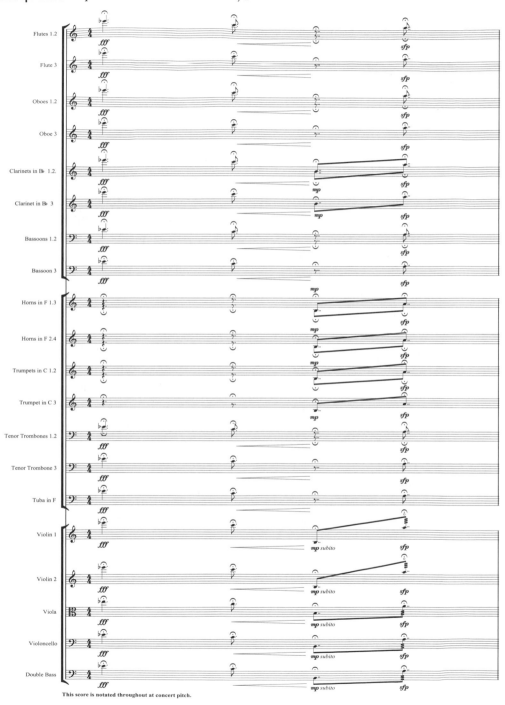

This score is notated throughout at concert pitch.

A few weeks after the premiere of *Metamorphoses on the name Schumann*, the Vogler Quartet gave the first performance of the composer's recently composed String Quartet No. 3. This ensemble, which was formed in East Berlin in 1985, had been quartet in residence in Sligo since 1999. Its members founded the Vogler Spring Festival, which still takes place in the town every May and features distinguished international artists. For the 2004 festival, which marked the conclusion of their residency, the quartet (with the assistance of Sligo County Council) commissioned Bodley to write a new work, which it played on 3 May in St. Columba's Church in Drumcliffe, Co. Sligo, in the famous graveyard in which the poet William Butler Yeats is buried. The quartet bears the motto 'Ave atque vale', a phrase from an ode by the Roman poet Catullus on the untimely death of his brother, which was subsequently used by Tennyson and Swinburne as the title of well-known poems and, in English translation, by George Moore as the title of his quasi-autobiographical prose work *Hail and Farewell!* Bodley alludes to these literary works in his programme notes and adopted the phrase to commemorate the Vogler's departure from the Sligo residency which 'like all leave-taking ... is both celebration and farewell'.[27]

The musical material of this three-movement quartet (*Adagio–Allegro–Largo*) is largely based on a sixteen-note row, which comprises a standard twelve-tone row, but with an extra four notes which can be used freely to liberate his row from any rigid employment — a device similar to that employed in *Metamorphoses on the name Schumann*. As in his first quartet, Bodley was clearly willing to allow his pen be guided by his ear, rather than adhere rigidly to serial procedures. This is particularly evident when he wishes to write fairly lengthy passages in thirds — for instance in the third movement from bars 278–83, where they are played by the violins over a pedal C and are answered by the lower strings from bars 284–92 (Ex. 47). However, despite these thirds, much of the material in the quartet is dominated by the sonority of a fourth. Rhythmic irregularity is generated across the piece by the use of double and triple dotting and other additive durations, such as minims tied to semiquavers and demisemiquavers. The slow movements display effective use of natural and artificial harmonics and the quartet alternates between contrasting homophonic and polyphonic textures. The central *Allegro* contains an extensive contrapuntal passage (from bar 101), preceded by a few bars of a passage marked *quasi cadenza* for the first violin. The main character of this subject is a sustained note over three bars set against a lively syncopated rhythm played *pizzicati*, which drives the music forward with some urgency. A quintuplet motif is introduced in bar 193, which evolves into a repeated note idea. At the very end of the quartet, Bodley requires the performers to observe a full bar's rest with a fermata, a pause which is anticipated by another full bar's rest four bars earlier to ensure that the final subtle silence is effective enough to maintain the listener's concentration. The work was warmly received: in his

---

27 Vogler Spring Festival 2004, programme booklet, 26 (reproduced in the prefatory remarks to the score in the Contemporary Music Centre, Ireland)

review of the concert for the *Irish Times*, Michael Dungan was struck by 'the extraordinary mastery which [Bodley] exerts over both material and technique in order to produce music of truly piercing sadness'.[28]

Ex. 47 String Quartet No. 3, III, 278–92

The years 2003–04 saw the writing of three vocal works to texts by Goethe. The first of these is a short song, *Wandrers Nachtlied* [Wayfarer's Night Song] for mezzo-soprano

28 *Irish Times*, 6 May 2004

(2003) which was then followed by a cycle of seven songs for soprano, baritone and piano entitled *Mignon und der Harfner* [Mignon and the Harper], commissioned for performance during a conference 'Goethe: Musical Poet, Musical Catalyst' which was organized by the Department of Music at the National University of Ireland, Maynooth, in 2004. In this work, Bodley sets the texts of songs sung by two characters in Goethe's novel *Wilhelm Meisters Lehrjahre*. These poems are amongst the most famous lyrics in the German language and have inspired many composers, including Schubert, Schumann and Wolf. The two vocal soloists, commencing with the baritone, alternate, each having three songs, and the final number, *Nur wer die Sehnsucht kennt* [Only one who knows what longing is] is cast as a duet. In the first song, *An die Türen will ich schleichen* [I will steal from door to door], the baritone intones a descending motif D–C sharp –A which pervades the cycle. Although the work features quasi-tonal references (with the sonority of the third featuring prominently), its harmonic vocabulary extends to some densely dissonant chordal aggregates.

The third work is slighter in nature, but was the first score of the composer's to feature the guitar as a solo instrument (if one excepts his orchestral work *Configurations* of 1967, which has a prominent part for electric guitar). *Zeiten des Jahres* (2004) is a setting of one of the *Venetianischen Epigrammen*, in which the poet expresses his contentment in love. It was first performed by mezzo-soprano Linda Lee and guitarist John Feeley on 25 November 2004, at the launch of a book of proceedings from the Maynooth Goethe conference, which was held in the Abbey Theatre Dublin. [29] The song is based on a note row which is introduced in its prime form in the vocal part after a guitar introduction which is based on the same form transposed up a tone. The disjunct vocal line is supported by a sparse and largely linear guitar accompaniment featuring few chords, the voice and guitar meeting appropriately on F sharp at the end of the word 'bedeckt' [sheltered] during the line 'seit mich Beglückten Amors Fittich bedeckt' [since I found happiness in the shelter of Love's wings]. The song ends with a *pianissimo* pentachord comprising the open strings of the guitar with the exception of the top E. Feeley, who is one of Ireland's most distinguished instrumentalists, has made a detailed study of guitar music by Irish composers and considers *Zeiten des Jahres* to be well crafted if in places technically demanding (highlighting the bars of semiquaver septuplets in particular).[30]

Two years later, Bodley composed a solo guitar work *Islands* for Feeley. Similarly, to the end of *Zeiten des Jahres*, *Islands* commences with the sonority of all the instrument's open strings repeated *fortissimo* and *pianissimo* thirteen times within the first eight bars (Ex. 48). This opening suggests an influence of minimalism, which is interesting in view of the fact that Bodley had previously expressed little interest in this stylistic trend, finding it 'frankly

29 Bodley, '*Mignon und der Harfner*' in Lorraine Byrne, ed., *Goethe: Musical Poet, Musical Catalyst* (Dublin, 2004), 294–345
30 John Feeley, *Classical Guitar Music by Irish Composers: Performing Editions and Critical Commentary*, unpublished dissertation, National University of Ireland, Maynooth (2007), 24

often a little childish'.[31] *Islands* is constructed around numerous repetitions of this sonority, which recurs, island-like, in the midst of other material. It is restated in its original form, in various transpositions and slightly truncated, all of these appearances framing the rapid running passages and spiky dotted motif sections. The importance of the ubiquitous thirds (presumably to counteract the prominence of the fourth in the recurring sonority of the open strings) is heightened towards the close, as this very intense piece closes with a gentle E major chord which was adumbrated in the preceding bars and also by means of a long series of low Es. Feeley had commissioned *Islands* with the assistance of the Irish Arts Council and gave the first performance on 28 June 2007 in St. Ann's Church, Dawson Street in Dublin. The *Irish Times* reported that it 'featured a noteworthy clarity in all the music's shifting and combining and juxtaposing, the result of which, in Feeley's committed performance, was something strangely human and persuasive.'[32]

Ex. 48 *Islands*, 1–12

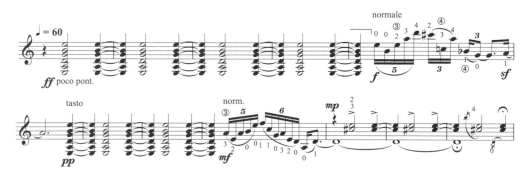

In August 2006, Bodley married for a second time. His wife, Lorraine Byrne (who adopted the surname Byrne Bodley after her marriage) is a musicologist and lectures in the Music Department at the National University of Ireland, Maynooth. Much of her research has focussed on Goethe and Schubert, and in addition to writing on these figures, she has prepared for publication editions of her husband's liturgical music and songs.

Bodley's most recent work suggests that his stylistic explorations have perhaps still not reached an end, and it is certainly possible that his idiom could undergo yet further change. The composer is untroubled by the apparent discontinuities and contradictions between the different phases of his development, and robustly defends his right as a creative artist to employ a wide variety of expressive means. He has articulated his views on this subject at considerable length in a number of recent talks and interviews. One of the most significant of these was a lecture 'The Claims of Conformity' given in Waterford on 29 January 2005 at

31 Dungan, 'An Interview with Seóirse Bodley'. Bodley also mentioned to Dungan that in the 1970s, although he found minimalism very interesting and singled out Reich's *Six Pianos* for praise, 'he never felt any temptation to go that particular route'.

32 *Irish Times*, 3 July 2007

a seminar 'Teaching the Unteachable? The Role of Composition in Music Education', which was jointly organized by the Waterford Institute of Technology and the Council of the Heads of Music in Higher Education. (This event was held during a festival of new music that was taking place in the city at the time, in which Bodley was the featured composer). His paper provides a useful summary of his views on the problems faced by contemporary composers, in particular that of evolving a personal compositional style. Bodley discusses the pressure to conform to the latest fashion which affects composers of all ages and the difficulty of sustaining an individual voice through stylistic change. He examines the trajectory of his creative path, considering works from various periods which are written in very different styles, such as String Quartet No. 1 (1968), *The Narrow Road to the Deep North* (1972), *The Tightrope Walker Presents a Rose* (1976), and *News from Donabate* (2001). His conclusion encourages young composers to resist external pressures to adopt any style that they find uncongenial:

> [This] feeling of compulsion ... is quite different in character from the inner excitement of taking a journey through uncharted waters in order to learn and expand. In one case the impetus for the change of direction is external, in the other the drive to learn is internal and to an extent self-directed. The ability to differentiate between the two types of motivation requires a degree of self-knowledge that is not so common among the young. Fortunately perhaps, many a young composer has another resource to call on: what I like to term 'the wisdom of youth'. The wisdom of youth is quite different from the wisdom of age, which, ideally, is a matter of mature considered reflection. The wisdom of youth consists in following a chosen path with fire and enthusiasm, almost regardless of the consequences ... . Today the contemporary composer is surrounded by other very different claims to conformity. There may be pressure to develop in terms of modernism, either of a more general kind or of the post-serial type. [But] finding your own voice is a matter of discovering which of your musical ideas feel as if they have the potential of having an independent life of their own. This feeling of life and potential in musical ideas can exist almost regardless of the style or idiom in which the music is written. [A composer] needs to see what musical ideas give him 'the feeling of rightness', regardless of style.[33]

Bodley has alluded to this 'feeling of rightness' many times previously. In 1969 he noted during a Radio Éireann 'Composer's Workshop' that, 'I have always worked in the light of a rather funny feeling of rightness when a work was going well and wrongness when it wasn't and it's largely by this criterion that I write at all.'[34] He has repeatedly emphasized his reliance on intuition and his inner ear (using the piano often as a point of reference),

33 Bodley, 'The Claims of Conformity', 32, 35–36
34 13 February 1969, RTÉ Recording Library

despite his frequent employment of strict compositional methods such as serialism.[35] Bodley has also stated that he does not adhere to a particular routine when composing, and compares his working methods to writing a letter:

> You sit down, you start, and you scribble it out. And what you write on Monday you might rub out on Tuesday. It doesn't really matter; it's all process, part of a process. And it's in that seeking that the idea comes.[36]

Around this time, Bodley had also begun to explore the writings of the Viennese philosopher, Karl Popper, which have exerted a considerable influence on his creative outlook. In his monograph *The Poverty of Historicism* (1957), Popper rejected the possibility of historical prediction in the social sciences, which, he contended, erroneously assumed that accurate predictions of future trends can be made 'by discovering the "rhythms" or the "patterns", the "laws" or the "trends" that underlie the evolution of history'.[37] Bodley has found in Popper's philosophies a way to clarify (and perhaps even validate) for himself, not only his own unpredictability in his many stylistic changes of direction over the years, but also his return to this neo-tonality in works such as *Islands* as described above. Bodley had discussed with Feeley the influence of Popper on the work reflecting on Popper's critique of the main tenets on which modernism is based. He explained that he was experimenting by trying to see what the effect might be if he were to bring his music closer tonally to an audience, but without jettisoning his own past.[38]

The influence of Popper's philosophies is apparent in one of Bodley's most recent works, the two-movement String Quartet No. 4 (2007), which was commissioned by RTÉ to celebrate the RTÉ Vanbrugh Quartet's twenty-first anniversary. It was premiered in the Aula Maxima of University College Galway on 28 November 2007 along with new quartets by Deirdre Gribbin (*Merrow Song*) and Ronan Guilfoyle (*Music for String Quartet*), and the programme was then taken on a short tour around Ireland. As in *Islands*, Bodley regards this work as an attempt to recover 'some of the ground that a composer has to cede in order to conform to the tenets of musical modernism' by means of a 'kind of personal "reverse experimentalism"'.[39] The quartet is pervaded by strong tonal references of a kind

---

35 See for instance 'Composers in Conversation', with Dermot Rattigan (23 July 1988), RTÉ Recording Library and an interview with Ciaran Carty, *Sunday Independent*, 15 May 1977.

36 Dungan, 'An Interview with Seóirse Bodley'. In another interview with Dungan, Bodley stated that his ideas 'come mostly in the act of composing', as he rewrites and revises the material he has already devised. Dungan, 'What's it like to be Seóirse Bodley?', Contemporary Music Centre, Ireland, website www.cmc.ie (2003). Accessed 27 December 2008.

37 Karl Popper, *The Poverty of Historicism* (London, 1957), 3

38 John Feeley in interview with Bodley, 12 September, 2006. I am grateful to John Feeley for providing me with the recording of this interview.

39 Bodley, RTÉ programme booklet, 28 November 2007, 4

that are almost unprecedented in his previous work, with deliberately strong statements of primary chords. In his programme note, Bodley remarked *a propos* of this stylistic shift:

> [It] is impossible not to 'express yourself' no matter what stylistic practices you adapt, since what you are is a trademark you carry with you in all that you do. In consequence, I do not feel that changes are of more than secondary importance in the greater musical scheme of things.[40]

When the present writer queried the use of the word 'adapt' instead of 'adopt' in this passage as being a possible misprint, Bodley explained that, for him,

> *adopting* a stylistic practice suggests taking one over wholesale and giving oneself totally to it. *Adapting* a stylistic practice is closer to what I have done and while it may be less usual to use the term in this way, I think it is closer to what I have actually done.[41]

The first movement, an *Adagio*, begins in G major in the viola and cello and the violins extend this in rising thirds (Ex. 49), an interval which permeates the entire quartet. Bodley aims to surround the listener symbolically with thirds (though not in a diatonic context) to depict 'the idea of music as being all around us, surrounding us always both from above and below'.[42] He contrasts this in bar 21 with a four-note quintal motif played *delicato* followed by a two-note idea C sharp–C (Ex. 49) — a motif which was anticipated prominently in *fortissimo* unison across all the parts in bar 92 of his String Quartet No. 3. From bar 34 there is a gentle pastoral feel provided by *pizzicato* triplets in the lower strings under some dialogue between the violins. This leads into two more short sections featuring a smooth semiquaver motif and a chordal passage respectively before the movement ends quietly (with bars 20–24 repeated almost identically) in D major. The second movement, *Allegro*, starts with this quintal motif developed over thirds in the viola and cello and ideas and moods from the first movement are revisited, expanded and elaborated on in a more intense and excited manner. Two *brillante* sustained statements in G major (bars 86–88) and C major (bars 131–33) are interpolated and the piece ends with a G major scale in thirds in the viola and cello leading to a plagal cadence in G major. Nothing could herald Bodley's reclaimed tonal territory more unambiguously as this quartet and these final two bars of dramatic G major with the concluding unison and accented Gs.

   After the Dublin performance in the National Gallery on 2 December, Andrew Johnstone recognized it as being 'an avowedly anti-modernist statement, particularly in its espousal of warmly consonant harmony. Yet its apparent exclusion of traditional formal and thematic processes places it firmly in the present.[43]

40   Bodley, RTÉ programme booklet, 28 November 2007, 4
41   Bodley, correspondence with author, 17 May 2007
42   Bodley, RTÉ programme booklet, 28 November 2007, 4
43   *Irish Times*, 6 December 2007

Ex. 49 String Quartet No. 4, I, 1–21

Shortly before this book was completed, an RTÉ Horizons lunchtime concert was held on 13 January 2009 in the National Concert Hall, at which the music of Bodley was played by the RTÉ National Symphony Orchestra with soprano Sylvia O'Brien and conducted by Colman Pearce. It was an excellent chance to hear again after many years two works from the mid-1960s and early 1970s, *Never to Have Lived is Best* and *Meditations on Lines from Patrick Kavanagh*. The composer was invited to introduce the works in a pre-concert talk and the concert was followed by the launch of a CD of three of his works. Bodley selected Stravinsky's *Dumbarton Oaks* to programme with his own works, a choice which allowed him to draw parallels in his introductory talk between the stylistic changes in his own output and that of the Russian composer.[44] The entire event was very well attended, highlighting not only Bodley's stature as one of Ireland's most prominent creative figures, but more importantly, reflecting his significance as a composer whose career has been followed by Irish concert-goers for many decades in his individual search for his own musical language and his quest for a collective national musical identity.

---

44 He chose *Dumbarton Oaks* because of 'the attitude of mind that it represents … . [A]ll through his life Stravinsky "changed style", when he wished to do so. Yet remarkably, compositions that might be considered stylistically different are clearly the work of the same composer.' Bodley, RTÉ programme booklet, 13 January 2009

Appendix I. Catalogue of Compositions

This list of works has been compiled from the following catalogues: 1. Edgar Deale, ed., *Catalogue of Contemporary Irish Composers* (Dublin 1973 [1968]); 2. Bernard Harrison, ed., *Catalogue of Contemporary Irish Music* (Dublin, 1982); 3. Catalogue of the Contemporary Music Centre, Ireland (published on the CMC website at www.cmc.ie and constantly updated); 4. Catalogue in Pádhraic Ó Cuinneagáin, *The Piano Music of Seóirse Bodley*, unpublished dissertation, National University of Ireland, Maynooth, 1992; 5. Seóirse Bodley, Personal Catalogue. The information contained in these various catalogues is occasionally both conflicting and inaccurate. The following list has been completed with the assistance of the composer, who has confirmed the details as correct. The music of Seóirse Bodley can be obtained from the Contemporary Music Centre, Ireland.

A. MUSIC FOR ORCHESTRA

Music for Strings (1952)
   Fp 10 December 1952; Dublin Orchestral Players, Brian Boydell (cond.); Metropolitan Hall, Dublin

Movement for Orchestra (1956)
   Fp 21 July 1956; Radio Éireann Symphony Orchestra, Milan Horvat (cond.); Phoenix Hall, Dublin

Salve, Maria Virgo (1957)

Fp 27 October 1957; Radio Éireann Symphony Orchestra, Milan Horvat (cond.); Gaiety Theatre, Dublin

Symphony No. 1 (1959)
Fp 23 October 1960; Radio Éireann Symphony Orchestra, Hans Müller-Kray (cond.); Gaiety Theatre, Dublin

Divertimento (1961)
Fp 15 June 1962; Radio Éireann Symphony Orchestra, Tibor Paul (cond.); Phoenix Hall, Dublin

Chamber Symphony No. 1 (1964)
Fp (broadcast) 6 October 1964; Radio Éireann Symphony Orchestra, Tibor Paul (cond.). Fp (public) 7 February 1965; Radio Éireann Symphony Orchestra, Tibor Paul (cond.). The composer made a recording of the work with the RÉSO in 1964 prior to the first broadcast performance, but it has not been possible to ascertain the exact date. This recording was made especially for the 1964 UNESCO International Rostrum of Composers in Paris.

Configurations (1967)
Fp 29 January 1967; Radio Telefís Éireann Symphony Orchestra, Tibor Paul (cond.); Gaiety Theatre, Dublin

A Small White Cloud Drifts Over Ireland (1975)
Fp 5 January 1976; Radio Telefís Éireann Symphony Orchestra, Proinnsías Ó Duinn (cond.); Francis Xavier Hall, Dublin

I Have Loved the Lands of Ireland (Symphony No. 2) (1980)
Fp 9 January 1981; Radio Telefís Éireann Symphony Orchestra, Colman Pearce (cond.); Royal Dublin Society, Dublin

Chamber Symphony No. 2 (1982)
Fp 17 June 1982; Ulysses Ensemble, Seóirse Bodley (cond.); Carroll's Building, Grand Parade, Dublin

Celebration Music (Orchestral Version, 1984) [See also Chamber Music below]
Fp 21 September 1984; Radio Telefís Éireann Symphony Orchestra, Colman Pearce (cond.); National Concert Hall, Dublin

Symphony No. 4 (1991)

Fp 21 June 1991; Orchestra Sinfonica dell'Emilia-Romagna 'Arturo Toscanini', Josè Ramon Encinar (cond.); Teatro Farnese, Parma, Italy

Symphony No. 5 (*The Limerick Symphony*) (1991)
Fp 4 October 1991; Radio Telefís Éireann Concert Orchestra, Proinnsías Ó Duinn (cond.); Jetland Festival Centre, Limerick

Sinfonietta (2000)
Fp 24 July 2000; National Youth Orchestra of Ireland, En Shao (cond.); University Concert Hall, Limerick

Metamorphoses on the name Schumann (2004)
Fp 23 April 2004; National Symphony Orchestra, Gerhard Markson (cond.); National Concert Hall, Dublin

B. CHAMBER MUSIC

Capriccio No. 1 for Violin and Piano (1951/2)
Fp 26 November 1954; Ruth Ticher (violin), Seóirse Bodley (piano); Trinity College Dublin

Capriccio No. 2 for Violin and Piano (1951/2)
Fp 26 November 1954; Ruth Ticher (violin), Seóirse Bodley (piano); Trinity College Dublin

Sonatina for Wind Quintet (1955)
Fp (broadcast) 14 December 1955; Les Amis de la Musique; Radio Éireann, Dublin

Sonata for Violin and Piano (1959)
Fp (broadcast) 2 November 1959; Margaret Hayes (violin), Seóirse Bodley (piano); Radio Éireann, Dublin

Scintillae (1968)
Two Irish harps. Fp 24 July 1989; Anne-Marie Farrell and Helen Davies (harps); Termonfeckin, Co. Louth. Pub *The Irish Harp Book*, Sheila Larchet Cuthbert, ed. (Dublin, 1975), 211–23; reprint (Dublin, 2004)

String Quartet No. 1 (1968)
Fp 6 January 1969; Radio Telefís Éireann String Quartet; Trinity College Dublin

In Memory of Seán Ó Riada (1971)
> Flute and piano. Fp 21 October 1971; Val Keogh (flute), Seóirse Bodley (piano); Royal
> Dublin Society

September Preludes (1973)
> Flute and piano. Fp 7 January 1974; Patricia Dunkerley (flute), John Gibson (piano); St.
> Patrick's College, Drumcondra

Celebration Music (1983) [see also Orchestral Music above]
> String quartet and three trumpets. Fp 11 November 1983; Testore String Quartet and
> trumpets [players unknown]; National Institute of Higher Education, Glasnevin,
> Dublin

Trio for Flute, Violin and Piano (1986)
> Fp 6 July 1986; Concorde Ensemble; Hugh Lane Gallery, Dublin

The Fiddler (1987)
> String trio and speaker [with optional choral and instrumental parts]. Fp 6 October
> 1987; Students of St. Louis Convent School, The Jupiter Ensemble; St. Louis Convent
> Post-Primary School, Monaghan

Phantasms (1989)
> Flute, clarinet, harp and cello. Fp 27 October 1989; Denise Kelly Ensemble; Douglas
> Hyde Gallery, Trinity College Dublin

String Quartet No. 2 (1992)
> Fp 21 May 1993; Degani String Quartet; National Gallery of Ireland, Dublin

Ceremonial Music (1995)
> Brass quintet. Fp 10 May 1995; Sovereign Brass (Colin Byrne, Neil O'Connor, Brian
> Daly, Gavin Roche, Patrick Kenny) Seóirse Bodley (cond.); O'Reilly Hall, University
> College Dublin

String Quartet No. 3: *Ave atque Vale* (2004)
> Fp 3 May 2004; Vogler String Quartet; St. Columba's Church, Drumcliffe, Co. Sligo

Islands (2006)
> Guitar. Fp 28 June 2007; John Feeley; St. Ann's Church, Dawson Street, Dublin

String Quartet No. 4 (2007)

Fp 28 November 2007; RTÉ Vanbrugh String Quartet; Aula Maxima, National University of Ireland, Galway

C. PIANO MUSIC

Scherzo (c.1953)
Fp 26 November 1954; Seóirse Bodley; Trinity College Dublin

Movement in B (c.1954)
Fp 26 November 1954; Seóirse Bodley; Trinity College Dublin

Four Little Pieces / Ceithre Píosaí Bheaga don Phianó (1954)
Fp 26 November 1954; Seóirse Bodley; Trinity College Dublin. Pub Feasta, January, March, June and September 1960. Reprinted by Waltons Music, 1985.

Rince [Dance] (1956)
(Fp Seóirse Bodley; private performance, date unknown; Dublin)

Prelude, Toccata and Epilogue (1963)
Fp 1964[?]; Deirdre McNulty; University College Dublin

The Narrow Road to the Deep North (1972)
Two pianos. Fp 17 February 1972; Raymond Warren and Evan John (pianos); The Whitla Hall, Queen's University Belfast

Planxty Rosen (1974)
Fp (broadcast) 11 October 1976; Seóirse Bodley; Radio Telefís Éireann, Radio

The Tightrope Walker Presents a Rose (1976)
Fp 11 September 1983, Patricia Kavanagh, National Concert Hall, Dublin. Pub Piano Album: Grade VII (Dublin: Royal Irish Academy of Music, 2009), 20–23

Aislingí (1977)
Fp 29 August 1977; John O'Conor; St. Canice's Cathedral, Kilkenny

The Narrow Road to the Deep North [version for solo piano] (1977)
Fp 29 August 1977; John O'Conor; St. Canice's Cathedral, Kilkenny. Pub Soundpost, 16, Oct/Nov 1983

Christmas Prelude (1986)
   (Fp Seóirse Bodley; private performance, date unknown; Dublin)

News from Donabate (1999)
   Fp 21 February 2001; Andrei Roudenko; Aula Maxima, National University of Ireland,
   Galway

Chiaroscuro (1999)
   Fp 14 May 2000, Lidija Bizjak, Kirill Gerstein [both played it in the finals of the AXA
   Dublin Piano Competition 2000]; National Concert Hall, Dublin. Pub CMC Editions,
   2000, CMC 1020, 2–12

In Quiet Celebration..., (2000)
   Fp (private performance) 19 April 2000; Seóirse Bodley; Dublin

An Exchange of Letters (2002)
   Fp 25 March 2002; Rolf Hind; John Field Room, National Concert Hall, Dublin

D. CHORAL MUSIC

Ring Out Ye Crystal Spheres (1950)
   Male octet. Text John Milton. Fp (broadcast) 25 December 1950; Radio Éireann Men's
   Octet, Hans Waldemar Rosen (cond.); Radio Éireann, Dublin

Song on May Morning (1951)
   Male octet. Text John Milton. Fp (broadcast) 26 May 1951; Radio Éireann Men's Octet,
   Hans Waldemar Rosen (cond.); Radio Éireann, Dublin

Trí h-Amhráin Grá [Three Love Songs] (1952)
   SATB choir. Text Seventeenth-century Irish poems. Fp 7 January 1953; Archbishop
   Byrne Hall, Dublin [details of choir unknown], Hans Waldemar Rosen (cond.).
   Published privately [date unknown]

Cúl an Tí [The Back of the House] (1954)
   SATB choir. Text Seán Ó Ríordáin. Fp (broadcast) 9 July 1955; Radio Éireann Singers,
   Hans Waldemar Rosen (cond.); Radio Éireann, Dublin

An Bhliain Lán [The Full Year] (1956)

> Tenor solo, SATB choir. Text Tomás Ó Floinn. Fp (broadcast) 1 February 1957; Radio Éireann Singers, Hans Waldemar Rosen (cond.); Radio Éireann, Dublin. Pub An Gúm, n.d.

An Bás is an Bheatha [Life and Death] (1960)

> SATB choir. Text Anon [Irish Proverbs]. Fp 22 January 1961; Radio Éireann Singers, Hans Waldemar Rosen (cond.); Gaiety Theatre, Dublin

Trí Aortha [Three Satires] (1962)

> SATB choir. Fp 18 May 1963; Culwick Choral Society, Seóirse Bodley (cond.); Aula Maxima, University College Cork

A Chill Wind (1977)

> SATB choir. Text Brendan Kennelly. Fp 12 January 1978; Radio Telefís Éireann Singers, Proinnsías Ó Duinn (cond.); Trinity College Dublin

The Radiant Moment (1979)

> SATB choir. Text Thomas MacGreevy. Fp 26 April 1979; Radio Telefís Éireann Singers, Eric Sweeney (cond.); Aula Maxima, University College Cork

Ceol: Symphony No. 3 (1980)

> SATB Soli, SATB choir, semi-chorus, children's choir, speaker, orchestra [with audience participation]. Text Brendan Kennelly. Fp 9 September 1981; Violet Twomey (soprano), Bernadette Greevy (mezzo-soprano), Louis Browne (tenor), William Young (bass), Aindreas Ó Gallchoir (speaker), Radio Telefís Éireann Symphony Orchestra, Radio Telefís Éireann Singers and Chorus, Our Lady's Choral Society, boys of St. Patrick's Cathedral Choir, Dublin, Colman Pearce (cond.); National Concert Hall, Dublin

GAA Song (1984)

> Baritone or mezzo-soprano solo, or vocal group, unison chorus, orchestra. Text Seóirse Bodley. Fp 7 October 1984; Martin Dempsey (baritone), RTÉ Concert Orchestra, Proinnsías Ó Duinn (cond.); Opera House, Cork

Frau Musica (1996)

> Mezzo-soprano, SATB choir, string orchestra, flute, [optional bassoon], organ. Text Martin Luther and Johann Walter. Fp 5 October 1996; Aylish Kerrigan (mezzo-soprano), Johann-Walter-Kantorei, Musica Juventa Orchestra, Ekkehard Saretz (cond.); Schlosskirche, Torgau, Germany

E. VOCAL MUSIC

O Mistress Mine (1950)
> Baritone and piano. Text William Shakespeare

A Cradle Song (1950)
> Soprano and piano. Text W. B. Yeats. Fp [details unknown]

Ná Déan Gáire [Do Not Laugh] (1953)
> Baritone and piano. Text Séamus Ó Néill. Fp 26 November 1954; Tomás Ó Súilleabháin (baritone), Seóirse Bodley (piano); Trinity College Dublin

Paidir I [Prayer I] (1953)
> Baritone and piano. Text Seán Ó Ríordáin. Fp 26 November 1954; Tomás Ó Súilleabháin (baritone), Seóirse Bodley (piano); Trinity College Dublin

Paidir II [Prayer II]: *Prayer for a Child in an Air Raid* (1953)
> Baritone and piano. Text Séamus Ó Néill. Fp 26 November 1954; Tomás Ó Súilleabháin (baritone), Seóirse Bodley (piano); Trinity College Dublin

Do Bhádhasa Uair [The Lament of a Bald Man for his Departed Hair] (1953)
> Baritone and piano. Text Anon (trans. Tomás Ó Súilleabháin). Fp 26 November 1954; Tomás Ó Súilleabháin (baritone), Seóirse Bodley (piano); Trinity College Dublin

Stróll [Stroll] (1953)
> Baritone and piano. Text Liam S. Gógan. Fp 26 November 1954; Tomás Ó Súilleabháin (baritone), Seóirse Bodley (piano); Trinity College Dublin

Cré [Earth] (1953)
> Baritone and piano. Text Anon. Fp 26 November 1954; Tomás Ó Súilleabháin (baritone), Seóirse Bodley (piano); Trinity College Dublin

Deire Fomhair [October] (1953)
> Baritone and piano. Text Séamus Ó Néill. Fp 26 November 1954; Tomás Ó Súilleabháin (baritone), Seóirse Bodley (piano); Trinity College Dublin

The Fairies (1953)
> Baritone and piano. Text William Allingham. Fp 26 November 1954; Tomás Ó Súilleabháin (baritone), Seóirse Bodley (piano); Trinity College Dublin

A Drinking Song (1953)
  Baritone and piano. Text W. B. Yeats. Fp [details unknown]

Never to Have Lived is Best (1965)
  Soprano and orchestra. Text W. B. Yeats. Fp 11 June 1965; Veronica Dunne (soprano), Radio Telefís Éireann Symphony Orchestra, Tibor Paul (cond.); St. Francis Xavier Hall, Dublin

Ariel's Songs (1969)
  Soprano and piano. Text William Shakespeare. Fp 7 January 1970; Marni Nixon (soprano), John McCabe (piano); Examination Hall, Trinity College Dublin.

Meditations on Lines from Patrick Kavanagh (1971)
  Contralto and orchestra. Text Patrick Kavanagh. Fp 30 June 1972; Bernadette Greevy (contralto), Radio Telefís Éireann Symphony Orchestra, Colman Pearce (cond.); St. Francis Xavier Hall, Dublin

Ceathrúintí Mháire Ní Ógáin [Máire Ní Ógáin's Quatrains] (1973)
  Soprano and orchestra. Text Máire Mhac an tSaoi. Fp 7 June 1974; Minnie Clancy (soprano), Radio Telefís Éireann Symphony Orchestra, Seóirse Bodley (cond.); St. Francis Xavier Hall, Dublin

A Girl (1978)
  Mezzo-soprano and piano. Text Brendan Kennelly. Fp 17 October 1978; Bernadette Greevy (mezzo-soprano), John O'Conor (piano); National Gallery of Ireland, Dublin

Transitions (1978)
  Two Speakers, piano and prepared piano. Text Brendan Kennelly. Cantata for radio adapted from A Girl. Fp (broadcast) 19 October 1978; Bernadette Greevy (mezzo-soprano), Máire O'Neill (speaker), Barry McGovern (speaker), John O'Conor (piano), Seóirse Bodley (prepared piano); RTÉ Radio

The Banshee (1983)
  SATB soli, electronics. Text Seóirse Bodley. Fp 25 April 1983; Electric Phoenix; Sonorities Festival, Whitla Hall, Queen's University, Belfast

A Passionate Love (1985)
  Mezzo-soprano or baritone and piano. Text Seóirse Bodley. Fp 5 May 1985; Aylish Kerrigan (mezzo-soprano), Seóirse Bodley (piano); Hugh Lane Gallery, Dublin

Canal Bank Walk (1986)

> Mezzo-soprano or contralto and piano. Version of Movement IV from *Meditations on Lines from Patrick Kavanagh*. Text Patrick Kavanagh. Fp 5 July 1986; Aylish Kerrigan (mezzo–soprano) and Seóirse Bodley (piano); National Concert Hall, Dublin

The Naked Flame (1987)

> Mezzo-soprano or baritone and piano. Text Micheal O'Siadhail. Fp 15 November 1988; Bernadette Greevy (mezzo-soprano), Miceal O'Rourke (piano); National Concert Hall, Dublin. Pub *A Hazardous Melody: Seóirse Bodley's Song Cycles on the Poems of Micheal O'Siadhail*, ed. Lorraine Byrne Bodley (Dublin, 2008), 1–59.

Carta Irlandesa (1988)

> Mezzo-soprano or baritone and piano. Text Antonio González-Guerrero. Fp 4 September 1988; Aylish Kerrigan (mezzo-soprano), Seóirse Bodley (piano); St. John's Cathedral, Sligo

By the Margins of the Great Deep (1995)

> Medium voice and piano. Text George William Russell (Æ). Fp 14 May 1995; Aylish Kerrigan (mezzo-soprano), Seóirse Bodley (piano); University of Bochum, Germany

Fraw Musica (1996)

> Mezzo-soprano and piano. Text Martin Luther and Johann Walter. Version of movements II and VIII from *Fraw Musica*. See Choral Music above. Fp private performance, date unknown; Aylish Kerrigan (mezzo-soprano), Seóirse Bodley (piano); Germany [venue unknown]

Pax Bellumque (1997)

> Soprano, flute, clarinet, violin and piano. Text Wilfred Owen and Thomas MacGreevy. Fp 2 May 1997; Concorde (Tine Verbeke (soprano), Madeleine Staunton (flute), Paul Roe (clarinet), Alan Smale (violin), Jane O'Leary (piano)); John Field Room, National Concert Hall, Dublin

Look to this Day! (1997)

> Voice and piano. Text Anon [Sanskrit]. Fp private performance, 21 December 1997; Aylish Kerrigan (mezzo-soprano), Seóirse Bodley (piano); Stuttgart, Germany

Earlsfort Suite (2000)

Voice and orchestra. Text Micheal O'Siadhail. Fp 17 September 2000; Bernadette Greevy (contralto), Radio Telefís Éireann Concert Orchestra, Proinnsías Ó Duinn (cond.); National Concert Hall, Dublin

After Great Pain (2002)

Mezzo-soprano and piano. Text Emily Dickinson and Walt Whitman. Fp 11 September 2002; Aylish Kerrigan (mezzo-soprano), Gabriele Schinnerling (piano); Landesbank, Königstrasse, Stuttgart, Germany

Wandrers Nachtlied [Wayfarer's Night Song] (2003)

Mezzo-soprano and piano. Text Johann Wolfgang von Goethe. Fp 6 May 2003; Aylish Kerrigan (mezzo-soprano), Seóirse Bodley (piano); Goethe Institut, Dublin

Mignon und der Harfner [Mignon and the Harper] (2004)

Soprano, baritone and piano. Text Johann Wolfgang von Goethe. Fp 27 March 2004; Kathleen Tynan (soprano), Sam McElroy (baritone), Dearbhla Collins (piano); National University of Ireland, Maynooth. Pub *Goethe: Musical Poet, Musical Catalyst*, ed. Lorraine Byrne (Dublin, 2004), 294–345

Zeiten des Jahres [The Seasons] (2004)

Voice and guitar. Fp 25 November 2004; Linda Lee (soprano), John Feeley (guitar); The Abbey Theatre, Dublin. Pub in *Goethe: Musical Poet, Musical Catalyst*, ed. Lorraine Byrne (Dublin, 2004), 360–64

Squall (2006)

Soprano and piano. Text Micheal O'Siadhail. Fp 20 April 2008; Sylvia O'Brien (soprano), Seóirse Bodley (piano); Hugh Lane Gallery, Dublin. Pub *Musics of Belonging: The Poetry of Micheal O'Siadhail*, ed. Marc Caball and David F. Ford (Dublin, 2007), 111–15

Earlsfort Suite (2000)

[Version for mezzo-soprano (or baritone) and piano] Text Micheal O'Siadhail. Fp 20 April 2008; Sylvia O'Brien (soprano), Seóirse Bodley (piano); Hugh Lane Gallery, Dublin. Pub *A Hazardous Melody of Being: Seóirse Bodley's Song Cycles on the Poems of Micheal O'Siadhail*, ed. Lorraine Byrne Bodley (Dublin, 2008), 61–78

E. LITURGICAL MUSIC

Mass of Peace (1976)
Celebrant [or cantor], unison voices [or SATB choir], congregation and organ. Text
Roman Liturgy. Fp 27 February 1977; Carmelite Conference Centre, Ballinteer, Co.
Dublin. Pub Irish Commission for Liturgy, 1976; reprinted in *Seóirse Bodley, Three
Congregational Masses*, ed. Lorraine Byrne (Dublin, 2005), 1–14

Hymn to St. John of God (1978)
Choir, congregation and organ [with optional instrumental descants]. Text Michael
Hodgetts. Fp King David Singers, Patrick Devine (organ), Seóirse Bodley (cond.) Pub
Dublin, 1979.

Mass of Joy (1978)
Fp 8 March 1979, Choirs of Clonliffe College & Mater Dei Institute of Education, Seóirse
Bodley (cond.), Patrick Devine (organ), St. Laurence's Church, Dublin. This work
incorporates *Hymn to St. John of God* (listed above). Pub Veritas, Dublin 1979 and in
Seóirse Bodley, Three Congregational Masses, ed. Lorraine Byrne (Dublin, 2005), 15–32

O Antiphons (1978)
O Antiphons is a collection of settings in English of seven antiphons by Bodley and
Gerard Victory [with an additional setting by P. Décha of the *Magnificat*]. Cantor,
small choir [or vocal group], congregation and organ. Text Roman Liturgy. Pub
Rain Magee and Fr. J. Threadgold, eds., Dublin, 1979.

Psalm 95: O Sing a New Song to the Lord (1979)
Cantor(s), choir [SA or TB or SATB], congregation, organ [with optional instruments].
Fp June 1979 [exact date unknown]; Knock Basilica, Knock, Co. Mayo

Hymn to Our Lady of Knock (1979)
SATB choir [or SSA choir, or soloists], congregation and organ [with optional
instrumental descants]. Text Michael Hodgetts. Fp June 1979 [exact date unknown];
Knock Basilica, Knock, Co. Mayo

Mass of Glory / Aifreann na Glóire (1980)
SSATBB [or SSA] choir [or soloists], congregation and organ [with optional instruments].
Text Roman Liturgy. Fp 15 August 1980; Sisters of Loreto Abbey, Dublin, Sr. Phillipa
(cond.); Loreto Abbey, Dublin. Pub Hyperion Books, Dublin, 1989

A Concert Mass (1984)

SATB soli, SATB choir, strings. Text Seóirse Bodley. Fp 4 May 1990; Radio Telefís Éireann Chamber Choir, Irish Chamber Orchestra, Seóirse Bodley (cond.); National Concert Hall, Dublin

Hymn for the Congregation of St. Louis (1980)
SSA choir [or SATB choir or solo voice] with instrumental or vocal descant, congregation, organ or string quartet [or string orchestra]. Text Michael Hodgetts

Amra Cholum Cille (2007)
SATB choir. Text: Anon [Old Irish, trans. Páraic L. Henry]. Fp 2 June 2007, Christchurch Cathedral, Dublin

F. FILM MUSIC

Athcuairt ar Ghabhla [Gola Revisited] (1977)
Incidental music (television). String Quartet and timpani. Fp (broadcast) 29 December 1977; Radio Telefís Éireann [performers unknown]

From Ireland's Past (1978)
Incidental music (television). Oboe, horn, 2 trumpets, trombone, tuba, string quartet. Fp (broadcast) 9, 16, 23 February, 2 March 1979; Radio Telefís Éireann. Georgian Brass Quintet, Testore String Quartet, Seóirse Bodley (cond.)

Michael Davitt and the Land League (1979)
Incidental music (television). Flute, oboe, clarinet, horn, bassoon, timpani, piano, string quartet. Fp (broadcast) 30 October, 6 November 1979; Radio Telefís Éireann; Ulysses Ensemble, Testore String Quartet, Seóirse Bodley (cond.)

James Joyce: 'Is there one who understands me?' (1981)
Incidental music (television). Flute, cornet, trombone, piano, string quartet. Fp (broadcast) 2 February 1982; Radio Telefís Éireann; Testore Ensemble, Seóirse Bodley (cond.)

Between the Canals (1983)
Incidental music (television). Chamber Ensemble. Fp (broadcast) 14 December 1983; Radio Telefís Éireann; [performers unknown]

Caught in a Free State (1983)
Incidental music (television). Fp (broadcast) 6, 13, 20, 27 October 1983; Radio Telefís Éireann; Testore Ensemble, RTÉ Concert Orchestra, Seóirse Bodley (cond.)

W. B. Yeats: *Cast a Cold Eye* (1988)
  Incidental music (television). Fp (broadcast) 24 January 1989 ; Radio Telefís Éireann; chamber ensemble; [performers unknown]

G. ARRANGEMENTS

Orchestra
  Ailliliú na Gamhna [Calling Home the Calves] (1956)
  Táim gan im gan ór [I'm without butter or gold] (1956)
  The Palatine's Daughter (1956)
  St. Patrick was a Gentleman (1956)
  Johnny Dubh [Black Johnny] (1957)
  The Connaught Heifer (1957)
  The Cat that Ate the Candle (1957)
  Gáire na mBan [The Laughter of Women] (1959)
  An Gaoth Aniar [The West Wind] (1973)

SATB choir and orchestra
  Who Fears to Speak of Easter Week? (1956)
  Rosc Catha na Mumhan [Battle Hymn of Munster] (1956)
  The Foggy Dew (1956)
  An Dord Féinne [The Chant of the Fianna] (1956)
  Amhrán Síodraimín [Sweet Little Song] (1959)
  An 'Habit Shirt' [The Habit Shirt] (1959)
  Rince Philib an Cheoil [Musical Philip's Dance] (1959)

 Solo voice, SATB choir, and orchestra
  An Spéic Seoigheach [The Joyce Spake] (1955/56)
  Tiocfaidh an Samhradh [Summer will Come] (1956)
  Tá mé 'mo shuí [I am awake] (1956)
  Réice Luimní [The Rakes of Limerick] (1956)
  Cill Aodáin [The Church of Aidan] (1956)
  Plúirín na mBan Donn Óg [The Flower of the Young Brown-Haired Women] (1959)
  Sliabh Gheal gCua [The Bright Mountain of Cua] (1959) [Also arranged for solo voice and orchestra (1983)]
  An Buachaill Caol Dubh [The Slim Dark Boy] (1959)
  Caoine na dTrí Muire [The Lament of the Three Marys] (1959)
  An Raibh tú ar an gCarraig? [Were you at the Rock?] (1959)

Solo voice and piano

    A Athair Dhílis [Faithful Father] (nd)

    An Spiorad Naomh Umainn [The Holy Spirit About Us] (nd)

    Be Thou My Vision (nd)

    The Bonny Boy is Young, But He's Growing Up (nd)

    Septembermorgen [September Morning] (nd)

    She Moved Through The Fair (nd)

    Brian O'Linn (nd)

    A Rí an Domhnaigh [O King of Sunday] (nd)

    The Limerick Rake (1951)

    Cuirfimid Deaindí [We will Make a Dandy] (1983)

    The Flower of Magherally (1983)

    The Enniscorthy Christmas Carol (1985)

    Danny Boy (1985)

    Moorlough Mary (1986)

    Dobbin's Flowery Vale (1986)

    On Raglan Road (1986)

    Who goes with Fergus? (1986)

    Waltzing Matilda (1986)

    Moreton Bay (1986)

    The Kilmore Carols (1986): (i) *A Carol for Christmas Day*, (ii) *A Carol for Twelfth Day* [piano or harpsichord or harp, with optional parts for cello and 2 flutes], (iii) *Song for Jerusalem*, (iv) *Carol for St. Stephen's Day*

    Hua Ku Ko [The Flower Drum] (1987)

    Jeannie with the Light Brown Hair (1987)

    The Shan Van Vocht [The Poor Old Woman] (1988)

    Freedom Triumphant (1988)

    Never Wed an Old Man (1988)

    Believe Me, If All Those Endearing Young Charms (1988)

    The Maid of Culmore (1989)

    Die Gedanken sind frei [Thoughts Are Free]

    Dia do Bheatha a Mhic Mhuire [Welcome, Son of Mary] (1995)

    Naomhtha Cearda Mhic Mhuire [The Accompanying Holy Spirit] (1995)

    Traditional German Carols (1997): (i) *Es sungen drei Engel* [There were three angels singing], (ii) *In dulci Jubilo*, (iii) *Maria durch ein' Dornwald ging* [Maria walked through a thorny forest], (iv) *O komm, o komm, Emmanuel*.

    Don Oíche úd i mBeithil [That Night in Bethlehem] (1997)

    An tAiséirí [The Resurrection] (2001)

    Balm in Gilead [Traditional American spiritual] (2002)

Solo voice and harp or piano

    My Boy Willie (1986)

    The Red-haired Man's Wife (1986)

    An Sagairtín [The Little Priest] (1986)

    The Royal Eagle (1987)

    The Green Linnet (1987)

    The Bonny Bunch of Roses, O (1987)

    Molly Malone (1988)

    Johnny Dhu' [Black Johnny] (1988)

    Upon my Lap my Sovereign Sits (1988)

    In Bethlehem City (1988)

    Suantraí na Maighdine [The Virgin's Lullaby] (1988)

    Dán Molta Dé [A Poem in Praise of God] (1988)

    Bí Íosa im Chroíse [Jesus Be in My Heart] (1988)

    Let Folly Praise What Fancy Loves (1988)

    Ar Éireann ní neosfainn Cé hÍ [For Ireland I'd not tell her name] (1988)

    Finnegans Wake (1988)

    Cruise of the Calabar (1988)

    The Burning Babe (1988)

    Pósadh Naomhtha Cána [The Holy Marriage of Cana] (1988)

    An Leanbhín Gléigeal [The Fairest Child] (2001)

SATB choir, SSA choir or SA choir unaccompanied

    Henry Joy McCracken (1953) SATB

    Famine Song (1953) SATB

    I Will Walk with my Love (1956) SSA soli or semi-chorus, SATB, Pub Cumann Náisúnta na gCór, 1982

    Bog Braon don tSeanduine [Pour a Drop] (1959) SSA, Pub *Feasta* (June 1959), 5

    Rince Philib an Cheoil [Musical Philip's Dance] (1959) SSA, Pub *Feasta* (July 1959), 10

    Cuirfimid Deaindí Deaindí [We will make a Dandy] (1959) SSA, Pub *Feasta* (September 1959), 5

    Amhrán Fíodóireachta [Weaving Song] (1959) SSA, Pub *Feasta* (August 1959), 5

    Deoíndí (1959), SSA. Pub *Feasta* (October 1959), 5

    Don Oíche úd i mBeithil [That Night in Bethlehem] (1959) SA, Pub *Feasta* (December 1959), 13

    An Habit Shirt [The Habit Shirt] (1959) SA, Pub *Feasta* (February 1960), 9

    Bruach na Carriage Báine [The Bank of the White Rock] (1959) SATB or unison, SSA, Pub *Feasta* (July 1960), 9

    Caoine na dTrí Muire [The Lament of the Three Marys] (1959) SSA, Pub *Feasta* (November 1959), 16–17

An Teicheadh go hÉigipt [The Flight to Egypt] (1960) SSA
Domhnall Óg [Young Donal] (1961) SSA
An Dreóilín [The Wren] (pre-1960) SSAA
Dilín Ó Deamhas (1959) SSA *Pub Feasta* (May 1959), 5

SATB choir and organ
Dóchas Linn Naomh Pádraig [Grant us hope, St. Patrick] (1960)

SATB choir and piano
Si le Roi m'avait Donné [If the King had given me] (1952)
Bonny Light Horseman (1953)
The Bold Belfast Shoemaker (1954)
Brídín Bán mo Stór [Fair Brigid My Love] (1954)
Johnny Dunlea (1954)
Ye Sons of Old Ireland (1955)
An Chéad Mháirt i Bhfoghmhar [The First Tuesday of Autumn] (1955)
Pride of London Derry (1955)
Buachaill ón Éirne [The Boy from Erne] (1955)
Follow me up to Carlow (1955)
The Jacket's Green (1955)
The Convict of Clonmel (1955)
The Dirge of O'Sullivan Beare (1955)
Dobbin's Flowery Vale (1955)
The Girl from Lord Blarney's Demesne (1955)
Bumper Squire Jones (1955)
Seachrán Cairn Tsiall [The Ramble of Carnteel] (1955)
Ballad of Ó Bruadair (1955)
Cuach mo Londubh Buí [My Darling Yellow Blackbird] (1955)
Glen Swilly (1955)
John McAnanty's Courtship (1955)
Pretty Susan, Pride of Kildare (1956)
Banks of Banna (1956)
An Bunnán Buí [The Yellow Hammer] (1956)
Hó Ró Do Bhuig, A Sheáin [Oh! Oh! your wig, Seán] (1956)
Na Géanna Geala [The White Geese] (1956)
Fanny Power (1956)
Mary Ann McHugh (1956)
Nóra an Chúil Ómra [Nora of the Auburn Hair] (1956)
Jimmy Murphy (1956)

Óró Mór a Mhórin [Oro Moreen] (1956)
Is a Éirinn ní Neósfainn cia hí [For Ireland I'd not tell her name] (1956)
Tá mo Ghrá-sa ar an Abhainn [My Love is on the River] (1956)
The Maid of Bunclody (1956)
The Wexford Massacre (1956)
Night of the Ragman's Ball (1956)
Iníon na Phailitínigh [The Palatine's Daughter] (1957)
An Spealadóir [The Reaper] (1959)

SSA choir and piano
Anach Cuain [Annaghdown] (1971)
SA and piano. English translation by Caoimhín Ó Conghaile. Pub McCullough Pigott
(Dublin, 1971)

An Fhalaingín Mhuimhneach [The Munster Cloak] (1971)
SA and piano. English translation by Caoimhín Ó Conghaile. Pub McCullough Pigott
(Dublin, 1971)

Miscellaneous
Caisleán Uí Néill [O'Neill's Castle]
Flute, viola and harp (nd)

De Bhárr na gCnoc [Over the Hills]
Flute, viola and harp (nd)

Gogaí-ó-Gaog [Guggy O'Geeg] (1959/60)
SATB or unison voices, clarinet, cor anglais and piano [or voice and piano]. Pub *Feasta*
(May 1960)

Battle Hymn of the Republic (1985)
Voice and piano [with optional 3-part chorus]

Appendix II. Discography

Music for Strings (1952)
> Decca (DL9843), LP (1958), *New Music from Old Erin*, Radio Éircann Symphony Orchestra, Milan Horvat (cond.)

An Spéic Seoigheach (1955/56)
> Angel Records, LP, Irish Festival Singers, Kitty O'Callaghan (cond.)

I will Walk with my Love (1956)
> Harmonia Mundi (HMS 30691), LP (1965), *Irische Volkslieder*, Der Kammerchor von Radio Dublin [Radio Éireann Singers], Hans Waldemar Rosen (cond.)
> New Irish Recording Company (DEB 002), LP (1974), Culwick Choral Society, Eric Sweeney (cond.)

Tá im gan im gan ór (1956)
> Gael-Linn (CEF001), LP (c. 1960), 'Ceol na hÉireann', Radio Telefís Éireann Light Orchestra, Eimear Ó Broin (cond.)

Alliliú na Gamhna (1956)
> RTÉ, LP (1980), RTÉ Concert Orchestra, Proinnsías Ó Duinn (cond.)

The Palatine's Daughter (1956/57)
> Gael Linn (CEF001), LP (1958), 'Ceol na hÉireann', Radio Telefís Éireann Light Orchestra, Eimear Ó Broin (cond.). Reissued Gael Linn (CEFCD001), CD (2009), 'Ceolta Éireann'

Trí Aortha (1962)
New Irish Recording Company (NIR 007), LP (1974), Radio Telefís Éireann Singers, Hans Waldemar Rosen (cond.) (Not released)
A Night at the Festival: Highlights of the 41st Cork International Choral Festival 1994, Corkfest Records, CD (1994), Cór Naomh Mhuire, Fiontán Ó Murchú (cond.) (No. 3, 'Laoi Cháinte an Tabac' only)

Prelude, Toccata and Epilogue (1963)
New Irish Recording Company (NIR001), LP (1971) Charles Lynch (piano)

Chamber Symphony No. 1 (1964)
New Irish Recording Company (NIR012), LP (1974), New Irish Chamber Orchestra, Seóirse Bodley (cond.)
RTÉ Lyric fm, CD (2009) Composers of Ireland Series, Vol. 3, RTÉ National Symphony Orchestra, Robert Houlihan (cond.)

String Quartet No. 1 (1968)
New Irish Recording Company (NIR006), LP (1973), Radio Telefís Éireann String Quartet (Not released)

A Small White Cloud Drifts Over Ireland (1975)
RTÉ Lyric fm, CD (2009) Composers of Ireland Series, Vol. 3, RTÉ National Symphony Orchestra, Robert Houlihan (cond.)

The Tightrope Walker Presents a Rose (1976)
Royal Irish Academy of Music, Grade VII Pieces, CD, 2009, Réamonn Keary (piano)

Mass of Peace (1976)
Network Tapes (NTO 55C), MC (1977) Clonliffe College Choir, Seóirse Bodley (cond.)

The Narrow Road to the Deep North (1977) [solo pf version]
Gael Linn (CEFO85), LP/MC (1980), John O'Conor (piano)

Hymn to St. John of God (1978)
Network Tapes NTO102C (1979) King David Singers, Patrick Devine (organ), Seóirse Bodley (cond.)

Mass of Joy (1978)
Network Tapes NTO102C (1979) King David Singers, Patrick Devine (organ), Seóirse Bodley (cond.)

I have Loved the Lands of Ireland (Symphony No. 2) (1980)
> RTÉ Lyric fm, CD (2009) Composers of Ireland Series, Vol. 3, RTÉ National Symphony Orchestra, Robert Houlihan (cond.)

Ceol: Symphony No. 3 (1980)
> RTÉ (RTÉ61) (limited release), LP (1981), Violet Twomey (soprano), Bernadette Greevy (mezzo-soprano), Louis Browne (tenor), William Young (bass), Aindreas Ó Gallchoir (speaker), Radio Telefís Éireann Symphony Orchestra, Radio Telefís Éireann Singers & Chorus, Our Lady's Choral Society, Boys of St. Patrick's Cathedral Choir, Dublin, Colman Pearce (cond.)

A Girl (1980)
> Gael Linn (CEFO85), LP/MC (1980), Bernadette Greevy (mezzo-soprano), John O'Conor (piano)

The Naked Flame (1987)
> Echo Classics Digital (LC7596), CD (1996), *Irish Vocal Music by Seóirse Bodley*, Aylish Kerrigan (mezzo-soprano), Seóirse Bodley (piano)

Carta Irlandesa (1988)
> Echo Classics Digital (LC7596), CD (1996), *Irish Vocal Music by Seóirse Bodley*, Aylish Kerrigan (mezzo-soprano), Seóirse Bodley (piano)

Symphony No. 4 (1991)
> Marco Polo (8.225157), CD (2001), National Symphony Orchestra of Ireland, Colman Pearce (cond.)

Symphony No. 5 (*The Limerick Symphony*) (1991)
> Marco Polo (8.225157), CD (2001), National Symphony Orchestra of Ireland, Colman Pearce (cond.)

String Quartet No. 2 (1992)
> Contemporary Music Centre, Ireland (CD02), CD (1997), *Contemporary Music from Ireland 2*, Degani String Quartet (third movement only)

By the Margins of the Great Deep (1995)
> Echo Classics Digital (LC7596), CD (1996), *Irish Vocal Music by Seóirse Bodley*, Aylish Kerrigan (mezzo-soprano), Seóirse Bodley (piano)

Sinfonietta (2000)
  NYOI, CD (2000), National Youth Orchestra of Ireland, En Shao (cond.)

String Quartet No. 3: *Ave atque Vale* (2004)
  Contemporary Music Centre, Ireland (CD06), CD (2006), *Contemporary Music from Ireland*
    6, Vogler String Quartet (second movement only)

RTÉ Recordings

On a CD ROM compilation of 'recordings of Works by Irish Composers in RTÉ Sound
Archives' included in the book *Music and Broadcasting in Ireland* (Dublin, 2005), Richard Pine
and Joan Murphy list 118 recordings of Bodley's compositions and arrangements. Copies
of most of these recordings are now available from the Contemporary Music Centre,
Ireland. Many of Bodley's works were recorded quite a few times, thus making for an
interesting comparative study of performance history and interpretation. *Music for Strings*
(1952), for example, was recorded by Brian Boydell, Douglas Cameron, Tibor Paul, and
Eimear Ó Broin; *Salve, Maria Virgo* (1957) by Milan Horvat, Constantin Silvestri, Tibor Paul,
and Eimear Ó Broin; the Symphony No. 1 (1959) by Hans Müller-Kray, Tibor Paul, Colman
Pearce, Proinnsías Ó Duinn, and Albert Rosen; and the Sonata for Violin and Piano (1959)
by various duos: Margaret Hayes and Bodley, Mary Gallagher and Veronica McSwiney,
Thérèse Timoney and John O'Conor, and Colin Staveley and Colman Pearce. There are
also numerous archive recordings of RTÉ radio programmes either partially or entirely
devoted to Bodley's music such as The Piano Music of Seóirse Bodley (1957), Composers at
Work (1958), Composer's Workshop (1969), The Music of Seóirse Bodley (1973), Music and
the Musician (1974), Profile of Seóirse Bodley (1976), Music Magazine (1976), Afternoon
Recital (1978), Composers in Conversation (1988), Concert Choice, as well as many Music
Room programmes. Bodley also presented a series of radio programmes on RTÉ in 1977
entitled A Change of Address, which introduced aspects of modern music to listeners.
These recordings are stored in the RTÉ archives and many of them are available at the
Contemporary Music Centre, Ireland, Fishamble Street, Dublin.

Appendix III. Published Writings (selected list)

'Cúrsaí Ceoil in Éirinn', *Comhar* (June 1954), 5–8

'An Chcolfhoireann agus na Gléasanna', *Comhar* (September 1956), 9–10

'Foirmeacha bunúsacha an cheoil', *Comhar* (January 1957), 21–22

'Ceol an Lae Inniu', *Comhar* (February 1957), 19–20

'Fadhb an Chumadóra Éireannaigh', *Feasta* (March, 1957), 3–4

'Ceol an Lae Inniu', *Comhar* (March 1957), 15–16

'Dialann Cheoltóra', *Comhar* (February 1958), 22

'Stair an Cheoil go hAchomair', *Comhar* (October 1956), 19–20

'A Composer's View', *Trinity News: A Dublin University Undergraduate Weekly*, 12, 5 (1964), 10

'The Uileann Pipes', *Ireland of the Welcomes* (May/June 1965), 6–10

'Report from Dublin: Curriculum at University College', *Current Musicology*, 7 (1968), 60–62

'Introduction', W. G. Grattan Flood, *A History of Irish Music*, 3rd ed. (New York and Washington, 1970 [1913]), v–x

'Introduction', Robert Bruce Armstrong, *The Irish and Highland Harps* (Shannon, 1969 [1904]), v–vii

'Remembering Seán Ó Riada', *The Capuchin Annual*, 39 (1972), 302–04

'Technique and structure in "sean-nós" singing', *Éigse Ceol Tíre*, 1 (1973), 44–54

'Bridging the Gap, *Irish Times*, 7 April 1977

'Boydell, Brian', in Stanley Sadie, ed., *The New Grove Dictionary of Music and Musicians* (London, 1980)

'Flood, Grattan', in Stanley Sadie, ed., *The New Grove Dictionary of Music and Musicians* (London, 1980)

'Ireland § 1: Art Music', in Stanley Sadie, ed., *The New Grove Dictionary of Music and Musicians* (London, 1980)

'O'Gallagher, Eamonn [Ó Gallchobháir, Éamonn]', in Stanley Sadie, ed., *The New Grove Dictionary of Music and Musicians* (London, 1980/1992)

'Ó Riada, Seán', in Stanley Sadie, ed., *The New Grove Dictionary of Music and Musicians* (London, 1980)

'Potter, A. J.', in Stanley Sadie, ed., *The New Grove Dictionary of Music and Musicians* (London, 1980/1992/2001)

'The Original Compositions: An Assessment', in Fryer, Grattan and Harris, Bernard, eds., *Integrating Tradition: The Achievement of Seán Ó Riada* (Ballina, 1981), 28–40

'The Music of the Carols' in *The Wexford Carols*, in Diarmaid Ó Muirithe, ed., [transcription with a commentary] (Mountrath, 1982)

'A Special Category', *Music Ireland* (May 1990), 10

'October 2001: A Journey to Japan', *aicnews* [Association of Irish Composers newsletter], November 2001

'Seóirse Bodley talking to Ann Fleischmann', in Ruth Fleischmann, ed., *Cork International Choral Festival 1954–2004: A Celebration* (Cork, 2004), 296–99. [An extract from this interview was also published in the *Journal of Music in Ireland*, 4, 3 (March/April, 2004), 16–17].

'The Claims of Conformity' in Patricia Flynn, ed., *Teaching the Unteachable? The Role of Composition in Music Education* (Waterford, 2009), 32–57

'"Bean an Fhir Rua" as Performed by a Master of Connemara Traditional Style, Seán Mac Donncha of Carna', in Anne Clune, ed., *Dear Far-Voiced Veteran: Essays in Honour of Tom Munnelly* (Miltown Malbay, 2007), 31–41

Bibliography

Acton, Charles. 'Seóirse Bodley', Music Supplement, *Hibernia*, September 1968

————. 'Interview with Seóirse Bodley', *Éire-Ireland*, 5, 3 (1970), 117–33

————. 'How to set about listening to Twentieth-Century Music', *Counterpoint* (September 1970), 15

————. 'An Irish Setting of the Mass', *Irish Times*, 10 March 1977

————. *Irish Music and Musicians* (Dublin, 1978)

————. 'An Irish Mass', *Irish Times*, 12 January 1980

————. 'Vision from the Past', *Irish Times*, 9 January 1981

Barry, Malcolm. 'Examining the Great Divide', *Soundpost*, 16 (October/November, 1983), 15–20

Bishai, Nadia Zaki. 'Further thoughts on Irish poetry set to music, with special reference to the Art Song in contemporary Irish music', in Patricia A. Lynch, Joachim Fischer, Brian Coates, eds., *Back to the Present; Forward to the Past: Irish Writing and History since 1798*, vol. I (Amsterdam/New York, 2006), 229–40

Boydell, Brian, ed. *Four Centuries of Music in Ireland* (London, 1979)

Bracefield, Hilary. 'The Northern Composer: Irish or European?' in Patrick F. Devine and Harry White, eds., *Irish Musical Studies IV: The Maynooth International Musicological Conference 1995, Selected Proceedings Part I* (Dublin, 1996), 255–62

Butler, Patricia and O'Kelly, Pat. *The National Concert Hall at Earlsfort Terrace, Dublin: A History* (Dublin, 2000)

Byrne Bodley, Lorraine, ed. *Goethe: Musical Poet, Musical Catalyst* (Dublin, 2004)

————, ed. with introduction, *Seóirse Bodley, Three Congregational Masses* (Dublin, 2005)

————. 'The Poetry of Musical Perception' in Marc Caball and David F. Ford, eds., *Musics of Belonging: The Poetry of Micheal O'Siadhail* (Dublin, 2007), 93–109

————, ed. with introduction, *A Hazardous Melody of Being: Seóirse Bodley's Song Cycles on the Poems of Micheal O'Siadhail* (Dublin, 2008)

Clare, Jane, O'Connell, Magdalen and Simmons, Jane, eds. *The Culwick Choral Society celebrates one hundred years 1898–1998* (Dublin: 1998)

Cleary, Joe and Connolly, Claire, eds. *The Cambridge Companion to Modern Irish Culture* (Cambridge, 2005)

Corcoran, Frank. 'New Irish Music', *Interface*, 12 (1983), 41–44

Cox, Gareth, ed. *Acton's Music: Reviews of Dublin's Musical Life 1955–1985* (Bray, 1996)

————. 'German Influences on Twentieth-Century Irish Art-Music', in Joachim Fischer, et al., *Deutsch-Irische Verbindungen: Irish-German Connections, Schriftenreihe Literaturwissenschaft*, 42 (Trier, 1998), 107–14

————. 'An Irishman in Darmstadt: Seóirse Bodley's String Quartet No. 1 (1968)' in Gareth Cox and Axel Klein, eds. *Irish Musical Studies 7: Irish Music in the Twentieth Century* (Dublin, 2003), 94–108

————. 'Darmstadt Revisited: Seóirse Bodley's *News from Donabate* (1999)' in *Proceedings of the 1st. Annual Conference of the Society for Musicology in Ireland, NUI Maynooth, 2–3 May 2003*, Barra Boydell, ed. (Maynooth, 2004), 137–42

Cox, Gareth and Klein, Axel, eds. *Irish Musical Studies 7: Irish Music in the Twentieth Century* (Dublin, 2003)

Cox, Gareth, Klein, Axel and Taylor, Michael, eds. *The Life and Music of Brian Boydell* (Dublin, 2003).

Cull, Gráinne. *Piano Music for Children by Contemporary Irish Composers: An Analytical and Pedagogical Study based on Applied Research*, unpublished dissertation, Mary Immaculate College, University of Limerick (1999)

Deale, Edgar, ed. *Catalogue of Contemporary Irish Composers* (Dublin 1973 [1968])

de Barra, Séamas. *Aloys Fleischmann* (Dublin, 2006)

De Paor, Paschall. 'The development of electroacoustic music in Ireland', in Gareth Cox and Axel Klein, eds. *Irish Musical Studies 7: Irish Music in the Twentieth Century* (Dublin, 2003), 29–38

Dervan, Michael. 'A Note of Change', *Irish Times*, 25 March 2002

Donoghue, Denis. 'The Future of Irish Music', *Studies*, 44 (Spring, 1955) 109–14

[Dungan, Michael]. 'Interview with Seóirse Bodley', *New Music News*, September 1996, 9–11

————. 'What's it like to be Seóirse Bodley' Contemporary Music Centre, Ireland, website http://www.cmc.ie/articles/article638.html (accessed 27 December 2008)

————. 'An Interview with Seóirse Bodley', on video with text on the Contemporary Music Centre, Ireland, website http://www.cmc.ie/articles/article639.html (accessed 21 April 2003.

Fadlu-Deen, Kitty. *Contemporary Music in Ireland*, unpublished dissertation, University College Dublin (1968)

Farrell, Hazel. *Aspects of Pitch Structure and Pitch Selection in Post-War Irish Composition: An Analytical Study of Tonal and Post-Tonal Referential Collections in Selected Works by Irish*

Composers, unpublished dissertation, Mary Immaculate College, University of Limerick (2002)

Feehan, Fanny. 'Seóirse Bodley: Astride Two Traditions', *Hibernia*, 13 February 1976 [with subsequent correction to the second paragraph in a letter to *Hibernia* on 27 February 1976]

————. 'Living Irish Composers', *Ireland Today (Bulletin of the Department of Foreign Affairs)*, 886, 7 May 1976, 6–8

————. 'The Importance of Being Seóirse', *Hibernia*, 4 January 1979

————. 'Seóirse's Second', *Hibernia*, 4 September 1980, 25

Feeley, John. *Classical Guitar Music by Irish Composers: Performing Editions and Critical Commentary*, unpublished dissertation, National University of Ireland, Maynooth (2007)

Fleischmann, Aloys, ed. *Music in Ireland: A Symposium* (Cork and Oxford, 1952)

Fleischmann, Ruth, ed. *Cork International Choral Festival 1954–2004: A Celebration* (Cork, 2004)

Flynn, Patricia, ed. *Teaching the Unteachable? The Role of Composition in Music Education* (Waterford, 2009)

Gillen, Gerard. 'Bodley, Seóirse', in Basil Blackwell ed., *Blackwell Companion to Modern Irish Culture* (Oxford, 1999), 74

Gillen, Gerard and Johnstone, Andrew, eds. *Irish Musical Studies 6: A Historical Anthology of Irish Church Music* (Dublin, 2001)

Griffiths, Paul. 'Bodley, Seóirse', in *The Oxford Companion to Music* (Oxford, 1983), vol. I, 229–30

Harris, Bernard. 'Contemporary Irish Music: A Survey', in Birgit Bramsback and Martin Croghan, eds., *Anglo-Irish and Irish Literature: Aspects of Language and Culture — Proceedings of the Ninth International Congress of the International Association for the Study of Anglo-Irish Literature* (Stockholm, 1989), 207–11

Harrison, Bernard, ed. *Catalogue of Contemporary Irish Music* (Dublin, 1982)

Häusler, Josef. 'David, Johann Nepomuk', in Stanley Sadie, ed. *The New Grove Dictionary of Music and Musicians*, 7 (London, 2001), 51–54

Hölzl, Peter. *Der Lehrer Johann Nepomuk David: Aus dem Unterricht bei Johann Nepomuk David an der Stuttgarter Musikhochschule* (Vienna, 1992)

Hughes, Anthony. 'Bodley, Seóirse', in Stanley Sadie, ed. *The New Grove Dictionary of Music and Musicians*, 2 (London, 1980), 838

Hunt, Edmund, 'Where is the Irish Bartók?' *The Question of Art Music and Its Relation to the Traditional Music Genre: A Study of Some Approaches and Contemporary Developments*, unpublished dissertation, University of Newcastle-upon-Tyne (2006)

Keary, Réamonn. *A Survey of Irish Piano Music from 1970 to 1995*, unpublished dissertation, National University of Ireland, Maynooth (1995)

Klein, Axel. 'Bodley, Seóirse', in Walter-Wolfgang Sparrer and Hans-Werner Heister, eds., *Komponisten der Gegenwart* (Munich 1992)

————. 'Aber was ist heute schon abenteuerlich?: Ein Porträt des irischen Komponisten Seóirse Bodley', *MusikTexte*, 52, January 1994, 21–25

————. 'Irish Composers and Foreign Education: A Study of Influences', in Patrick F. Devine and Harry White, eds. *Irish Musical Studies 4: The Maynooth International Musicological Conference 1995, Selected Proceedings Part I* (Dublin, 1996), 271–84

————. 'Bodley, Seóirse', in Ludwig Finscher, ed., *Die Musik in Geschichte und Gegenwart (MGG)*, second revised edition, 3 (Kassel, 2000), 194–96

————. *Die Musik Irlands im 20. Jahrhundert* (Hildesheim, 1996)

————. 'Bodley, Seóirse', *Irish Classical Recordings: A Discography of Irish Art Music* (Westport CT, 2001), 12–14

————. 'Bodley, Seóirse', *The New Grove Dictionary of Music and Musicians*, Stanley Sadie, ed., (London, 2001), 774–75

————. 'Roots and Directions in Twentieth-century Music', *Irish Musical Studies 7, Irish Music in the Twentieth Century* in Gareth Cox and Axel Klein, eds. (Dublin, 2003), 168–82

————. 'A twentieth-century Irish music bibliography', in Gareth Cox and Axel Klein, eds., *Irish Musical Studies 7: Irish Music in the Twentieth Century* (Dublin, 2003), 183–204

————. 'Mirror Imagination: Cultural Reflections between Irish and German Music, 1930–1970', in Christa Brüstle and Guido Heldt, eds. *Music as a Bridge: Musikalische Beziehungen zwischen England und Deutschland 1920–1950* (Hildesheim, 2005), 205–24

Klein, Rudolf. *Johann Nepomuk David: Eine Studie* (Vienna, 1964)

Komma, Karl Michael. 'Johann Nepomuk David, Mensch und Musiker: Erinnerungen an seine Stuttgarter Zeit', in *Mitteilungen der Internationalen Johann-Nepomuk-David Gesellschaft*, 11 (Wiesbaden, 1996), 1–23

Lawrence, Ian. *Transformations: The String Quartet in Britain and Ireland since 1885* (Dorset, 2004)

Le Govic, Tristan. *The Development of the Contemporary Repertoire for the Irish Harp*, unpublished dissertation, University College Cork (2002)

Loveland, Kenneth. 'Composers in Search of a National Identity', *Counterpoint* (October 1972), 10–11

Murphy, Daniel, et al. 'Seóirse Bodley' in *Education and the Arts: The Educational Autobiographies of Contemporary Irish Poets, Novelists, Dramatists, Musicians, Painters and Sculptors: A Research Report* (Dublin, 1987), 230–38

Ó Canainn, Tomás. *Seán Ó Riada: His Life and Work* (Cork, 2003)

Ó Cuinneagáin, Pádhraic. *The Piano Music of Seóirse Bodley*, unpublished dissertation, National University of Ireland, Maynooth (1992)

O'Connor, Honor. 'Sounds and Voices: Aspects of Contemporary Irish Music and Poetry' in *Anglo-Irish and Irish Literature: Aspects of Language and Culture*, 2 (Uppsala, 1988), 211–17

O'Donoghue, Patrick. 'Music and Religion in Ireland', in Gerard Gillen and Harry White, eds. *Irish Musical Studies 3: Music and Irish Cultural History* (Dublin, 1995), 116–52

O'Flynn, John. 'National Identity and Music in Transition: Issues of Authenticity in a Global Setting', in Ian Biddle and Vanessa Knights, eds. *Music, National Identity and the Politics of Location* (Aldershot, 2007), 19–38

O'Kelly, Pat. *The National Symphony Orchestra of Ireland 1948–1998: A Selected History* (Dublin, 1998)

O'Leary, Jane. 'Dublin Festival of Twentieth Century Music', *Perspectives of New Music*, 17, 2 (Spring–Summer 1979), 260–67

Page, John. 'A post-war "Irish" Symphony: Frank Corcoran's Symphony No. 2', in Gareth Cox and Axel Klein, eds. *Irish Musical Studies 7: Irish Music in the Twentieth Century* (Dublin, 2003), 134–49

Phelan, Helen. '*Roma locuta, Causa finite?* —The Perception, Interpretation and Implementation of Conciliar and Post-Conciliar Directives regarding Liturgical Music in the Republic of Ireland, 1962–92', in Patrick F. Devine and Harry White, eds. *Irish Musical Studies 4: The Maynooth International Musicological Conference 1995, Selected Proceedings Part I* (Dublin, 1996), 119–26

Pine, Richard. *Music and Broadcasting in Ireland* (Dublin, 2005)

Stuckenschmidt, Hans Heinz. *Johann Nepomuk David: Betrachtungen zu seinem Werk* (Wiesbaden, 1965)

White, Harry. 'The Need for a Sociology of Irish Folk Music: A Review of Writings on "Traditional" Music in Ireland, with some Responses and Proposals', *International Review of the Aesthetics and Sociology of Music*, 15, 1 (June 1984), 3–13

————. 'Musicology in Ireland', *Acta Musicologica*, 60 (Sept.–Dec. 1988), 290–305

————. 'The Preservation of Music and Irish Cultural History', *International Review of the Aesthetics and Sociology of Music*, 27, 2 (Dec. 1996), 123–38

————. *The Keeper's Recital: Music and Cultural History in Ireland, 1770–1970* (Cork, 1998)

————. 'Irish Art Music in the Twentieth Century' [review of Axel Klein, *Die Musik Irlands im 20. Jahrhundert*], *Irish Review*, 24, 1999, 139–43

————. 'The divided imagination: music in Ireland after Ó Riada', in Gareth Cox and Axel Klein, eds. *Irish Musical Studies 7: Irish Music in the Twentieth Century* (Dublin, 2003), 11–28

————. *The Progress of Music in Ireland* (Dublin, 2005)

Zuk, Patrick. 'Words for Music Perhaps? Irishness, Criticism and the Art Tradition', *Irish Studies Review*, 12, 1 (2004), 11–27

————. *Raymond Deane* (Dublin, 2006)

Index